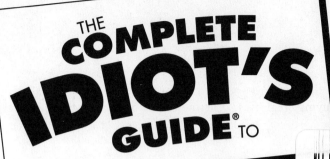

THE COMPLETE IDIOT'S GUIDE® TO

Going Back to College

WITHDRAWN

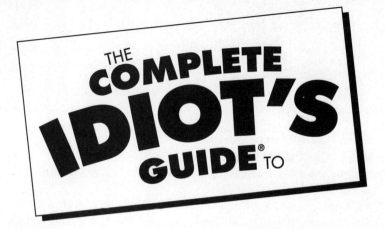

THE
COMPLETE
IDIOT'S
GUIDE® TO

Going Back
to College

by Dolores A. Mize, Ph.D.

ALPHA

A member of Penguin Group (USA) Inc.

ALPHA BOOKS

Published by the Penguin Group

Penguin Group (USA) Inc., 375 Hudson Street, New York, New York 10014, U.S.A.

Penguin Group (Canada), 10 Alcorn Avenue, Toronto, Ontario, Canada M4V 3B2 (a division of Pearson Penguin Canada Inc.)

Penguin Books Ltd, 80 Strand, London WC2R 0RL, England

Penguin Ireland, 25 St Stephen's Green, Dublin 2, Ireland (a division of Penguin Books Ltd)

Penguin Group (Australia), 250 Camberwell Road, Camberwell, Victoria 3124, Australia (a division of Pearson Australia Group Pty Ltd)

Penguin Books India Pvt Ltd, 11 Community Centre, Panchsheel Park, New Delhi—110 017, India

Penguin Group (NZ), cnr Airborne and Rosedale Roads, Albany, Auckland 1310, New Zealand (a division of Pearson New Zealand Ltd)

Penguin Books (South Africa) (Pty) Ltd, 24 Sturdee Avenue, Rosebank, Johannesburg 2196, South Africa

Penguin Books Ltd, Registered Offices: 80 Strand, London WC2R 0RL, England

International Standard Book Number: 978-1-59257-571-8
Library of Congress Catalog Card Number: 2006930730

09 08 07   8 7 6 5 4 3 2 1

Interpretation of the printing code: The rightmost number of the first series of numbers is the year of the book's printing; the rightmost number of the second series of numbers is the number of the book's printing. For example, a printing code of 07-1 shows that the first printing occurred in 2007.

Printed in the United States of America

Note: This publication contains the opinions and ideas of its author. It is intended to provide helpful and informative material on the subject matter covered. It is sold with the understanding that the author and publisher are not engaged in rendering professional services in the book. If the reader requires personal assistance or advice, a competent professional should be consulted.

The author and publisher specifically disclaim any responsibility for any liability, loss, or risk, personal or otherwise, which is incurred as a consequence, directly or indirectly, of the use and application of any of the contents of this book.

Most Alpha books are available at special quantity discounts for bulk purchases for sales promotions, premiums, fund-raising, or educational use. Special books, or book excerpts, can also be created to fit specific needs.

For details, write: Special Markets, Alpha Books, 375 Hudson Street, New York, NY 10014.

Publisher: *Marie Butler-Knight*
Editorial Director: *Mike Sanders*
Managing Editor: *Billy Fields*
Senior Acquisitions Editor: *Randy Ladenheim-Gil*
Development Editor: *Jennifer Moore*
Production Editor: *Kayla Dugger*
Copy Editor: *Tricia Leibig*

Cartoonist: *Richard King*
Cover Designer: *Bill Thomas*
Book Designers: *Trina Wurst/Kurt Owens*
Indexer: *Angie Bess*
Layout: *Brian Massey*
Proofreader: *John Etchison*

Contents at a Glance

Appendixes

Contents

Introduction

One of the obvious benefits of a college degree is the increase in pay you're likely to receive. People with college degrees in the United States earn a million dollars more over a lifetime, on average, than people who hold only a high school diploma. This statistic explains why going through life without a college degree is often called "the million-dollar mistake."

But there are many less-obvious plusses to a college degree, among them better job benefits such as health insurance and a pension plan, a healthier lifestyle, and even a longer life!

Earnings and Workplace Benefits

Over the past two decades, people without Bachelor's degrees or higher have seen dramatically decreased earnings when compared to people with Bachelor's degrees. And even though there is still a gap between male and female wages among Bachelor's degree holders, women are making gains in earnings at a faster rate than men, and are thus narrowing the wage gap. If you don't have a high school diploma, your earning potential is very low. You earn only slightly more if you have just a high school diploma.

If you have a Bachelor's degree or higher, you're more likely to be working in a job that provides health insurance. Not only does having health insurance help you stay healthy, you're also in a position to make sure your children stay healthy. With good health insurance and a good job, you never have to worry if you have enough money to take yourself or your children to the doctor—it's covered!

In addition, adults with Bachelor's degrees or higher are also much more likely to work in jobs with good pension benefits, whether those are traditional pensions, 401k programs, or benefit programs that allow you to save for retirement through mutual funds, stock options, and so on. Having a college degree can help you spend your retirement years doing what you've always wanted to do!

Education Level and Health Factors

By itself, having a college degree doesn't make you healthier. However, when you have a college degree, you're more likely to be more informed about how to live a healthy lifestyle. You're less likely to be at risk for heart disease because you're less likely to smoke and live a sedentary lifestyle. You're more likely to exercise because you know its importance in keeping you healthy. Consequently, you're less likely to be obese. In this case, what you don't know *can* kill you.

Benefits for Your Children

Your children benefit from your college degree, too, and it's not only through the example you set by stepping back into a learning environment. Studies show that, time after time, the best predictor of whether or not a child will attend college and earn a degree is whether one or both parents hold a college degree. Parents with college degrees, or at least some experience in college, are better able to help their children go through the process of selecting colleges, careers, and academic programs. Parents with college degrees also earn more money and are in a better position to help support their children through college.

Finally, parents with degrees are more likely to have saved for their children's education. Even if you are in the process of getting your own degree when your children are entering college and are not yet in a financial situation where you can directly support your children, you're savvy about financial aid and how to maximize the financial aid your children can earn.

In 2003, children of parents with a Bachelor's degree or higher were almost twice as likely to be enrolled in college right after high school than children whose parents did not complete college. Children of parents with at least a Bachelor's degree were approximately 30 percent more likely to attend college than children of parents holding only a high school diploma. Even if you've had some college or vocational training, your children are more likely to go to college. What you do with your education after high school matters to your kids' futures!

The good news is that it's not too late to avoid the million-dollar mistake. There's never been a better time in higher education for adults to take part in the American dream!

This book is written to help you achieve that dream by getting a college degree.

I show you the ropes, especially the ones that you're not likely to learn from college catalogs, websites, or promotional materials. In this book, you will learn …

- How to think of yourself as a college student again.

- Why a college degree is important to increase your earning potential.

- What steps you need to take to prepare for and apply to college.

- How to choose the right college and degree program for you.

- How to identify colleges that serve adult students well.

- The options available for paying for college and reducing your college costs.

- How to manage family, work, and college all at the same time.

Don't worry if it's been years since you last stepped foot on a college campus. I fill you in on what has changed as well as what's stayed the same. For instance, technology now makes it easier for you to take classes, interact with your professors, and complete projects for class. Because computers are a big part of today's college experience, colleges expect you to have some basic computer skills. Fortunately, they offer computer literacy programs to get you up to speed.

You have more options than ever before for getting your degree. Not only are there more degree programs, but there are also more ways to get that degree. Whether you are sitting in a traditional college classroom, taking a televised course, or taking an online class from a college clear across the country, college is an exciting endeavor for adult students today.

More than half of all students enrolled in college are just like you—adults—with children, spouses, work responsibilities, and any number of competing interests. And although not all colleges have taken the steps to make their campuses adult-friendly, I help you identify the ones that are.

The Complete Idiot's Guide to Going Back to College contains five parts:

Part 1, "Thinking Like a Student Again," reacquaints you with the world of higher education and tells you what colleges are like for adult learners. You'll learn how to make sure your academic and career goals work together and find out what skills colleges expect adult students to have as they begin taking classes.

Part 2, "Choosing the Right College," guides you through the steps of selecting the right college and academic program. Learn about resources that help you compare colleges. And decide what kind of academic program and teaching/learning structure works best for you.

Part 3, "Paying for College," introduces you to the items you'll see on a college account bill. Learn how to lower some of your college costs and how to obtain all forms of financial aid. See how federal and state governments, as well as the campus you choose, support adult students with aid, tax benefits, and savings programs. Gain skills for deciding the best way for you to pay for your college experience.

Part 4, "On-Campus Survival Skills," guides you to the people and departments on campus that will help you with the enrollment process. Make your return to class stress-free with some commonsense strategies. Learn ways to interact in today's college classroom and build academic support systems. Also, find out where to go when you need help.

Part 5, "Managing College, Work, and Family," helps you prevent unexpected conflicts within your family as you return to college. Learn about your family responsibilities as a student and how to make your children a part of your college experience. See how adult students who have successfully made it through college managed to study for class, write papers, and prepare for exams. Learn the subtleties involved in resolving work-school conflicts.

Extras

Within each chapter, you'll see the following sidebars:

def•i•ni•tion

The world of higher education is full of jargon. These boxes help you make sense of all the academic mumbo-jumbo you'll encounter on campus.

Cautionary Tales

These boxes contain the "fine print" of going to college. These are the sorts of cautions I wish someone had shared with me when I went to college.

Extra Credit

Here you'll find tips for succeeding in college.

Office Hours

Find out what advice college faculty and staff have to offer adult students.

Student Center

Other adult students are probably your best source of information on succeeding in college. These boxes contain their stories.

Acknowledgments

Many people have shaped what I know about succeeding in college as an adult student. I thank my husband, Richard Mize, historian by night and journalist by day. I also thank my daughter, Ashley Buckbee. A special dedication goes to the late Hans Brisch, Chancellor Emeritus for the Oklahoma State Regents for Higher Education. I thank all of the state regents, especially Chairman John Massey and former regent Marlin "Ike" Glass; colleagues Joe Hagy and Marvanna Millican; John Hensley; Arthur L. Coleman; Ruth Ann Dreyer; Beth Bailey Jones; Pam Tate; Karen Pennell,

Jon Erickson, Cyndie Schmeiser, and Dick Ferguson (as much family as they are colleagues); Paul Lingenfelter; Carroll Wilson; parents Jerry and Nelda Jansen; my sister Sandra Jansen Dilbeck; Norma Lee Eckelkamp; Renee Wilmeth; Don Pitchford; and finally, former U.S. Secretary of Education Richard Riley, whose belief that all students deserve the life-changing benefits of a college degree motivates me and my work.

In addition, I want to offer a special debt of gratitude to development editor Jennifer Moore, who handled my questions and concerns with the perfect blend of diplomacy and helpfulness.

My acquisitions editor, Randy Ladenheim-Gil, is not only one of the finest professionals I've had the opportunity to work with, but also a fellow survivor and true believer when it comes to helping adults get their college degrees.

Special Thanks to the Technical Reviewer

The Complete Idiot's Guide to Going Back to College was reviewed by an expert who double-checked the accuracy of what you'll learn here, to help ensure that this book gives you everything you need to know about going to school as an adult. Special thanks are extended to my good friend and colleague Kristin Conklin, Senior Counselor to the Undersecretary, U.S. Department of Education.

Trademarks

All terms mentioned in this book that are known to be or are suspected of being trademarks or service marks have been appropriately capitalized. Alpha Books and Penguin Group (USA) Inc. cannot attest to the accuracy of this information. Use of a term in this book should not be regarded as affecting the validity of any trademark or service mark.

Part 1

Thinking Like a Student Again

Your "inner student" is starting to assert itself again! You have this uncontrollable urge to buy school supplies—clean notebooks, new pens and pencils, and maybe a big pink eraser just for old time's sake.

Thinking like a student is more than just having all the right supplies in hand, but it's a fun way to start. Going to college as a grown-up will be a whole different animal than when you were 18 and fresh out of high school. The good news is that you're not alone. As a matter of fact, adults are quickly becoming the majority on a number of campuses.

The first part of this book will help you jump-start your journey to a college degree. You'll want to gather up your credentials, find out about what opportunities are out there, and think about your career goals. I'll tell you what you can do to brush up your math and writing skills, help you make sense of all the jargon associated with colleges, and steer you toward a school that fits your needs.

## Chapter 1

College Orientation for Grown-Ups

In This Chapter

- Appreciating today's diverse college population
- Interacting with students and faculty who are younger than you
- Looking at what has changed about college in the last several years
- Considering how long it will take to get a degree
- Reviewing your degree program options

Adult students who are considering college sometimes talk themselves out of the idea because they think it's been too long since they had to "learn" anything. Don't fall into that kind of thinking! You have been learning and teaching yourself every single day, whether at work or at home. You're learning chemistry when you try a new recipe. You're learning critical thinking skills when you solve a problem in the office. You're learning management skills when you head up a committee at church. You're learning education skills when you teach your own children to read.

After you start taking classes, you'll be surprised by how quickly you start thinking like a student again. Words and phrases that you haven't heard or read in years—*credits, final exams, office hours*—will resurface and help you start thinking of life in terms of semesters.

Going back to college is a lot like riding a bike. You might feel shaky at first, but it won't take you long to get back into the groove. The role of being a student will come back to you quickly; all you have to do is open yourself up to the possibility of thinking and learning. And you'll probably find that you're a much better student now than you were when you were younger. You'll be a better student not only because you have a specific goal in mind, but also because you have been learning in real-life situations every day. You're an experienced learner, and you've been learning in the biggest classroom of all—the world around you.

Get Ready for a Wild and Rewarding Ride

If it's been a while since you've stepped foot on a college campus, prepare yourself for some changes. For one thing, the cafeteria that used to offer diners a choice of meatloaf or spaghetti now serves up a wide range of meal options, often including national franchises such as Subway, McDonald's, and Little Caesars. And for you caffeine junkies, there's probably a coffee counter where you can order your daily double skinny latté to keep you awake during that 3-hour geology lecture.

Cautionary Tales

Though you'll quickly get comfortable being back in class, guard against the temptation to challenge a faculty member simply because he or she is younger than you. Your professor is the expert in the classroom. A better way to share your experience is to illustrate an academic concept with a real-life example. When you do that, your fellow students learn from you as well.

You'll also probably see more—in some cases, *a lot more*—older students on campus than you remember. That's not just your eyes playing tricks on you. Colleges across the country are enrolling more adult students than they used to. As a matter of fact, as of the year 2000, half of all undergraduate college students in the United States were 26 years old or older. That means you'll find plenty of people just like you in college. In fact, the "traditional" students in the 18-to-24 age range occupy fewer of the seats in classrooms today than they did even a decade ago. Welcome to the new college majority—you and your fellow adult learners.

The following are some traits that are common among "nontraditional" students. See if you can find yourself among them. They are:

- ◆ Over the age of 25 and increasingly minority group members.

- Older teenagers with children.

- Military wives or husbands who have had to attend colleges in many locations as they work toward a degree.

- Former military members who are making a career change.

- Businessmen and -women seeking to upgrade their skills for advancement in the workplace.

Extra Credit

As you start this book, ignore the echoes of your finger-waving elementary school librarian about not writing in books. Write in this book! Take notes, write in the margins. Take your yellow and pink and orange highlighters and mark this book up from cover to cover. You'll get used to writing in books again, something everyone has to grow accustomed to when going to college.

When you're among people who have shared memories and similar life experiences, you'll be more likely to perceive your campus as a familiar and friendly environment. You'll be more likely to stick with college and earn your degree. As an adult student in college, your rich life experiences are assets! Bring those assets with you to class because it's a great time to be an adult student in college working toward a degree.

When it comes to technology, colleges have been advancing by leaps and bounds. For instance, chalk and chalkboards are being replaced by PowerPoint slides and screens. Instead of using pens and pencils to scribble lecture notes, many students type their notes into laptop computers. And whereas you used to have to go to a professor's office to get help, now your professor is as close as an e-mail address.

Colleges used to be static learning environments; they were places you *went* to learn and gain knowledge. Today, although colleges still have physical campuses, the delivery of academic content is anything but static. Courses or units of study within courses are offered in flexible ways, including on the Internet, on television, or by *podcasting*.

All these changes have made being an adult student a lot easier. That's good for you as a returning adult student because professors will often post their presentations on their website for you to download after class. You can listen to what your professor says more carefully while you're in class, rather than worrying about writing everything down.

def•i•ni•tion

Podcasting is the process of "broadcasting" digital video, audio, or visual content over the Internet to be viewed or heard on a computer or any small device that can store audio files and visual data.

Cautionary Tales _____

Technological improvements make it too easy for you to slip into bad habits. For example, don't skip class and download the lecture from the class website and think you've gleaned everything that took place in class. You'll miss valuable student-teacher interaction and illustrative examples of the material. What you learn in class isn't just in writing; it's experienced as part of the classroom environment.

Working full-time no longer prohibits you from learning multiple subjects or taking more than one class at a time. Courses that have at least part of their content delivered electronically allow you to review lessons, read ahead, study for a test, or interact with faculty or other students. You can do this while wearing your pajamas late at night at home, or using your lunch break at work.

You may not feel up to tackling all the latest technological innovations at the same time as you're working to learn your subject, though. No problem. If you prefer a traditional classroom with a professor lecturing to students, you can find plenty of those courses as well. Nothing, in fact, stands in the way of your being able to complete a college degree. You can learn any academic content you wish, at any hour of the day, no matter where you happen to be.

So forget any blanket assumptions that colleges are ivy-covered brick buildings with clock towers and bells. Your college today is as likely to be in a refurbished downtown office building as it is a standalone campus. And the educational experience is often enhanced by electronic interface between and among students and professors. College today is both a place and a process.

Breaking the Traditional Student Mold

As more adults are returning to college or going to college for the first time, they are challenging colleges to break many of the educational molds created long ago for a very *traditional* student population. So many adult students are returning to college campuses all over the United States that the word used to describe adult students, *nontraditional*, doesn't really apply anymore—though you'll still see it used regularly. On many campuses, especially in community colleges, adult students make up more than half the students enrolled.

Higher education has been moving in an adult-friendly direction for some time now. The increase in college access for women and minority students that happened because of civil rights actions has helped set the stage for colleges to meet a wider variety of college student needs.

def•i•ni•tion

A **traditional** college student is a student who attends college directly after graduation from high school. Traditional students start college at 17, 18, or 19 years of age. **Non-traditional** students are all the others; students who worked a few years before starting college or who began as a traditional student, left, and returned as an older adult.

When you add recent technological advances to the college equation, especially the flexibility of college course delivery and the sheer speed of give-and-take in the learning environment, you end up with a system that is primed to serve adult learners and meet their unique needs.

Courses and degree programs are more demand-driven than when the college population was more homogenous, and with more adult students on campuses, the supply of adult-friendly courses and campuses is on the rise and getting better all the time.

Colleges have also retooled their courses and class schedules to make sure they are serving the adult student demographic. In some cases, this means that colleges are offering classes on a 24-hour schedule or building shorter courses that a student can start at any time during the school year and finish at a pace that suits his schedule.

Your Peers: The "Over 25" Crowd

Of course, adult students still represent a very small minority on some college campuses. Some colleges are more likely to have adult students enrolled, while other colleges in the United States have chosen to focus on the traditional college student as their bread and butter. Large, traditional universities, where research is the biggest game on campus, tend to have more younger students. These also tend to be the campuses with the most well-known sports programs, with football and basketball teams playing games you'll find on your local TV channels.

Extra Credit

Just as the term "adult" means something different when you're talking about drinking age or voting eligibility, in higher education, an adult student is one who is 25 years of age or older. There are a number of reasons why the age 25 was chosen, but the most practical one is that the federal government uses this age when gathering data about adult college students.

If you feel more comfortable learning in an environment with the "over 25" crowd, you are more likely to find your peers in regional liberal arts colleges, community colleges, career colleges (where the focus of learning is on a specific career, such as nursing or business), and in for-profit universities that have made adults their focus. You'll also tend to find more adult students taking courses at night, on weekends, or through computer or televised distance learning. Some colleges even create courses specifically for adult learners.

But no matter where you choose to go to college, you're going to find like-minded adult peers who are going through college just like you. Your peers will have full-time or part-time jobs. They will be married, single, or divorced, and many will still have children at home.

Adult students, by nature of their ages and life experiences, are more likely to have more in common with each other than traditional students who come from all walks of life. Knowing this as you prepare to go to college may help give you a sense of security—you're not in this quest alone.

Faculty Views on Adult Students

College professors appreciate having adult students in their classrooms. It's not a hard-and-fast rule, but adult students tend to take their studies more seriously than traditional students. Adults are typically in college for a very specific reason, whether it's to improve their earning potential or make a midlife career change.

Office Hours
A faculty member in a large university appreciates adult students in her classroom: "In general, I find nontraditional students better because they value their education more for a variety of reasons: 1) it's usually out of their pockets, not Mom and Dad's; 2) students who balance families tend to be better because they understand the importance of focusing when given the chance; 3) they are there because they want to be, not because they have to be."

Traditional students are usually still in the process of deciding what they want to be when they grow up. And they also have a lot of "growing up" to do. Because adult students come to campus for more goal-oriented reasons, they tend to take the entire college experience more seriously. Adult students are more likely to attend class and not skip out. And adult students' genuine interest in the academic content is affirming for professors.

At the same time, adult students are often less sure of themselves and their ability to learn than younger students fresh out of high school. Faculty members find that adult students are more likely to seek individualized help through office hours or electronic interaction. Combine the adult student desire to learn with a lower self-confidence, and adult students are sometimes considered "high maintenance" by faculty. It's important to have a balance between seeking individual faculty assistance and the need to figure some things out on your own—or with a little help from your fellow students.

Even if you feel like you're slipping into the high maintenance category, rest assured that teachers prefer students ask questions and seek their assistance rather than allow confusion to fester. You and your professors have the same goal—to make sure you learn.

Extra Credit

Make use of faculty office hours and other forms of communication to keep pace in class. Keeping quiet when you don't understand a concept is counterproductive. Faculty members will help you outside of class time, but you have to ask for help to receive it.

My friend John, who is a community college professor, sent me a list of all the things he likes about having adult students in class. He's taught adults and young students alike for a long time, and he's collected some fun stories through the years. Here's what John has to say about adult learners:

- They're more serious students. They don't view class as play time—they don't goof around.

- They have life experiences that contribute to the class and their academic success.

- They're better students. A colleague of mine several years ago showed that the grade point averages for nontraditional students were higher than the younger students. That's a trend I've seen myself as well.

- They're more respectful. I've yet to see a nontraditional student put his head on the desk and try to take a nap while I lecture. They are far more likely to call me "Doctor," affording me the respect of the academic title.

- They come to class more regularly, even though they usually have more potential conflicts in their daily routine.

- Adult students actually study and take responsibility for their grades. A young man in one of my introductory classes this semester sits in the front row without a pencil, pen, textbook, or notebook. His desk is totally bare. He can't understand why his grades are so bad!

◆ Older students seem to enjoy classes. Younger students tend to see them as a chore.

◆ Older students seem to have been better prepared in high school than current students are.

◆ Older students are also more likely to actually study at home.

John, like many other college faculty, has had positive experiences with adult students. His experiences and sentiments are commonly held among college faculty: adult students are wanted in class, and are welcome.

How Long Will It Take to Get a Degree?

The time it will take you to complete a degree depends on the type of degree you seek and if you have any prior college experience. It will also depend on whether you attend school full-time or part-time.

If you took college courses right out of high school and not too many years have passed, you might be able to pick up where you left off. If you haven't taken any college courses or you're returning to college to earn a completely different degree than you had planned when you first went to college, you'll probably need to start from scratch. The time frame depends on whether you return to college full-time or part-time, the type of degree you seek, and whether you need a few refresher courses before you return to college-level academic work.

Even though the answer to the question "How long does it take to get a college degree?" is "It depends," there are some trends and basic parameters associated with each type of general degree program. For example, no matter what degree area you choose, you will be required to take general education courses. These are the kind of classes that are required of all college graduates and are typically taken during the freshman and sophomore years in college. You might remember these courses as "the basics." The basics may differ slightly, however, depending on whether your focus of study is liberal arts-oriented or science-oriented.

Associate's Degrees and Certificates

Associate's degrees are often referred to as "two-year degrees" because, traditionally, students attending college full-time could complete such a degree in two years. Associate's degrees are typically offered at community or junior colleges and include general education courses plus courses specific to your Associate's degree require-ments. In general, you can choose among an *Associate of Arts* degree (A.A.), an *Associate of Science* (A.S.) degree, or, if your program is primarily technical or technological, you can obtain an *Associate in Applied Sciences* (A.A.S) degree.

def•i•ni•tion

An **Associate of Arts** degree is a degree you typically earn because you plan, eventu-ally, to seek a four-year Bachelor of Arts degree. Similarly, an **Associate of Science** degree prepares you for a Bachelor of Science degree. Think of those two Associate degrees as a certified midpoint of your college career, though some students earn only an Associate degree and enter the workforce with two years of college study. An **Asso-ciate in Applied Sciences** can allow you to jump right into the workforce with your new credentials. For example, you can obtain an A.A.S. in manufacturing technology or heat-ing and air conditioning and immediately use that credential to find a job.

Careers and professions that require only an Associate's degree were once more com-mon than they are now. More and more, today's jobs require a Bachelor's degree. A good example of careers that still require an Associate's degree include many health careers, such as lower-level nursing or radi-ology technicians. Teacher's aides and other *paraprofessional careers* require Associate's degrees as well.

def•i•ni•tion

Paraprofessional careers are those in which you help profes-sionals in your field with their professional duties. For example, a paralegal helps attorneys in their professional endeavors and an intake counselor in a hospital helps the licensed counselors with their work. Lower-level degrees are required for paraprofessional careers.

Certificates and industry certifications are often also earned during the process of obtaining an Associate's degree. For example, you may earn an A.A.S. degree in an automotive field and also take the Automotive Service Excellence (ASE) certification test. ASE certification is a quality assurance certification based on automotive service industry standards, as opposed to an academic certificate. Or you might earn academic certificates concurrently with your degree. For example, if you pursue an A.S. degree in a business field, you might be awarded an academic certificate for proficiency in one or more business-related software applications.

Today's students working toward Associate's degrees are typically taking courses at community colleges. Many students attend a community college first because it is, literally, a part of the community. For adult students, the community college is often the closest campus to home and work. The convenience of the community college makes it an ideal place for adult students to get started toward a degree.

> **Cautionary Tales** _____
>
> If you are working on a degree at a community college and choose to transfer to a four-year college or university before completing an Associate's degree, you should look into what degrees and courses will transfer. The last thing you want to do is take classes for a year at a community college only to find that you have to start from scratch at your new four-year college or university. Work closely with an academic advisor to ensure that you are choosing courses and programs that will transfer if you plan to eventually earn a higher degree than an Associate's degree.

Many Associate's degrees are accepted by four-year colleges and universities that have articulation agreements with the community college that awarded the degree. An articulation agreement is an agreement between colleges that allows for transfer of degree credits between two partner colleges or among colleges within a system or state.

It now takes students an average of three years to obtain an Associate's degree "on time." It's not that there are more classes than there used to be, or that it's more difficult to get an Associate's degree. Rather, it's because more students of all ages are working at least part-time and have less time for school.

Bachelor's Degrees

Most students, traditional and adult alike, attend college for the purpose of earning a Bachelor's degree. Unlike the decline in the demand for associate degrees in many professions, the demand for Bachelor's degrees has actually increased. Bachelor's degrees are earned in colleges that range from small liberal arts schools to large research universities.

The path to a Bachelor's degree begins with general education courses, normally completed during the freshman and sophomore years of college. At some point during your general education courses, you will declare a major and a minor. Your major is your major course of study; the minor is generally a related course of study to your major, but it can also be an entirely different field altogether.

The major is the academic content area in which you expect to earn a degree. For example, a philosophy major will earn a Bachelor's degree in philosophy. An education major will earn a Bachelor's degree in education.

Extra Credit

Depending on your goals and how much time you have to dedicate to college, consider whether you can manage to earn a double major or additional credentials or certificates. The double major makes you more marketable in multiple career fields. The added certificates also make you more marketable because you hold industry-standard credentials that are respected by employers. Many states and community colleges offer state-specific, industry-recognized certifications that can help you secure a good job.

Your minor field of study indicates a second academic area in which you choose to take more courses or learn more content. If you choose a closely related field as a minor, you may be able to count courses in your major area as meeting the requirements for completing your minor. An example of a closely related field would be a business major and a marketing minor. Many courses you take could potentially meet the requirements for either your major or minor, or in some cases, both.

If you choose a complementary field as a minor, you'll probably need to take more courses; however, doing so is also likely to expand your knowledge base and also give you more flexibility in the work world. An example of a complementary field would be a computer science major and a mathematics minor. When selecting a complementary minor field of study, you should also investigate how many more courses would be required for you to have a double major. Using the computer science and math example, if you took just a few more mathematics courses, you might have enough credits to earn a double major of computer science and mathematics.

Student Center

A colleague in his 40s, working in a second career, told me, "After eight years as a professional writer and editor, I did an about left-face and jumped back into school for a second B.S. in the sciences to change careers. I found that nothing and everything had changed since my first degree … my confidence in small group discussions inevitably wins me a leadership role … my motivation was much, much higher for schoolwork because I no longer had dating and dorm life to distract me."

Taking the same example a step further, you also have the option to earn *two* Bachelor's degrees if you meet the course requirements in both academic areas. With an additional investment of time, you can have a Bachelor's degree in computer science *and* a Bachelor's degree in mathematics. How you choose to structure your academic plan and choose your major and minor is an individual decision that is based on your career and academic accomplishment goals.

Extra Credit

Your choice of degree program will often dictate whether the degree you seek is an arts degree (A.A. or B.A.) or a science degree (A.S. or B.S.). Some degree programs allow you to choose either an arts degree or a science degree, giving you the flexibility to take courses in subjects you prefer.

Your choice of academic major will also dictate the *kind* of Bachelor's degree you will earn. A major in computer science and minor in mathematics, for example, would fall under a Bachelor of Science (B.S.) degree. Earning a Bachelor of Science degree means that you have taken more science courses as you worked toward your degree than humanities or liberal arts courses. An English major, however, is most likely to earn a Bachelor of Arts (B.A.) degree; that's because a person choosing to become an English major is more likely to take more humanities-related and liberal arts courses.

The act of *declaring a major* also helps guide the elective courses that you will take for the purposes of completing your general education requirements. The earlier in your college career that you declare a major, the less likely you will choose to take classes that won't "count" toward your degree requirements.

def•i•ni•tion

Declaring a major is a formal process that you undertake with the assistance of your academic advisor. As you work with your advisor on planning your college experience, she will help you choose not only the right major for your academic and career goals, but also the right time to declare a major.

Just as the Associate's degree is no longer, in reality, a two-year degree, the Bachelor's degree is rarely completed in four years. Only students who have the luxury of taking full course loads all year long will complete their degree in four years.

The majority of students, adult and traditional students alike, works at least part-time and cannot complete their Bachelor's degree within four years. As a working adult, you should be realistic about how long it might take you to obtain a Bachelor's degree. You'll be in the majority if you take longer than four years. In fact, the standard in higher education for the receipt of a Bachelor's degree is now six years, not four.

Cautionary Tales

Don't set expectations for yourself too high; you will only end up disappointing yourself. Be realistic about how long it will take you to complete your degree. Few students complete a Bachelor's degree in four years. Mentally, grant yourself plenty of time to finish your degree.

The added accessibility of college to more people, no matter their gender, race, ethnicity, or age, has made time to degree completion longer than when colleges were only populated by young students from families of means. Among adult students—and even among a greater number of traditional students—work and family are now an everyday part of the college completion equation.

Some Careers Require More Than a Bachelor's Degree

Although most of the careers you are considering require only a Bachelor's degree, some fields require a graduate degree or other coursework beyond a Bachelor's degree. In other fields, graduate degrees aren't required, but can help you earn more money or advance to higher levels within your profession. As you are choosing which degree program to complete, make certain that you know what the expected *terminal degree* is.

def•i•ni•tion

A **terminal degree** is the lowest college degree required for a certain profession. Without paying careful attention to the interrelationship between professions and required college degrees, you could easily find yourself with a nonterminal Bachelor's degree that won't help you within your chosen profession.

In accounting or education, for example, you can leave college with a Bachelor's degree and immediately enter those professions. However, psychology requires graduate degrees to enter most professions. In part, degree requirements are dictated by state and/or national licensing or certification criteria for certain professions. For example, if you want to be a licensed marriage and family therapist or a licensed professional counselor, you must complete at least a *Master's degree*. Not only is this requirement a function of licensing requirements, it's also required by health insurance companies for payment of health benefits.

def•i•ni•tion

A **Master's degree** is a graduate degree that involves two or more years of full-time graduate study. This graduate degree is often needed to work in fields requiring licensure and is also available for certain fields such as education to increase earning potential or to prepare students for management or administrative positions.

Some fields require *doctoral degrees*, such as a Ph.D. (Doctorate of Philosophy) or an Ed.D. (Doctorate in Education). High-level professions such as medicine (Medical

Doctorate, or M.D.), pharmacy (Pharmacy Doctorate, or Pharm.D.), or law (Juris Doctorate, or J.D.) also require higher graduate degrees.

Graduate school and professions requiring graduate degrees are specific enough to warrant a complete book just on graduate school. For now, as an adult college student planning your college career, it's important to know up front if the degree program you are choosing has the Bachelor's degree as a terminal degree or whether graduate school is required.

You're Never Too Old to Go Back to School

Every May, newspapers across the country are peppered with wonderful stories of older Americans obtaining a college degree. Some of these graduates are in their 70s or 80s when they attend their commencement ceremonies! These stories prove that college is possible for everyone.

No matter your age or stage, American colleges and universities have something to offer that will enrich your lives, expand your thinking, and even help you earn more money and advance in your job. Knowing the basics about your choices in college degrees is just the first step to preparing for your return to college.

Checklist of actions that will prepare you to be a student again:

❑ Buy a few school supplies. Nothing makes you feel more like a student again than a new set of pens or pencils, a five-subject spiral notebook, or a shiny new laptop computer. Use these supplies to create your road map back to college, drawing from what you learn in this book.

❑ Talk to a friend or colleague who has returned to college as an adult and draw lessons from his experiences. Learn what to do and what *not* to do!

❑ Write down why you want to go to college again and what you hope to gain. At this point, you're writing this from your heart—you can fill in the details later, after you've read subsequent chapters in this book.

❑ Talk to your family about your thoughts of returning to college. Later, you'll sit down and talk specifics. For now, use conversation with your family as a means to keep you motivated to go through the process and the paperwork you'll need to do.

❑ Refer to yourself as a student. You may also be a mom or dad; you might be a nurse or bank teller or automotive mechanic. But you can add "student" to your list when you refer to yourself.

The Least You Need to Know

- ◆ You'll find many other adult students on campus.
- ◆ College courses are flexible and can be completed on campus or online.
- ◆ Investigate the type of degree you will need for the career you wish to enter.
- ◆ Be realistic and know that earning a college degree will take time.
- ◆ Starting now, think of yourself as a student.

Matching Your Career with a College Degree

In This Chapter

- ◆ Going for your dream job
- ◆ Making a midlife career change
- ◆ Advancing in your current career path
- ◆ Combining college and career

Few people go to college simply for the sake of earning a degree. College students of all ages are working toward a degree for the express purpose of gaining skills and knowledge that will help them have a rewarding career.

One of the most popular reasons adults return to school is that they can't move up into higher positions in their own career without further education. Others go back to college to get the kind of job they've always wanted but never had before. This chapter explores both of these reasons for going back to college, and also offers advice for juggling your current job while going back to school.

It's Time to Pursue Your Dream

Life events may have forced you to take a job you didn't really want. Millions of Americans, particularly those with families, have put their career goals aside to meet more pressing obligations. Even though you've never lost your childhood desire to be a veterinarian, you go to work every day to sell insurance. You might like selling insurance just fine, but deep within you, you know there is a veterinarian waiting to emerge.

Maybe your dream job didn't offer the kind of health benefits you needed, or perhaps the hours made it impossible to raise your family. Or maybe your dream job required a college degree that you didn't have the time or the money to earn. But that doesn't mean you have to work in an unfulfilling job until the day you die.

Many adults are working in jobs because that's the path life dished out to them, while all the time, they've been suppressing their true career desires. Take the lid off any suppressed desires for learning and career. College awaits you.

Extra Credit _____

Colleges understand the unique needs of people changing careers in the middle of their work life. Make sure college personnel you work with know that you're changing careers. It will help them help you through the process.

It's never too late to change your path, to change your job, to move back to what you wanted to be when you grew up. You should temper your enthusiasm with realism, of course, because you really can't go back to college at age 45 and be a star on the college football team. For most dream careers, though, your age is not an obstacle; your drive and enthusiasm for learning are all that matter!

Can you really get your dream job by going back to college? Absolutely!

Student Center

In her early 50s, Margaret decided to go to college and get her degree so she could have her dream job. A single mother of five teenage children, Margaret never stopped working toward her dream. She moved her family from Montana to Kansas so she could attend the college of her choice. There, Margaret earned her undergraduate degree. She then moved her family again and earned her Doctoral degree in yet another state. Margaret kept going until she became a professor. She now lives in the northeastern United States and helps students of all ages reach their own degree and career goals.

Why Working Adults Are Returning to School

Adult students between the ages of 25 and 34 have typically already been in the workforce for a number of years. They might be working in the same job since they graduated from high school. However, they realize that their ability to move up in their current job is limited. They also realize that their marketability in other jobs or careers is hampered by their lack of a college degree. In short, there is a career "ceiling" for people who don't possess a college degree. Growth in earning potential may also be limited by the lack of a college degree.

Office Hours

A friend of mine who holds a full-time job but also chooses to spend his evenings as a part-time faculty member shared the following insights with me: "I'm teaching a night class right now, and most of my students are nontraditional ... I actually love it and find the students are warm and engaged in a way that I don't usually encounter. One way I find they differ most is in their time management. Most of them work full-time and are a) more skilled in managing their time and b) more realistic about what can get done and what obstacles they'll have to work around."

Although older adult students may be returning to college for the same reason as those in the 25 to 34 age range, it is more likely that students returning to college when middle-aged are doing so for the purposes of a midlife career change. Many have worked in a job for 20 or more years, are ready to do something new, and are young enough to enjoy a full and satisfying second career.

Even older students, especially those who have retired, are most likely to be returning to college for the enrichment experience.

Increased Earning Potential

Regardless of why adult students return to college, all data show that their earning potential increases greatly with more education. Men and women who only have a high school diploma earn much less than those who have completed some college or an Associate's degree. If you have a Bachelor's degree, you are likely to earn more than someone with an Associate's degree, on average. And because of the nature of careers requiring graduate degrees, the earning potential of Master's and Doctoral degree holders is greater than all other categories of educational attainment.

The following figure illustrates the average earnings by level of education. Note the difference just between the high school graduate and the Bachelor's degree holder. In addition to the expected increase in annual salary, Bachelor's degree holders will earn, on average, a million dollars more in a lifetime than people who only completed high school.

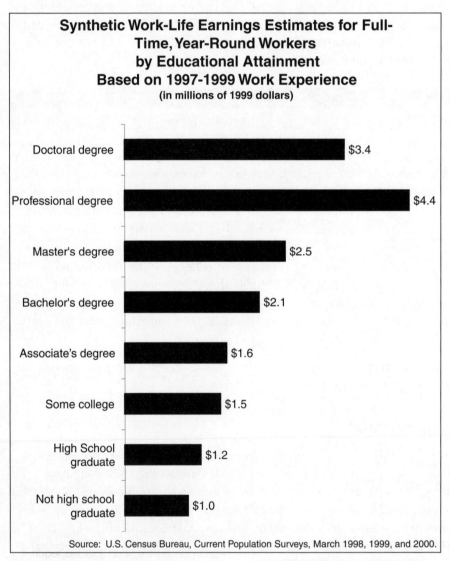

Synthetic Work-Life Earnings Estimates for Full-Time, Year-Round Workers
by Educational Attainment
Based on 1997-1999 Work Experience
(in millions of 1999 dollars)

Doctoral degree	$3.4
Professional degree	$4.4
Master's degree	$2.5
Bachelor's degree	$2.1
Associate's degree	$1.6
Some college	$1.5
High School graduate	$1.2
Not high school graduate	$1.0

Source: U.S. Census Bureau, Current Population Surveys, March 1998, 1999, and 2000.

This chart shows that the more education Americans get, the more likely they are to earn higher wages.

Moving Up in Your Current Job

Before you make a *degree program* decision, take stock of what opportunities for advancement exist in your current place of employment. Can you reasonably expect to move up in your company or business by getting a college degree? Are the requirements for upper-level positions in your company such that a college degree would give you a competitive advantage if you sought a higher position? Is the additional salary in place to adequately reward you for your new level of responsibility and education?

def•i•ni•tion

A **degree program** is a program with a specified sequence and number of courses required to obtain a degree in a particular academic content area. Degree programs are typically regulated by a state-level higher education entity and/or by licensing requirements for specific professions.

If you aren't sure which college degree will help you advance in your current job, visit your Human Resources director or your company's employee training director. These professionals can give you practical information about your company's priorities for degreed workers before you seek academic advice on a college campus. When seeking a college degree to help you advance within your current career field, the more communication with Human Resources officers, supervisors, or management, the better. Not only will your desire to move up in the company be recognized by decision-makers, you'll enter a sort of partnership with your employer that can help you gain the support and time you need to complete your degree.

Making a Mid-Career Switch

One career/college degree area that sees a large number of students making mid-career changes is education. Men and women who have worked in private business or who have retired from the military often find teaching a highly rewarding second career.

States and individual colleges also develop special programs in their education departments for those making mid-career changes to teaching because some areas of teaching are in short supply. States and colleges also create incentives for career areas that either

Extra Credit

The federal government encourages retired military personnel to become teachers through the Troops to Teachers program. Through the program, the government offers special incentives to retired military members and to those who were discharged honorably so they can join the teaching force as a second career. You can learn more about this program at www.ed.gov.

def•i•ni•tion

enhance the state's workforce or help the state meet economic development goals. Pay attention to these sorts of incentives, as they are a good barometer of careers that are in short supply of employees in a state.

Other career areas are experiencing shortages in available personnel because of aging Baby Boomers. To promote college degrees in shortage areas, employers and colleges are offering incentives, scholarships, signing bonuses, and more. Careers with dramatic shortages are in the health professions. Not only are the shortages a result of retiring Boomers, they are also a result of Boomers requiring more health-care services than when they were younger.

Nationwide, the shortage of nurses and medical support personnel is reaching critical levels. Health providers, in partnership with vocational and higher education leaders, are helping students interested in health careers attend college and earn a health-related degree. In some cases, hospital groups will pay all education costs in return for the agreement that the student work at the same hospital after graduation.

These are just a few examples of career paths for jobs in which there are few qualified people to fill empty slots in the workforce. You can learn about more career areas from the *career center* on your campus.

Negotiating with Your Employer for School Time

At some point in your journey toward a degree, you will probably need to take one or more courses that are only offered when you're supposed to be on the job. This will require some planning and negotiating on your part.

If you're seeking a degree to advance in your current job, you may be able to get your employer to consider the time you spend in school in part or in full as "work time." You may also be able to create a more flexible work schedule around your classes.

The further in advance you can talk to your employer about your needs for flexibility, the better. Most employers will do what they can to help you earn a college degree.

If you work in a field in which flexibility is not possible, your best strategy for blending work and college is to seek the assistance of academic advisors on campus; they may be able to help create opportunities for fulfilling course requirements with alternative classes or independent study. Even if your degree program requires a prescribed sequence of courses before you obtain your degree, *policy exceptions* are always possible. College personnel will not generally offer a petition for a policy exception up front; you need to ask for such exceptions.

Extra Credit

If you use a computer in your current job, negotiate with your employer to use your work computer after hours for school purposes. Some employers allow workers to use computers to write papers or download information from class. The best employers know that benefits like these generate loyalty and goodwill among their employees.

def•i•ni•tion

Policy exceptions are granted on a case-by-case basis. Your academic or faculty advisor can request a policy exception for alternate courses for your degree program if your work interferes with your ability to take the traditional sequence of courses. Use policy exceptions as a last resort, after all other options have been exhausted.

How College Benefits Employers

Your employer has made an investment in you. Whether you have been on the job for 2 years or 10, your supervisor has been teaching you to become better at your job. Your employer has supported you and invested salary and benefit packages in return for your work. Your company may have also provided you with on-the-job training.

Employers sometimes also invest in their employees by helping pay for college education. Some employee tuition assistance

Extra Credit

Tuition assistance programs are becoming more common as a benefit that employers provide for their employees. Tuition assistance programs also come with tax benefits for the employee, provided that the tuition assistance is for the purposes of obtaining a Bachelor's degree or below.

programs cover college expenses in any college degree area, while others provide funding for college only in degree areas related to an employee's current job. Take advantage of this option if it's available to you. (See Chapter 9 for more on this topic.)

By investing in their employees' education, employers not only add an attractive option to an employee's benefit package, they also "grow" their own managers and/or executives. Paying for employees' education also instills employee loyalty to the company. And degreed employees can also help train others who join the company or business, thereby reducing the time it takes new employees to learn all aspects of the job. It's simply a good business practice for companies to provide tuition support for their employees.

Cautionary Tales

You are less likely to receive monetary or career support from your current employer if you are seeking a college degree in a field unrelated to your current job. Companies prefer to invest in employees who are going to stick around.

Employers aren't stupid. They know that the more educated their workforce is, the fewer employees they'll need. When a company has a highly degreed workforce, the company is populated with employees who can perform multiple skills and more efficiently solve problems and think on their feet.

Companies are eager to help their employees seek additional education if it will yield a benefit for them. However, don't be afraid to negotiate time for your college classes with your employer even if you are making a wholesale career change, especially if a generalized tuition assistance program is one of your benefits. As long as you are getting your current job done and meeting the requirements of your position, your employer can become an ally for your dream job and college degree.

How Your Job Will Benefit Your Studies

Even if you've never set foot on a college campus and are taking your first steps toward a degree, you may be bringing more to your college studies than you think. Depending on what your current job is, it's likely that you've had some form of training, certification, or professional development for your job.

All those experiences, from one-day seminars on preventing harassment in the workplace, to studying complicated manuals for new equipment, to taking phone calls and organizing your work, involve skills that will help you in college! Those skills may not stand out to you as activities that prepare you to enter college as an adult, but they do. Think of your seminar at work on preventing harassment as analogous to a sociology class. If you can study a complicated manual and use the equipment as the directions indicate, then you can conduct a chemistry lab assignment, or even write a rudimentary computer program. If you're accustomed to organizing, filing, planning events, or scheduling personnel, then you are already adept at managing tasks and time in such a way that you can step into the role of a college student with very little trouble.

Far too often adult students don't realize that they are bringing critical skills with them to the college campus—skills that younger peers right out of high school don't have. Use these life experiences and skills and translate them into the college environment. Don't be intimidated by the college bureaucracy or the fact that you might have to go to five different places on a college campus to arrange classes, seek advisement, create your class schedule, or even pay for classes. If you've had a job and a family, you are more than prepared to conquer these tasks!

The following items should appear on your "to do" list when it comes to matching career and college choices:

Checklist of actions for meeting your college and career goals:

❏ Explore options for college degrees to help you advance in your current job. Talk to your Human Resources director and your supervisor, and get specific information on what it will take for you to move into positions with more responsibility and higher salary.

❏ Find out if college tuition benefits are available at your workplace. If tuition assistance is available, check to see if the benefits only apply for degrees directly related to your career area, or if your company will support your college experience regardless of your degree choice.

❏ Study the priorities for jobs in your state. The main website for your state's governor is a good place to start looking for your state's economic and workforce priorities. Ask college personnel about incentives in priority career areas, particularly those in which shortages are evident. Or check America's Career Information Network at www.acinet.org for a national perspective.

❏ Make an appointment to talk to your supervisor about your plans to return to college. Use this meeting to inquire about the flexibility of your work schedule and how willing your employer might be to help you manage college and work at the same time.

The Least You Need to Know

- ◆ Making a drastic career change in middle age is common and rewarding.

- ◆ A college education can greatly increase your earning potential.

- ◆ Many employers understand the value of a college education for their employees and are willing to be flexible when classes conflict with work.

- ◆ Your time in the work world has already given you important skills needed in college.

Basic Skills, Common Fears

In This Chapter

- ◆ Overcoming reading, writing, and mathematics anxieties
- ◆ Improving your skills
- ◆ Speaking up in class
- ◆ Getting computer savvy

If you're worried about your level of proficiency when it comes to basic academic skills, welcome to the club. It's very common for adult students to lack confidence in their reading, writing, and math abilities. And the thought of having to speak up in class sends shivers down the spines of college students of all ages—even that hip 19-year-old sitting in the back row of Psychology 101.

Though these fears are common, many adults sell themselves short when it comes to basic skill readiness. This lack of confidence keeps large numbers of adult students from re-entering college. The purpose of this chapter is to help you overcome your anxieties and to tell you what you can do to brush up on your skills. Sure, you might need to exercise parts of your brain that haven't had any action since your senior year of high school, but a little mental workout never hurt anyone!

Reading

You'll be doing a lot of reading in college. In the following sections I offer some ideas for assessing and improving your reading skills.

Reading for Information Versus Reading for Pleasure

Reading a passage for the purposes of extracting information is a lot different than reading for pleasure. Reading for information is more purposeful and active. Reading for pleasure is a more passive form of reading.

When reading to extract information, you must be able to discern the relative importance of the facts presented to you and later, perhaps on a test or in an essay, reproduce those facts in your own words. Although this might sound difficult, you probably read for information all the time without even thinking about it. You're doing so right now, in fact! You're also reading for information when you read the instructions for putting together a bookshelf, or figuring out how to run your DVD player, or assembling your children's new swing set.

Cautionary Tales

It's okay to use CliffsNotes or other literary summaries to help you recall important points in your reading. But it's essential that you also read the assigned book from cover to cover. Doing so will help you improve your comprehension of the text as well as your overall literacy.

An excellent set of resources for testing your ability to read for information is available at www.act.org, the website for the not-for-profit company that delivers the ACT college admissions test. On this site, you can take a practice ACT assessment and see how you perform on the reading subtest on the ACT. For the reading portion of the test, you read through passages and answer questions on their content.

Extra Credit

While you're at the ACT website, take a few minutes to explore their workforce development services section. This section can be valuable for assessing your basic skills in reading, listening, applied mathematics, and other areas that are important in the work world. WorkKeys assessments, developed by ACT, allow you to assess your skills in the context of work environment scenarios and real-world problems. For example, when you test your reading skills, you will be given questions that are relevant in the work world, as opposed to literary or hypothetical reading passages.

Nothing instills confidence like *really* knowing what you know and are able to do. Before convincing yourself that you're not a proficient reader, take the time to assess your abilities.

Improving Your Reading

The best way to improve your reading is to read. Of course, how you read is important, as is what you read. The following activities can help improve your reading speed and comprehension as well as your ability to retain that information for longer periods of time:

◆ **Read newspapers.** Read newspapers in a new way—read *purposefully*. Read so you can remember facts or story points with a level of detail that would allow you to write a paragraph summarizing what you've read. Test your ability to comprehend and retain what you've read by telling friends and colleagues about the story or stories.

Pay particular attention to straight news stories, which are largely factual. Also read feature stories, which usually have a human interest component. Some of the best writers in the world are journalists, so you might even improve your writing skills by reading newspapers.

◆ **Read instructions or instruction manuals.** Read instructions in such a way that you can picture steps or activities in your mind as you read. It's a good test of your ability to turn words into actions—can you see in your mind what the instructions are telling you? Once you've read the narrative description of the tasks outlined in the manual, compare what you envisioned with illustrations of the actions if they are included in the manual.

◆ **Read poetry and interpretations of the poems.** Reading poetry, even if you don't consider yourself a poetry "buff," will hone your interpretive skills and also show you how spare language can communicate large-scale themes. Compare what you believe a certain poem means with formal, published interpretations of the work. How is your interpretation similar or different?

Many adult learners are concerned with their reading speed. Before investing money in programs or services that make big promises about improving the speed of your reading, know that comprehending what you read is far more important to success in college than all-out speed. You don't have to be a speed-reader to be successful in college; you do, however, need to remember what you've read and be able to discuss it or write about it intelligently.

Writing

Being able to write is such an integral part of a college education that most colleges require students to complete some form of writing assessment before being placed in college-level courses.

Although early life experiences and early schooling play a key role in people's writing abilities, even marginal writers can improve their writing skills. All they have to do is practice!

Improve Your Writing Daily

You can improve your writing by writing often. Write something every day, if you can, and write about different topics. Describe things you see—a game-winning home run, a breathtaking sunset, your dog's pursuit of a squirrel. Summarize a magazine or newspaper article you've read. Write a letter to a relative you haven't talked to in a while, sharing the latest family news.

Build your confidence, your ability to reflect, and your writing skills at the same time by starting a journal. Write in your journal at the end of each day. Act as if you are a famous person whose writings might be published someday. This will make you more careful about word selection and punctuation, and also help you use more descriptive language.

Technological advances have made spelling less of an issue in writing, as most people now use word processing software that checks and catches spelling errors. Some of the brightest people and the best writers confess that they're not good spellers. Fortunately, technology allows you to focus on the quality of your writing without worrying about your spelling ability.

Extra Credit _____

Don't rely completely on a computer to catch your spelling errors. One weakness of spell-check programs is that they cannot spot typos that are actually words. For example, if you mean to write "by means of" but instead write "my beans of" (a real example from my own academic history), the computer won't catch the error. Missing such errors can lead to some amusing reading, but won't earn you points in the classroom.

Get Feedback on Your Writing

With writing, though, it's not only important that you write, it's also important that you get constructive feedback on your writing. And to get feedback, you need to be willing to accept constructive criticism. This is a very hard thing for most people to do. The important thing to remember is that when people are giving you feedback on your writing, they are giving you feedback on what you *do*, not who you are!

When you write, it's perfectly natural for you to feel as if you've taken something deep inside and exposed it for the whole world to view. But to learn how to write better, you must take a dispassionate view of your writing. Accept criticism as a means to make your writing better; it's not a criticism of you or your character, just your writing.

Find people who write well and ask them to critique your writing. Ask a friend or your spouse to read short passages and give you feedback.

A good way to critique your own writing is to read what you've written aloud. You will be able to hear when ideas aren't expressed fully or when you've expressed a concept awkwardly. When you read your work aloud, you'll hear noun-verb disagreements and any run-on sentences. After a while, you'll be able to see and hear whether you are writing well.

Extra Credit

Lose the ego when you're submitting your writing to friends or colleagues for review. Ask them to be brutally honest about your writing. Not only will this prepare you for the kind of feedback you'll get from college professors, it'll help you be a better writer overall. You can't shy away from constructive criticism if you want to be a better writer.

Techniques to Make Writing Easier

When it comes to sending off a quick e-mail to a colleague or writing a letter to your mother, you rarely find yourself worrying about your punctuation or sweating over word choice. One way to make writing easier is to view formal writing as something you might do informally as a matter of course.

For example, suppose you're given the assignment to write a paper on wind-powered energy. You wouldn't automatically be an expert on the topic, so your first step would be to compile research on the topic. You would build a set of facts about this form of energy and possibly assert a position on environmental or societal impact.

But after you do your research, where do you start writing? You've already learned all your parts of speech; you might remember what a "thesis sentence" is, or a topic sentence. You can probably still hear your high school English teacher in your head as you sit in front of the blank page.

Beginning to put words on that blank page will be easier if you do a simple mental trick: pretend that you are writing to your mom or dad, to your spouse, or to a friend. If it helps, include "Dear Mom" at the top of the page and write as if you're telling someone you know well about wind-powered energy. Write with the same enthusiasm you use when writing to people close to you.

This simple technique has helped many college students break through their mental blocks about writing for class. When you tell yourself that you're writing for someone you know, it becomes much easier to put the first word on the blank page and then tell your story.

Math

Few subjects cause as much anxiety as mathematics. Adult students aren't alone in being concerned about their math proficiency when they go to college. The majority of students who graduate from high school are not prepared to do college-level math.

Colleges have instituted systems to improve and/or restore mathematics skills for adult and traditional students alike by creating what are called developmental or remedial courses. They serve as "refresher" courses for students who need to hone basic math skills before taking college-level math classes.

Regaining Forgotten Math Skills

Math skills are of the "use it or lose it" variety. If you're not using math skills regularly, you probably won't remember how to complete some of the more abstract mathematics you learned back in high school. Because of this, it's common for returning students to take a refresher, or developmental, course before enrolling in college-level math.

Developmental courses, which are often called *zero-level* courses, rarely "count" for college credit. Don't be surprised if you have to take two or three semesters of developmental mathematics before entering an official college algebra course.

def•i•ni•tion

Zero-level courses are developmental or remedial courses that traditional and adult students take to strengthen skills in core academic areas. The courses cost money and will delay your entry into college-level courses in the content area in which your skills are weak. They can, however, help you regain forgotten skills and ensure that you're ready to succeed in credit-bearing college courses.

Be realistic about your math skills and be willing to accept that you might need to take one or more refresher courses to get yourself up to speed. Many colleges will give you a mathematics placement assessment, though this will depend on how long it has been since you were last in college and also on local college policies. A placement assessment will help you determine which math course is the best first course for you.

After you have taken developmental courses in math or sought math *tutoring* to rebuild your forgotten math skills, you should be ready to enter a college-level math course.

def•i•ni•tion

Tutoring is one-on-one instruction between a student and someone proficient in a particular field. On campus, organized tutoring centers are usually paid for with student fees and are available to you at no charge. However, if you engage a tutor before you enroll in college to help you regain your math skills, you will be expected to pay for the tutor's time.

Algebra Is Not a Dirty Word

You said it in high school. Your friends said it, and your children will probably say it, too. It's the question that math teachers hear hundreds of times a year: "When am I ever going to use this in the real world?"

Algebra teachers hear this more than any other math teacher because college students, no matter what their chosen field, are expected to take college algebra or a similar course as part of their general education courses. When a student goes on to trigonometry or calculus, they're not asking that question because they're obviously students who are planning a degree for which higher-level math skills are important. Algebra instructors, however, hear the moans and groans about their subject's utility almost daily.

A recent study by ACT shows that algebra skills are needed for the kind of jobs necessary to earn a salary that is sufficient to support a family of four. It's not just scientists and algebra teachers who need to know algebra skills, either. Algebra skills are critical for people working in manufacturing and related fields. People who need algebra for work include electricians, pipe fitters, sheet metal workers, draftsmen, and surveyors.

No, you probably won't be asked to factor polynomials as part of your job. But the kind of thinking and problem-solving that you do in your job is likely to be enhanced if you're able to do the kind of abstract exercises required in an algebra course. No, algebra is not a dirty word, though it might seem so at times. As an adult student, don't look at the word "algebra" as a hurdle; look at it as a way of problem-solving that will help you throughout your life.

You'll use algebra in the real world, but most likely, you won't even know when you're using it because the skills become so automatic.

Finding Your Inner Math Whiz

Adult learners returning to college are often surprised to find math more interesting than when they were in high school. You might say that they've discovered their inner math whiz.

Not everyone will find something meaningful in their math class. But you might. After all, you've lived life since you were last in school, you've worked in the real world, and the problem-solving benefits that math gives you might be more apparent when you return to college this time. Be open to considering yourself a math person. You might find that the label sticks!

Speaking Up in Class

When it comes to speaking up in class, adult students often have an advantage over younger students. Adult students have more life experiences than students just out of high school. They've voted in more elections, witnessed more current events, and have spent time out in the real world. They draw upon these experiences when contributing to class discussions.

You will have something valuable to contribute in many of your classes, so do it. Even if you start college feeling unsure of yourself, it won't take long for you to get comfortable and feel sure enough to say your piece.

Computer and Technology Skills

A computer can save you time in college. Therefore, you should have some basic technology skills before you return to college.

You'll want to use a computer (a laptop will give you the greatest flexibility) in college to write papers for class, to take notes in class, and to study for tests. You can also use the software on your computer to organize your college life by using calendar and spreadsheet software. For instance, at the beginning of the semester you can take all of your class syllabi and enter assignments, tests, and other important dates into your calendar software. This will allow you, at a glance, to see where you might have two tests during the same week, or help you plan your writing schedule.

Before you return to college, you should be able to …

- Use a computer. You don't have to be a computer whiz or a speedy typist, but you should have a basic grasp of how to operate a computer.

- Use basic word processing software. You'll use word processing software such as Microsoft Word on an almost daily basis to prepare papers for class, convert notes you take in class into electronic format, and share notes back and forth will fellow students.

Extra Credit

Don't have a computer of your own? Almost all colleges have computer labs available for student use. Computers are available for public use in public libraries, in some coffee houses, and in retail copy centers. Short courses on basic computer skills are offered through many community adult education programs. Colleges also have zero-level computer courses.

◆ Use e-mail. You will use e-mail to communicate with your professors. Professors also like to gather all e-mail addresses and send additional materials and assignments to their students. They also use e-mail to write students in advance if they're going to miss a class. If you're not proficient in e-mail, you might find yourself sitting in an empty class when your professor is sick, while all the other students are at home enjoying the day off!

◆ Search the Internet. You'll do much of your research for school assignments online, so the more experience you have, the better prepared you'll be.

> **Extra Credit**
>
> When it comes to learning basic computer skills before you return to college, a good place to look for help is your children. Even many kindergartners use computers regularly in class. Elementary school children usually know how to send e-mails, do research on the Internet, and use word processing programs.

You may still prefer to take notes in class by hand, but you'll notice that many students carry laptops and take their notes on their computer. As a matter of fact, some campuses are "laptop universities," meaning that all students are required to have a laptop for the purposes of interacting with professors and their classmates.

Depending on the course, you might need to have more advanced computer skills. Always be sure to check the requirements for the courses you are taking. If you are not sure whether you have the required skills, talk to the professor.

The Least You Need to Know

◆ Read to remember.

◆ Accept constructive criticism on your writing and learn from it.

◆ Read your writing aloud to hear what others will read.

◆ Set realistic expectations for what kind of math you're ready for.

◆ Be comfortable speaking up in class.

◆ Learn basic computer skills before starting college.

## Chapter 4

Getting Ready

In This Chapter

- ◆ Preparing to apply for college
- ◆ Researching admissions requirements
- ◆ Taking admissions or placement tests
- ◆ Transferring old college credits
- ◆ Applying for college
- ◆ Creating an action plan

By now, you've already decided to at least consider a return to school. It's okay if it's taken a while to reach that decision. You might have had a bad experience with college when you were first out of high school, or maybe you've had doubts about your ability to "learn" anymore. Get past the negative thoughts. This time college will be different.

Even if you've decided you're ready to hit the books again, you should take some time to research prospective colleges and prepare to enroll. Suppose you decide at Christmas that you want to go back to college. Although you might be able to enroll at your local community college in January, I encourage you to take some time to get ready for all the changes that going back to college entails.

Studies on college students show that, regardless of age, being prepared academically is the best predictor of a student's ability to stay in college and get a degree. And that's a statistic you *want* to be a part of!

Student Center

Brad is a physical therapist who returned to college to gain additional credentials to increase his earning potential. Married and with a baby on the way, he was at first quite hesitant about hitting the books. One of Brad's patients was instrumental in getting him to make the move. While Brad helped her learn to walk again, she helped him see his way back to college, telling him about an online program he could enroll in from home. He recently received his doctorate in physical therapy and wrote a note of thanks to his patient: "Your encouragement was a big part of my decision." You never know who might be the voice of support.

Researching Your College Options

Teenage students heading to college right out of high school look at their college options in a completely different way than returning adult students. You might remember as a senior sending test scores to all your dream colleges just to see if you could get in. The world was your oyster. You probably had the freedom to pick up and go anywhere in the country that you wanted.

This time around, you're probably not interested in getting into the best party college or concerned whether your school of choice has top-rated faculty in your area of study. You're going to take a more pragmatic approach this time. Now, college has to fit in with your son's soccer practice schedule and your work schedule. This time, you've got more to consider than your degree program, classes, and career goals.

With more variables affecting your choice, you'll find that choosing the best college is paradoxically both more complicated and easier. It's more complicated because you need to select a school that is either near where you live or else has a sophisticated online education component. You also want to find a college or university that fits in with your busier and more complicated life.

Selecting a college is easier because your choices are much more limited than they were before. You simply can't pick up and move across the country and live in a dorm or join a sorority or fraternity. The motto for most adult students is "convenience, convenience, convenience." Convenient location and convenient scheduling is more important than the school's academic ranking, proximity to the ski slopes, or the success of its football team. You have a life now—likely with a job, family, and other obligations.

Extra Credit

If you have a computer and a good Internet connection, you don't have to choose the community college in your home town or the university a short commute away. You can choose online universities or colleges that were created specifically for adult students. Technology has opened up college opportunities that were unheard of even a decade ago. You've picked a great time to return to college. See Chapter 7 for more information on online learning and distance learning options.

Talking to Adult Students or Graduates

After you decide to return to college, sit down and outline a list of questions or concerns you have about returning. Don't leave any of your questions off the list. Perhaps you want to know if the desks in colleges look different nowadays than they did 15 years ago, or what kind of clothes students wear to class. At this stage, no question is too stupid to ask. Is there a good place on campus to do your homework between work and class? Do you have to pay for parking on campus? What time does the cafeteria open? All these are legitimate questions! For too many adults, it's all these little things added up that create doubt about whether they can actually do it.

Talk to friends or acquaintances who are either in college right now or who have recently obtained a college degree and ask them the questions on your list.

Cautionary Tales

Talk to a wide range of friends—male and female—about their college experiences. Get multiple views on college from all different perspectives. Don't rely only on one good friend or relative for information. The more perspectives you get, the more likely you'll be ready for anything that comes your way.

As you talk to friends about college, keep in mind that they'll be giving you *their* take on the college experience. This is why you should get multiple viewpoints. One friend may have had a hard time making it through college algebra; he will view his college experience through that lens. Another friend may have found it difficult being in class with younger students, while another may have found the diversity in ages a positive experience. Draw on multiple experiences and see what fits best with your own situation. No one's college experiences will be exactly the same.

Knowing What You're Ready to Learn

What holds adult students back from making the decision to return to college more than anything else—even money—is fear of failure. When it comes to formal academic content, students are definitely in a "use it or lose it" situation. Don't talk yourself out of going back to college because you can't remember when the *Magna Carta* was signed (it was 1215, by the way—see, you're already ahead of the game!). Formal learning skills will come back to you after you get back in the swing of things.

You can practice the basics as a way to see just where you are in terms of your readiness for college-level learning. Review the basics (math, sciences, literature, history) if you need to take general education courses. Take a practice ACT assessment on the ACT website or a practice SAT on The College Board website (see Appendix C).

Cautionary Tales

The ACT has measured achievement for more than 40 years, and the College Board recently retooled the SAT to be achievement-oriented as well. Achievement is a measure of what you know and are able to do. Because admissions exams are achievement-based, it's difficult to increase your scores on them just by practicing the test. You have to know and understand the concepts. Yes, you can pick up some test-taking skills to help you rule out wrong answers and eliminate test anxiety, but the best way to approach an achievement test is to simply know your stuff.

Even if you don't have to take an admissions test to return to college, by taking practice tests in advance, you will at least be able to show *yourself* what you're ready to learn. Knowing exactly where you are in terms of college readiness can help take away much of the fear that you're beyond the ability to learn.

You're never too old to learn. In fact, you'll be surprised at how quickly you feel like a bona-fide student again.

The Shelf-Life of High School Assessments

Many colleges require prospective students to take a college entrance exam, such as the ACT or SAT, to assess their readiness for college.

Even if you've already taken the ACT or SAT, you might have to retake the exam. That's because these tests have a shelf-life, and many colleges won't accept test scores if too much time has passed. That's because an ACT that you took 15 years ago isn't going to be a good test of what you know and are able to do now.

If the thought of taking a standardized test strikes fear in your heart, relax. Most campuses have special policies for adult students that provide alternate ways of meeting the entry requirements, so you might be able to avoid taking one of these exams. Community colleges and vocational-technical colleges that are called "open admissions" colleges are also likely to waive entrance exams for prospective students. In many cases, the only requirement for enrolling in community college is a high school diploma or its equivalent.

If you're applying to a four-year college, you'll probably have to take the ACT or SAT, and you'll probably have to get at least a pre-determined minimum score to be admitted. Appendix A lists the main higher education systems in each state. Find the website for your state's system and you're likely to find either state-level or campus-level testing and admissions policies and requirements. If you know the website for the college you're interested in attending, you can go directly to that site; however, if you don't know the address, the state system lists the campuses in your state, and you can link to your college through them.

Extra Credit

Adult students may not have to take college admissions assessments to get into college. Many colleges have separate admission policies for nontraditional, or adult, students. Still, you may be required to take tests to see if you're ready to be placed in college-level work.

Cautionary Tales

Don't take offense at terms colleges use to describe their adult admission standards. For example, I've seen younger students' admission referred to as a "regular admit," while adult students' admission are called a "provisional admit" or a "special admit." These labels don't mean you're any less qualified than younger students.

Many states have these policies listed, word for word, on their websites. Some states' sites are more easily navigated than others, so if the policies aren't immediately evident, use the main phone number for the agency and ask to have the policies sent to you. If you are contacting a state agency, you can ask to have the state requirements and the campus-level requirements sent to you.

State higher education agencies have different levels of authority when it comes to the colleges in their system. The U.S. Department of Education identifies official agencies in each state to oversee public colleges and universities. These agencies oversee the accreditation of the colleges and universities as well. Accreditation is important because, if a college isn't accredited, it can't offer you any form of federal financial aid or federally subsidized student loans. If you can't access these forms of financial aid, your wallet will feel it.

Extra Credit _____

Cutoff scores are scores on standardized assessments at which certain decisions are made. For example, a college may have a cutoff score of 20 on the ACT for admission into college-level classes. The ACT is on a 1 to 36 score range; a cutoff score of 20 (if a college chose the cutoff score based on scientific research) means that the college has determined that a 20 is necessary for the student to have a 75 percent chance of making a "C" or better and a 50 percent chance of making a "B" or better in an entry-level college course. Similar cutoff scores are used on placement exams to help make sure you are placed in the best math class, for example, for your current level of skill.

If the state agency you've located in Appendix A doesn't have authority over the community colleges in your state and you're interested in testing and admissions requirements for your local community college, see Appendix C for community college-specific websites. Additionally, if you're searching for information on private/ independent colleges, Appendix A lists private systems when those systems are large ones and/or are in partnership for *accrediting* purposes with the state higher education agency.

def•i•ni•tion _____

Accrediting (or accreditation) is the process of establishing that a college or university meets certain expected requirements for quality in academic programs. Independent accrediting agencies assess the quality of campus programs at regular intervals. Accrediting also occurs at the state level. State laws and policies determine which agency accredits colleges. If you are unsure about the accrediting body for a college you've selected, check with your state's higher education agency.

If you don't find your selected private college listed in the system noted in Appendix A, check out Appendix C for the National Association of Independent Colleges and Universities (NAICU) website. NAICU's site is an excellent portal for finding private colleges across the United States.

Placement Tests

Even if you choose a college with an open admissions policy, you'll probably still have to take placement tests to help determine what level of classes you're ready to take. In other words, you're "in" when it comes to the whole college, but the placement tests tell you what classes you'll be eligible to take.

Placement tests are given in traditional academic content, such as reading, English, mathematics, and writing, as well as other academic areas that individual campuses deem important. Many colleges administer placement tests created by ACT or The College Board, but others administer tests developed by their own departments. Most higher education systems are trying to get away from these "home-grown" kinds of tests, but they're still being used in great numbers. If the college you choose uses locally developed placement assessments, it may be harder for you to practice for them. You can always ask at the campus assessment office if practice versions of locally developed placement tests or study guides are available.

These placement tests aren't just important for making sure your academic journey begins at the right place. The results of your placement tests can have a financial impact as well. If, for example, the placement test determines that you need one or more refresher courses in a content area, you will need to take—and pay for—classes that don't count toward your degree.

Extra Credit

During the process of researching colleges, see if their websites describe what kind of placement tests are used. Many colleges use placement tests that are linked to or created by ACT and The College Board, the two major college admissions test companies. If so, practice tests on the ACT and SAT websites can be helpful in preparing you for the placement tests you'll have to take.

As I noted in Chapter 3, you shouldn't feel bad if you have to take some refresher courses; it's common for adult students to have to take these "catch-up" courses first. Developmental courses are designed to help students get fully ready for their first college-level class in that content area, and help prevent them from failing the college-level work.

If you're planning to attend a liberal arts college or a research university to obtain a four-year degree, don't feel bad if you're asked to take the developmental classes elsewhere. Many states have assigned the role of delivering developmental courses to the community colleges. In most cases, this arrangement is the result of a formal partnership with the higher-level college or university.

Test-Taking Skills

Even though most of the tests you will take for admissions and/or placement in college-level classes are achievement-based and therefore difficult to study for unless you know the content well, there are some things you can do to feel more confident about your test-taking abilities.

The idea of taking a test, especially after years of not having to sit down with paper and a #2 pencil, can be pretty scary. It can be even scarier if the college you're attending uses computer-based testing and you've never taken a test on a computer before.

The practice tests identified earlier can help you re-familiarize yourself with the format of most assessments you will encounter, but you need to have both body and mind in good shape on the day you take one or more assessments for college.

Here's some test-taking advice:

◆ Get a good night's sleep the night before you take any assessment for college admission or placement.

◆ Even if you aren't a breakfast person, eat breakfast! And make it a balanced breakfast; a meal of just carbohydrates (bread, cereal, bagels, etc.) might leave you feeling sluggish.

◆ Don't cram. If you've taken practice tests and prepared, cramming won't improve your ability to perform well.

◆ Read test items carefully while also keeping in mind that most tests have a time limit.

◆ With multiple-choice tests, you can often eliminate two answers as "wrong" while searching for the right answer.

◆ Don't spend too much time on any one question. If a question is giving you trouble, move on to the next question, saving problem questions for last.

◆ Don't second-guess yourself. If you've finished your test in the time allotted, go back through and make sure you've filled everything out correctly, but don't obsess over one or two answers.

◆ Don't talk negatively to yourself before or during the assessment. Approach each problem/question individually and give it your undivided thought. This is no time to allow self-doubts to creep into your head.

◆ Do something nice for yourself when the test is done.

◆ If you aren't pleased with your results, see if you can take the test again. Sometimes you can, sometimes you can't, but it's worth asking.

Putting Your Credentials Together

Applying for college will be a lot easier if you've kept records on your high school and previous college experiences. As you prepare to apply, gather the following items:

◆ Official high school and college transcripts. Most colleges require that your transcripts have the official seal of the school or institution affixed to them. Although you might be able to get one copy for free, subsequent copies generally cost money. After making initial inquiries, send formal requests along with any money required. If you've never attended college, all you'll need is your high school transcript.

◆ Certificates or official education information you have obtained through your workplace. In some cases, colleges will evaluate a portfolio of your learning and training and grant you course credit for life or work experiences.

◆ Information on previous financial aid you have received and/or loans you are currently paying or have paid. Your student loan information is likely already held in a national database, but it doesn't hurt for you to retain these records. If you cannot locate these records, ask financial aid officials how to locate this information or contact your lender or guarantor (on your student loan bill).

◆ A resumé that outlines your work and educational experiences.

◆ Letters of recommendation from previous college teachers, employers, supervisors, or community leaders. This will help primarily if you're seeking to enter a college that has limited space and is more selective.

You might also consider putting together a portfolio that describes any work-based learning and formal training you've had. You may have the chance to earn course credit for work and life experiences. Just because you've never been to college doesn't mean you're walking onto a campus empty-handed. You may be able to begin college farther ahead than you think.

Applying for College

Many states and college systems within states have developed portals that allow you to do everything from managing your transcript delivery to applying for college on-line. In fact, you can apply for one college in your state and never have to retype the information again. Once you have an "account" (which is free), your information will pre-populate any form in your state's portal. This means that you can apply to multiple colleges almost with the touch of a single button!

The majority of student portals that have emerged have been developed by Xap. You can visit www.xap.com and select your state or college system from a menu on Xap's home page. Think of the Xap site as a portal for portals!

Another positive feature of the Xap portals is this: not only can you apply for colleges in your own state once you create an account, you can also apply for other colleges in states where a Xap portal is being used. Xap's portals also pre-populate your personal information to the Free Application for Federal Student Aid (FAFSA; see Chapter 10) should you choose to use this feature of the portal system in your state.

When You've Been out of College for Several Years

If you've been in college as recently as five years ago, then you are less likely to be surprised by the changes that new technologies have brought to college campuses and classes. If you've been gone from college a decade or more, you should know that most college campuses are now technologically sophisticated and many are using cutting-edge equipment, not just in research laboratories, but also in professor-student interactions, enrollment and fee payment processes, and in the delivery of courses.

Cautionary Tales

Don't be surprised if the college doesn't accept credits on your transcript from 20 years ago. Think about it. You've probably forgotten what you learned long ago, so it makes sense for you to take such a class again. In the end, you'll be glad you re-took the classes, as they can help you get back in the swing of things before tackling more advanced classes.

It's not unusual for professors to have a bulletin board for student questions and also have a way to interact electronically with other students in your classes. A decade ago, you had to wait for formal office hours to see your professor for assistance. Now, that assistance is as close as an e-mail address. Professors often post class syllabi, reading material, and practice tests on their class websites.

Although the mechanisms for teaching and learning have grown more technologically sophisticated, the basic teaching and learning processes are still the same.

The most important thing you can do when preparing to return to college is to give yourself plenty of time. Take time to gather your credentials and to develop a means of presenting yourself and what you know to your prospective college(s). If you do, you'll slip back into college life like it's a comfortable pair of jeans.

Creating an Action Plan

At the beginning of this book, I encouraged you to write in it. Go back now and build yourself a plan for returning to college. Remember, if you give yourself more time to get all your preparatory work done, you will be more likely to slide into your college experience smoothly.

Whether you draw out your plan on a yellow legal pad with blue lines or use a spreadsheet program, outline what you need to do first, second, third, and so on. Use a format that makes sense for you and also one that you *know* you will follow!

- Make a list of the credentials you need to gather; write to the schools and colleges you've been to before and have them delivered to you.

- Build a chronological timetable on all that you need to do and check off each action item as you complete them. With a plan, one you've written down, you will feel more obligated to finish it. Keep your plan close at hand, either in your briefcase, on the passenger side of the car, or as a file on your computer. Refer to it often, check your progress, make changes as you need to. With each task you complete, know how much closer you are to starting and finishing college.

- Spend some time researching schools and academic programs when you get to that part of your action plan. Visit campuses that you are considering. Check out all the characteristics of the college that you've read about. Find out if classes are offered on days and times that are convenient to you. Determine whether it's an adult-friendly college.

- Set up a time to visit with a student services person, whose job is to work with students who are thinking about attending their respective campus.

- Find out what financial aid is available to you. Send your FAFSA results to several of the colleges that you are considering and see which ones offer you the best aid packages.

- Find out how many credit hours you will need to complete a degree.

- See which of the campuses you're considering will provide you with credit for life and work experiences, or if you can get credit in advance by testing out of some classes.

Go through all the steps suggested here, make them all part of your action plan, and then make a decision. Choose to return to college. Choose the right college for you with the best financial aid whose services appeal to you as an adult learner.

Get the whole family on board with you, and divide household responsibilities differently, if you need to, so you can continue to be a parent and a spouse and add the title of student to your life.

Put an item on your action plan that includes work. Make time to talk to the Human Resources director to learn about employer benefits for college. Examine the potential for alternative schedules in case classes are offered during traditional work hours for you.

Add anything else that's unique to you and your individual circumstances to your action plan.

And when you're done with all the elements in your plan, guess what? You've already started down the path of being a student. You've organized yourself and you've done your homework. Congratulations!

The Least You Need to Know

- Don't rush back into college. Give yourself plenty of time to prepare for the experience.

- Research the admissions and placement policies for the colleges you're considering.

- Prepare yourself to take placement assessments before enrolling in classes.

- Don't feel bad if you have to take a "catch-up" course or two; it'll help you in the long run.

- Accept the fact that you might have to re-take courses that you took the last time you went to college.

Part 2

Choosing the Right College

You can still find plenty of traditional college campuses complete with ivy-covered buildings and beautifully landscaped grounds, but college has outgrown this traditional image.

Today's adult college student has more choices than ever before. You can take courses over the Internet, enroll in your local community college, or go to your state university full-time. And because so many more adult students are going back to school, colleges are beginning to offer services and schedules with adults specifically in mind.

When you think about the college you want to attend, you should consider your life and career goals.

This part will help you navigate the myriad degree programs and colleges available to you. Bottom line: you will learn how to choose what's best for you.

## Chapter 5

The Best Colleges for Adult Learners

In This Chapter

- Finding out what colleges can do to increase your chance for success
- Determining how flexible the school is when it comes to scheduling classes and paying tuition
- Reviewing the school's approach to the adult learning experience
- Looking into support services, financial aid, and technology support available to adult students

Whether you're considering a college that's around the corner from your house or accessible only via the Internet, you should evaluate how "adult-friendly" it is.

Some colleges have made it their mission to focus their attentions on their fastest-growing demographic—adults. Good for them! Unfortunately, many colleges still treat their students as if they are all just out of high school, even when adults make up the majority of their student population. It's essential that you find out whether the colleges you're considering have made the effort to make adult students feel welcome.

Finding an Adult-Friendly College

There's no question that adults have unique educational needs, especially if they are working students. According to the Council for Adult and Experiential Learning (CAEL), these unique needs "reflect how the experience, knowledge, skills, and attitudes of adult learners are different from the traditional-aged student." When researching colleges, look for those that make an extra effort to accommodate the unique needs of adult students. Adult-friendly colleges …

- Reach out to adults via advertising aimed at their unique needs.

- Are flexible and offer classes and student support services at convenient times for adults.

- Pair each student with an academic advisor who personalizes the college experience to match the students' career goals.

- Allow more of a student's on-the-job learning to count for college credit.

When you know what to look for, you can determine whether the colleges you're considering are adult-friendly. The following sections delve more deeply into these and other adult-friendly traits.

Extra Credit

The Council for Adult and Experiential Learning (CAEL) is one of the nation's best organizations for helping institutions of higher education meet the needs of adult learners. CAEL's mission is focused on adult learners and their unique needs in education and training. Part of their mission is to make sure adult learners don't run into unnecessary red tape when making their return to school. They also highlight colleges who do the best job of serving adult students.

One initiative that CAEL undertook recently is called the *Adult Learner Focused Institution* initiative, in which they identified educational principles that best serve working adults. This chapter draws heavily on these principles.

Outreach

Sure, you might have lived across town from a community college all your life, and your first inclination might be that this is the school for you. But has this school ever made an effort, via direct mail, public service announcements, or other means, to reach out to adult students? If not, what does that say about the college's adult student outreach capabilities?

An adult-oriented institution …

◆ Uses a variety of special methods and venues to attract adult learners—for example, on-campus and off-campus information systems, ad campaigns, online information, and so on.

◆ Addresses the needs and concerns of adults who are unaccustomed to viewing themselves in the role of a student.

◆ Helps adults identify and overcome barriers that keep them from returning to learning.

◆ Assists adult learners in making informed decisions about how well the colleges match their interests and goals.

◆ Employs faculty who do not limit themselves to the traditional role of lecturer in the classroom. They might perform in blended roles that include administrative duties, advising, teaching, and facilitating.

To get a feel for whether a college is one that particularly reaches out to adults, check their websites for areas devoted to adult students. See if the student services portion of the site outlines advising structures at the college that will help you return to school. Read the profiles of the faculty, either in the course catalog or on the website. In addition, take note of whether they advertise to adult students.

Life and Career Planning

College, life, and career planning can't be done in isolation from each other. At least, they can't be done in isolation and do you any good. You've got to think of all three at once: how career impacts your college and choices of programs; how family impacts college life; and how your career goals will help shape your future earning potential.

The campus you choose should be a partner with you in planning for these elements of your life. The best campuses will actually tell you straight out if their offerings aren't for you and will help you find a college that does meet your needs.

An adult-oriented institution …

◆ Engages the adult learners in a thorough process of education and career planning to determine their level of educational development upon entry, their educational and career goals, and to establish a plan for reaching those goals as efficiently as possible.

◆ Uses education and career planning as a method of establishing long-term relationships with adult learners and encouraging them to take greater responsibility for their own learning.

◆ Engages adults as active partners in planning, delivery, and evaluation of their learning.

◆ Promotes opportunities to gain credit through *prior learning assessment.*

def•i•ni•tion

Prior learning assessment involves a college reviewing your life experiences and work credentials to see if you can be granted course credit for non-academic experience. If you can demonstrate proficiency in certain academic areas and are granted course credit in advance of your return to school, you can move on to classes that you're more suited for, and save money by not taking classes you don't need.

◆ Creates pathways for adult learners to gain credit for learning from a variety of sources so that college-level learning acquired prior to enrollment can be accepted toward institutional credentials and degrees.

As you check out colleges and their offerings, see if the advisement process involves both academic and career planning. Check websites for prior learning assessment opportunities that will allow you to get credit for life and work experiences. See how individualized the campus process is for test taking and placement. Is there flexibility in course choices for you based on your assessment results, or are you herded into certain courses because of a single test score? Interview college staff about opportunities to earn college credit outside the college's walls by applying academic concepts in the real world.

Financing

College financing is often more challenging for adults than it is for younger students. Colleges and states tend to reserve large portions of local aid for students who live on campus and come directly from high school.

Student financial aid sources often also require that recipients take a full load of courses, leaving adults who attend school part-time out of the aid circle. How a college handles financing tells you a great deal about how well their practices support adults.

An institution focused on adult learners …

- Informs adult learners about convenient payment options available to them.

- Assists adult learners through deferred payment options when tuition reimbursement programs do not make funds available until course completion.

- Makes financial aid and scholarships available to part-time students.

- Assesses charges to learners incrementally during the course of a program and establishes equitable refund policies.

- Helps adult learners develop strategies for locating external funding sources to assist them with college costs.

Don't assume that payment options are set in stone and due in full within 30 days of the first day of class. Ask for policy exceptions or for bridge loans to help you through class until your employer reimbursement takes place. When you visit with financial aid professionals, make sure you ask about outside financial aid sources (such as local scholarships) even if no one brings up the topic first.

Assessment of Learning Outcomes

Colleges in the United States are struggling to come up with good measures of what students know and are able to do when they graduate from their campuses. It's not an easy task, especially when there are so many options for college degrees. Still, campuses are agreeing more and more on what students should know after having taken all the "basics" or "general education" courses.

Adult students, even more so than younger students, need colleges that account for and can demonstrate that graduating students have attained certain skills and knowledge. For you, this can mean the difference between getting a better job or not.

The college or university that is "walking the walk" when it comes to assessing what's being learned …

- Designs educational experiences with learning outcomes in mind.

- Finds ways to integrate the perspectives of a range of stakeholders, such as businesses and the community, in defining learning outcomes.

- Embraces a variety of assessment techniques for measuring learning outcomes and assigning credit for prior learning.

- Documents what learners know and what they can do as a result of their educational experience.

- Uses learning outcomes to establish a foundation for those who wish to pursue subsequent degrees.

- Promotes the opportunity to gain credit through organizations' instructional programs to adult learners.

- Initiates a dialogue with community-based organizations to learn what knowledge, skills, and abilities are needed by organizations and the community, and then develops learning outcomes based on these needs.

- Regularly re-evaluates external instructional programs to ensure their relevance and rigor in relation to the institution's offerings.

- Creates pathways for adult learners to gain credit from a variety of sources so that college-level learning acquired prior to enrollment can be accepted toward institutional credentials and degrees.

- Promotes opportunities to gain credit through prior learning assessment.

In your academic area of interest, see if a campus shows that they're measuring learning outcomes that are relevant to your business or industry area. Many programs are accredited or go through a program review to make sure they're offering the up-front requirements to have a high-quality academic program. But this doesn't tell you about what value the college experience adds to the learner.

Ask to see graduation rates, job placement rates, and other statistics showing what students have done or where they've gone after graduation. Look for evidence of partnerships with local employers to blend classroom and workplace learning opportunities.

The Teaching-Learning Process

You will enhance your potential for success by choosing a college that meets your specific learning needs. Nowhere will this be more evident than in the classroom and in the interaction between student and faculty.

Although some campuses are doing a great job of matching student learning styles with faculty teaching styles, it's still rare to find this process in place for every faculty member in every department on campus.

Practices that are the most friendly to adults and adult learners occur at colleges that ...

◆ Employ a teaching-learning process that includes a high degree of interaction among learners and between learners and faculty.

◆ Consider adult learners as co-creators of knowledge. Therefore, learning experiences and projects are often designed in cooperation with the learner and directly relate to the adult learner's work and personal world.

◆ Offer multiple methods of instructional delivery to enhance convenient access to education and provide choices that fit learning styles.

◆ Use assessment as an integral part of the learning process and in ways that enhance competency and self-confidence.

◆ Encourage faculty to build on the knowledge, interests, and life situations that adults bring to their education to develop learning experiences. When working in partnership with businesses and/or unions, faculty members strive to present material in a framework that incorporates issues and language of the learners' workplace and communities.

◆ Support faculty members' work with adult learners, staff, adjunct faculty, and local community resources in developing collaborative learning experiences.

For academic programs and/or classes that you're considering taking, review the class syllabi to see if the course is taught by lecture or whether students are encouraged to actively participate in discussion (some courses use both teaching styles). Is there group work involved? Are there choices in assignments for credit? Do you have the chance to blend what you do at work with what you're doing in class?

Student Support Systems

Adult-friendly campuses realize that grown-ups need a little help from their friends, too. Adult students need advisement, tutoring, mentoring, and other services on campus just as much as younger students. As a matter of fact, adults who have been out of college for a while may require even more support systems on campus than students who just graduated from high school and are familiar with structured school settings.

You will know you're in an adult-friendly college if you find the following activities and services on campus:

◆ Support systems are activated by an adult learner's initial inquiry.

◆ Flexible time frames for enrollment, registration, and program participation are part of the academic and administrative structure.

◆ Faculty and staff provide individual attention to adult learners to inform them of the institution's programs and services designed to provide them with academic and personal support.

◆ Support services address the life circumstances of the adult (for example, child care, support networks, adult-centered orientation, and advising).

◆ Faculty members are encouraged to participate in professional development activities related to adult learning theory and application.

◆ Staff and faculty work with employers and/or unions to develop mentoring and advising programs.

The student support services on a campus can make or break your decision to return to college. So go armed with knowledge, and make sure that a support system is in place.

Cautionary Tales

You might encounter defensiveness from front-line staff on college campuses when asking about specific services for adult learners. Some staff truly don't "get" the difference between an 18-year-old freshman and a 38-year-old freshman. Be persistent about your needs and let your academic advisor or counselor know when you meet with resistance in another part of the campus.

Above all, ask questions and see what happens when you ask. Are your questions answered right away? Or are you handed off from one department to the next?

Do you have the ability to enroll in a class at 2 A.M. in your pajamas, or do you still have to line up and register on-site?

Even if the campus itself doesn't provide a particular service that you need (such as daycare, for example), are they in partnership with a local organization that can give you advice or help you find what you need?

Are faculty members involved in any portion of the advisement process, or do you only see them in their classrooms at their appointed times?

Technology

Technology on college campuses is generally quite advanced, and includes more than just computers. Students might be expected to use video teleconferencing, podcasting, and advanced calculators.

Computer technology used to be a tremendous barrier for adult students because adults didn't use computers in their everyday lives. Because more adults use computers in the workplace, today many adult students often come to campus computer-savvy. However, if you are not used to working with computers and other technology, you need to make sure that the college you're planning to attend can help you get up to speed.

A college that employs adult-friendly technology practices ...

- Uses technology to build community among adult learners living in remote geographical areas.

- Uses information technology to provide flexible and timely education and administrative services (for example, web registration centers and call centers).

- Uses technology to empower adult learners to better manage their learning process both inside and outside the classroom (for example, partial and full Internet-based courses and technology-rich on-campus instruction).

- Employs technology in the learning experience in ways that mirror the technology-rich environment many adults work in.

The most important question you can ask is whether the technology you have will be sufficient to participate in and complete all the courses you wish to take.

Do you and fellow students have the chance to participate in a bulletin board where you can help each other by asking or answering questions of one another?

Are faculty expected to have an e-mail relationship with their students?

Technology itself has allowed many more adult students to gain college credentials. Technology is not the only benchmark of a college's adult student focus, but it's a good indication of a college's understanding of flexibility in delivering classes and also understanding the variety of ways that students, adult and young alike, learn.

Strategic Partnerships

At first you might wonder why you should care what partnerships with the private sector a campus has in place. Well, it does matter, especially to adults, because many of the strategic partnerships can later lead to employment opportunities.

An example of a great partnership is one in which a college's business partner has experts in the field come to the campus to deliver a class. Combining the academic expertise of a faculty member with the real-world expertise of a professional in the business world can create a learning environment through which you could jump from the classroom to the workplace!

Think about it: if a college has good community and business partners, it means that the college cares that their students leave with the kind of skills that employers want. You can only gain from such partnerships.

A college that engages in profitable strategic partnerships ...

◆ Helps establish learning goals that include the organization's future job opportunities and skill needs.

◆ Works with employers and/or unions to develop mentoring and advising programs.

◆ Helps organizations develop ways to encourage employees/members to pursue their education (trains supervisors to communicate to employees the importance and relevance of learning; develops internal promotional programs to alert employees/members of learning opportunities).

◆ Provides support for adult learners at times and places that are congruent with work schedule—such as establishing education extension centers at or near work locations.

◆ Encourages employers to make telephones, computers, Internet access, and video conferencing available to employees for engaging in education-related activities during hours when technology is not used for business-related activities.

◆ Develops options for using learning technology at work sites and on desktop computers.

◆ Works with organizations to measure the impact of educational programs on an organization's goals.

Extra Credit

Some colleges offer courses to employees at their work site. Strategic partnerships make these more innovative educational opportunities possible. Imagine finishing your work for the day and, instead of fighting traffic, going down the hall to a conference room where you and 10 of your colleagues take an algebra class!

You've got opportunities to bridge college and work if you choose a college that is accustomed to working with employers for the benefit of students/employees. The most adult-focused colleges are those open to discussion with employers, whether it's for using computer equipment in the workplace or providing training for employees outside the campus arena.

The Least You Need to Know

- You can find a college whose mission is to make college life as easy for adults as possible.

- The best colleges for adults are those that meet adult needs for flexibility.

- You have every right to expect special student services for adult students.

- The best colleges have multiple financing options.

- With good partnerships between college and community, you can benefit from convenient academic options.

## Chapter 6

Bricks and Mortar: Choosing a College

In This Chapter

- ◆ Taking a closer look at community colleges, four-year colleges, and research universities
- ◆ Researching colleges online
- ◆ Finding a college close to home
- ◆ Being a cautious consumer

It's time to start thinking about the kind of college you'll attend. You're probably already aware of at least one or two colleges within easy driving distance of your home. Perhaps one is a community college and the other is a large research university. How do you decide which one is better suited to your needs? Before you enroll in the nearest school, you should consider whether it offers the kind of educational experience you seek. Not all colleges are created equal.

Classifications of Colleges

Different kinds of colleges offer different kinds of programs, degrees, and overall educational experiences.

The following sections outline the general academic and student services you can expect from different kinds of colleges and universities.

Community Colleges

As their name implies, community colleges play an important role in their communities. A community college system is normally in an urban or suburban area (or a combination of the two). Stand-alone community colleges can also be found in rural areas.

Community colleges offer two-year degrees as their highest academic credential in all but some very rare cases in which higher degrees are awarded. They offer the kind of programs for jobs that only require two-year degrees—such as some of the support functions in the medical community—and also provide general education courses for students who plan to transfer to a four-year college or university.

Some students don't obtain a two-year degree before moving on to a four-year college. Others seek an Associate's degree before transferring to another campus to obtain a higher degree.

Many community colleges work with nearby universities to offer 2 + 2 programs, in which the community college offers the first two years of programming and the four-year college or university provides the final two years of work. Upon completion of the program, students are awarded a four-year Bachelor's degree.

Extra Credit

Many community colleges used to be called "junior" colleges, so schools in your area may have undergone name changes in the past decade to replace the word "junior" with "community."

Student services at community colleges are generally very adult-friendly, and many adults start by taking classes at community colleges. Community colleges often have more flexible hours and offer more sections to meet the needs of students who work full-time.

Four-Year Colleges and Liberal Arts Schools

Four-year colleges typically offer Bachelor's degrees as their highest degree, though some also offer degrees at the Master's degree level as well. Many also fit the description of liberal arts schools because they provide a good, general preparation of core knowledge across their curricula. Some four-year colleges also offer two-year degrees, but usually the role of providing the two-year degrees is left to community colleges.

Four-year colleges can vary widely in their services to adult learners. Some of these colleges serve young students almost exclusively; others, particularly those in urban areas, offer convenient courses for adults.

Though not all four-year colleges have taken steps to address the needs of adult students, many colleges are at least trying to transition their student services to meet their needs.

Universities

Universities generally offer all levels of degrees, up to a Ph.D. Universities are typically larger than four-year and community colleges, have a larger student body than other types of institutions, and occupy a larger campus space than other colleges in their state. Research is a big part of the faculty's work, often over and above their teaching duties. For students, universities are less likely to contain a significant number of adult students, but adults have, over time, increased in numbers in the university setting.

University "systems" often contain multiple campuses under the same university heading. Medical schools or law schools may be attached to the university, as well as other programs that provide professional degrees, such as pharmacy.

Universities generally have the most stringent admission standards for traditional students, but adult students rarely have to meet the same standards as students entering directly from high school.

Vocational/Technical Institutions

Vocational/technical institutions are designed to impart knowledge and skills of a more technical or applied nature. For instance, many of these institutions offer certificates or degrees in auto body, heating and air conditioning, and computer repair. Some also provide certificates in cosmetology, massage, and other less technical areas.

They are often affiliated with community colleges, but there are also stand-alone vocational and technical institutions.

Searching for a School Using COOL

By now you should have a pretty good idea of the kind of college you'd like to attend. But how do you find those schools? And how do you know if they even offer the degree program you seek? The answer is as close as your computer.

The College Opportunities Online Locator system (COOL) is a national online database of more than 7,000 colleges—public and private, two-year and four-year, vocational and proprietary schools. COOL enables you to make real "apples to apples" comparisons of what colleges have to offer you. How cool is that?!

The following section shows you how to compare colleges using the COOL system, while also recommending other strategies for evaluating the best school for you.

The COOL Home Page

The COOL home page is at www.nces.gov/ipeds/cool. When you go to this page, you will see a couple of different search options.

For a Quick Search, you search using the name(s) of a college or university. If you know the name of a handful of colleges that you want to review or compare, the quick search function will save you time.

The Search by Criteria option allows you to search by location, by program of study you're interested in, or both. Because most adult students are interested in convenient locations, the location function will help you quickly narrow your search. You can also limit your search to a specific state.

Let's take a closer look at some of the other COOL search criteria.

COOL Search Criteria

For now, skip the box at the bottom of the COOL home page that asks you to enter your preferred program of study. Click the More Options button at the lower-left side of the page. You will be taken to a second page on which you can enter any number of search criteria, including the following:

- ◆ **Institution name:** Leave this field blank if you don't have a particular institution in mind.

- ◆ **Institutional characteristics:** You can select any number of characteristics that interest you. Characteristics in the first section include institution type (public versus private) and the kind of degree offered (Associate's, Bachelor's, Master's, Ph.D.). If you select nothing in the institutional characteristics section, your eventual search results will contain all kinds of institutions.

- ◆ **Students enrolled:** This is a drop-down menu that allows you to select institutions based on size, as indicated by the number of students enrolled. You may prefer smaller institutions, or you may not care about size. If the size of the student population is not something you are concerned about, you need not select anything on this drop-down menu; all sizes will be considered in your eventual search results.

◆ **Religious affiliation:** If you're searching for a college that aligns with a particular religion, use this feature to narrow your search according to a number of different denominations. Again, if you leave this option blank, institutions of all affiliations (provided that you left the institution type indicator at the top of the page blank or selected private institutions to narrow your search) will appear in your search results.

◆ **Location:** Choose from a drop-down menu of all the states and U.S. territories. If you already clicked a state on the home page, you don't need to do so again on this drop-down menu; the state you selected on the home page will already be highlighted.

◆ **Region:** You can narrow your search to the far west, Rocky Mountains, southwest, plains, southeast, Great Lakes, mid-east, and New England.

◆ **Distance from my ZIP code:** For adult students, this selection feature is often the most important. Enter your ZIP code in the appropriate space and then select the maximum number of miles (as the crow flies) from your ZIP code that you would be willing to drive to school.

◆ **Program or major:** Finally, at the bottom of the search page, you can search for programs or majors. You search by major as well as degree level. For level of degree, you can select from Certificate, Associate's, or Bachelor's and Graduate.

◆ **Title IV:** If you want to make certain that the colleges you search for are eligible to deliver federal financial aid to their students, you can limit your search to only schools that are "Title IV eligible." This means that the college or university can offer you need-based grants and federally guaranteed student loans.

At the bottom of the second page of criteria, click the Results button. The search engine will generate a list of colleges that fit the criteria you identified.

Sample COOL Search

Let's do a sample search so you can see how it works before trying it on your own.

Our sample student, Sandra, lives in Lebanon, Ohio. Lebanon is an expanding bedroom community that lies almost equidistant from Cincinnati and Dayton. Lebanon is north of Cincinnati and north of Mason, one of Cincinnati's fastest-growing suburbs. The town of Lebanon itself doesn't have a college or university, but the proximity of large cities and small towns means that Sandra likely has a lot of options for colleges.

Sandra prefers a public college, is concerned about college costs, and doesn't want to travel more than 60 miles from her home to take classes.

Student enrollment isn't a concern for Sandra, and religious affiliation won't come into play because she's searching only for public colleges. She wants to leave her options open in terms of the level of degree offered at any of the schools she gets in her results, so she will leave that section blank.

She does, however, have a major or degree program in mind. Sandra wants to be a kindergarten teacher, so she needs to search for programs in elementary education.

Sandra accesses the COOL website. On the first page of the site, she skips down to the map of the United States and clicks the state of Ohio. In the section at the bottom of page one that asks for her choice of program or major, she types **Elementary Education** into the field, but leaves the choices of degree level (Certificate, Associate's, Bachelor's, or Graduate) blank because, although she will be working toward a Bachelor's degree now, she wants to know what her local options look like should she consider graduate school in the future.

Now Sandra clicks the More Options button at the bottom of the COOL home page and is taken to the second page to enter additional criteria that she wants to use to search for Elementary Education programs.

She clicks the check box beside the word Public on the Institution Type option and then skips all the other criteria to get to the criterion that's the most important to her—the distance from home. She enters her ZIP code, 45036, and then indicates that 60 miles is the maximum distance from that ZIP code that she is willing to travel. Sandra is also hoping to qualify for financial aid, so she limits her search to Title IV-eligible schools.

The Program or Major section at the bottom of the page has already been prepopulated with the Elementary Education choice she made on page one, so she doesn't need to enter that information again. When she clicks the Results button at the bottom of the page, a page pops up asking her to either deselect her program choice or to check the program choice of Elementary Education and Teaching. Sandra chooses Elementary Education and Teaching and then clicks the Results button again.

The results page identifies five institutions that match her search criteria. All these institutions are able to offer her an Elementary Education program and all are public colleges within 60 miles of her ZIP code.

For each institution, the COOL site gives its name, the city where it's located, and the number of students enrolled. When you click the name of each college, you're taken to a page that provides information about the college—information elements that are the same for each college in the COOL site, so Sandra can not only read more about the college, but compare them side by side.

Sandra clicks the Wright State University option, the last option in her alphabetical listing. When she clicks the university's name, she is taken to a page with detailed information about the campus in Dayton, Ohio.

The following figure shows the General Information results page for Wright State University. From this page, you can get every piece of information you could possibly want about any college you're comparing. Each college in the COOL database contains all the same indicators that you will find in the Wright State University example.

An example of the kind of search results the COOL database can generate.

As Sandra begins to explore the General Information page for Wright State University, she finds the following information:

- Mailing address, telephone number, and website for the college.

- A description of the type of institution Wright State University is, as well as its official Carnegie Classification and its mission statement. You can view the mission statement for each college using the COOL site—these are typically general, overall statements about the purpose of the college or university.

- The kind of financial aid that is offered.

- The degrees and certificates that are offered.

- The student services that are offered.

- Special learning opportunities, such as study abroad, ROTC, and distance learning.

From the General Information page, you should be able to establish whether the institutions you have selected to review meet the basic needs you have for your college.

Links listed on the left side of the General Information page take you to a more detailed analysis of the university's offerings and services, as follows:

- **Estimated Student Expenses:** Describes the in-state and out-of-state expenses for the past three years, as well as estimates for books and room and board.

- **Financial Aid:** Shows the proportion of students who received financial aid, with other figures describing what kind of aid the students received.

- **Admissions:** Lists the admissions fee and provides a link to all the steps in the admissions process at Wright State University.

- **Enrollment:** Indicates the percentage of part-time and full-time students, the race and gender of the students enrolled, and the number of undergraduate and total student enrollments.

- **Retention/Graduation:** Indicates how many full-time and part-time students came back to the university after the first year (this is the retention rate). Graduation rates are provided for four-, five-, and six-year durations. From these, you can get an idea of how long it takes the typical student to obtain a degree from this university.

◆ **Awards/Degrees:** Provides the most recent information on how many degrees were awarded within an academic content area. You can also view the Master's and Doctoral degrees awarded by the university.

Three other criteria appear on the General Information page. One is a link to accreditation information, another is a federally required campus security report, and the third is an estimate of loan default rates.

How to Use the COOL Site to Your Benefit

Sandra was able to locate good choices in campuses using the COOL website. The data on each of the five colleges yielded from her search gave her a way to compare each of the colleges through which she could get her Bachelor's degree in education within an hour drive from her home. She was able to see how many students are full- and part-time and also the amount of financial aid students receive.

To do more in-depth research on the five colleges in her list, the COOL site provides a direct link to each of the colleges' websites. After you go through the information in the COOL site, you will want to "visit" each college by going to their own websites. On many sites, you can take virtual tours and learn more about the precise curricula involved in getting a degree.

Extra Credit

For adult students, the COOL site has one important variable that many other college and university information portals don't have: the distance from your home. Because location and convenience are often as important as the degree programs offered to adult students, the ability to locate schools close to home is a real plus.

College Ads on TV

You can't turn on your TV these days without seeing commercials for colleges. Some of the ads are very good; if they capture your attention, they're obviously reaching something in you that's important.

As with any other "product" you see advertised on TV, though, you need to be a cautious consumer. Many college commercials, particularly ads run during the workday, are designed to appeal to stay-at-home moms, to people who are out of work, or to people who have been injured or disabled and can no longer do the work their previous job required of them. Before you pick up the phone and dial the toll-free number, you need to take note of the following cautions:

◆ Look for the words "financial aid for those who qualify." In many cases, colleges that use this phrase are not Title IV-eligible, meaning that you won't have access to free, federal financial aid. Loans, especially private loans, may be your only option.

◆ In the fine print along the bottom of your TV screen, you may see an indication of what agency or entity licenses the school. Write it down, and do some research on the entity before you choose one of these colleges.

Appendix A lists contact information for every state's agency for higher education. You can call and ask questions about any college you see advertised on TV. You can also use the COOL system to look up the college you see advertised and determine if they meet all the criteria you're looking for in a college.

The Least You Need to Know

◆ A school's classification indicates the types of programs and degrees it offers.

◆ Evaluate colleges for their best fit with your learning and your career goals.

◆ The College Opportunities Online Locator (COOL) system is a quick and easy way to compare colleges.

◆ COOL allows you to compare colleges using the same kind of data across the board.

Chapter 7

Online Learning Options

In This Chapter

- ◆ Understanding what distance learning is about
- ◆ Determining whether distance learning fits your learning style
- ◆ Considering the pros and cons of distance learning
- ◆ Mixing and matching online and traditional courses

Up to this point I've only mentioned online learning as one among many college options. It's now time to look deeper into the vast, virtual world of online learning.

Depending on your learning style and the kind of degree you seek, online learning might be an ideal option for you. However, although there are a number of high-quality universities that enable students to earn degrees entirely or partly via online courses, there are also several questionable degree mills out there that care more about their bottom line than the quality of your education. And, of course, online courses only make sense if you don't mind learning on your own and have the appropriate computer equipment and Internet access.

This chapter considers some of the pros and cons of online courses and how to make sure that if you choose to pursue your degree online that you get what you pay for.

Distance Learning and Online Learning

Distance learning merely means that you're taking a class while not on campus. In the past, colleges offered correspondence courses in some degree areas. Today, distance learning involves taking classes via the Internet. Some of these classes are fully online, and you never actually meet your professor or fellow students in person. Other courses blend in-person test dates with online lessons.

Cautionary Tales

The phrase *distance learning* is somewhat misleading because you could be taking an online class from a college a block from your house. *Online learning* is a more appropriate name for the type of courses I talk about in this chapter.

In some online classes, professors hold virtual discussion boards where class members can pose questions to the professor and other classmates. This is as close as you'll get to interacting with others in your virtual classroom. Of course, just as in a traditional class, you can e-mail questions to your professor at any time. No matter the format of your online course, you may still have to purchase books and other materials, although in some online classes everything you need will be available online.

Many traditional colleges and universities offer online programs in addition to their on-campus classes. For instance, you can enroll in academic programs in a traditional university that offers online classes that count toward your degree. Many adult students find this blended option works well because they get a degree from a college they know but can reduce the amount of time they spend on campus by taking some online courses on their own schedule.

Extra Credit

In their most recent report on distance learning, the National Center for Education Statistics found that more than half of all public, Title IV-eligible, degree-granting institutions offer online learning options.

Most students who take classes online take traditional classes as well, but a few universities make it possible to earn a degree exclusively through online courses. You can make sure that these completely virtual colleges meet all your needs by evaluating them in the same manner that you would a traditional college. For instance, you can also use the COOL system (see Chapter 6) to evaluate colleges that deliver all of their content online.

Is Online Learning for You?

Before you search for an online university, I encourage you to consider whether you're a good candidate for it. Is your personality a good match for this type of education? Are you self-directed enough to make sure you can keep pace with expected benchmarks for progress? The following sections will help you decide if online learning would work for you.

Are You Task-Oriented?

When you start a project at home or at work, do you tend to focus on it and finish it? If so, online learning might be a good option for you.

If, on the other hand, you're more of an idea person, who has multiple projects going on at once and can't seem to finish any of them, or they now bore you, you might do better in a traditional learning environment—one that has set deadlines and people to nudge you along the way.

Do You Prefer to Study or Learn Alone?

When you're working on something new, do you usually work through it on your own with no one else's input? If so, you might be a good candidate for online learning.

On the other hand, if you often seek the help or advice of others, you might prefer learning in the more social environment that the traditional college offers.

Do You Tend to Work Ahead of Others?

On team projects are you constantly done with your task before your colleagues? If so, you might prefer the freedom to work ahead that you have with online learning.

However, if you prefer more structure and tend to keep pace with your peers, the traditional classroom might be a more comfortable place for you.

You know yourself better than anyone else does. Ask more questions of yourself than just these. It's as important when you're making the decision to return to college to select the right college *format* as it is to select the right college.

Extra Credit _____

Think about your preferred learning style before you begin an online learning program.

Do You Have Good Computer Skills?

Chapter 3 outlined the basic computer skills you need to succeed in a traditional college setting. For online classes, you need a more advanced level of computer proficiency to succeed.

Most online universities describe the type of computer and web browser you need to access their sites and inform you of any other hardware or software needed to complete their coursework.

You'll probably also need a high-speed Internet connection such as DSL or cable to download materials in a timely fashion and efficiently navigate course websites. In all cases, check with the school you're attending for specific guidelines.

The Pros and Cons of Online Learning

Aside from figuring out if you are the kind of person who would do well in an online learning environment, you need to also consider the pros and cons of this type of education.

Pros

Some of the pros of online courses include the following:

◆ You can do your schoolwork on your own schedule.

◆ You can often earn an online degree more quickly than you can in a traditional college setting.

◆ Online courses are less disruptive for your family.

◆ Most online universities are very generous about granting credit for courses you have taken in other colleges.

◆ You are in charge of your own classroom.

◆ No one is there to mark you tardy or absent.

◆ Even if you choose to attend a completely virtual university, your diploma will look the same as one from a traditional university.

◆ You can go to school in your pajamas!

Cons

As with anything in life, distance learning has its downsides, too:

◆ Online programs can be more costly than traditional programs; convenience often costs more.

◆ Not all financial aid sources may be available at all online universities. Federal and state laws govern the financial aid that is available just as it governs traditional universities and colleges.

◆ Some academic content areas aren't easy to learn in an online format.

◆ You're a classroom of one, and you alone are responsible for what you learn.

◆ Not all degree programs are available online. However, advances are taking place that allow even laboratory experiments to take place virtually, using virtual chemicals, for example, to yield a virtual chemical reaction.

◆ It's harder to learn those "soft skills" that employers are looking for in prospective employees.

Deciding if online learning is for you requires that you take a close look at yourself, your style of learning, what you want out of your college education, and what you'd like to do with it when you're done.

How Employers View Online Degrees

Employers care about what you can do, how well you learn new skills, and how adaptable you are to change and to doing multiple tasks. Put simply, when you're hired, you're hired for what you know and are able to do. Your diploma is your credential saying you can do what people with similar degrees are able to do.

Just as most employers are unlikely to ask you for your college transcript, they're equally unlikely to ask to see your diploma. If the university you list on your resumé is an online university, you might be asked

Extra Credit

If you're taking a distance learning course or have made the decision to "attend" an online university, your employer may allow you to use your work computer for the purposes of "going to class." If you don't have a good computer at home, the use of a work computer is a great way that employers help support their employees in furthering their education.

some questions about the legitimacy of the program. However, if you received a degree from a quality program, you should be able to assuage their fears. On the other hand, if you got your diploma from an online university—even one with a good reputation—while another candidate steps up with a diploma from a well-known school, the employer might very well choose the other candidate because she has a traditional degree.

As distance learning becomes more popular and more online universities prove themselves, the value of an online degree will likely gain ground on traditional college degrees.

Which Online Schools Are Reputable?

Caveat emptor! Let the buyer beware. When you begin your search for online universities, you should be on high alert for empty promises and inflated prices. You want to make sure that you get good value for your money. But you should also expect to pay more for convenience and a degree from a school with a good reputation.

Electronic Campuses

Each state has some form of virtual university or list of virtual learning opportunities. Contact your state higher education agency (see Appendix A) to find out what courses are approved for online learning in your state. You're going to find that some academic areas have only one or two courses available, whereas other degrees can be earned by taking online courses exclusively.

Extra Credit

If you don't live in a state covered by the SREB, talk with your academic advisor and/ or the department head for your academic division about whether your school will allow a course on SREB's electronic campus to "count" toward your own degree program.

For efficiency in online delivery, and for the purpose of making more online courses available to more students, 16 southern states that comprise the Southern Regional Education Board (SREB) created the Electronic Campus at www.electroniccampus. org, a resource for locating online learning opportunities in the participating states (see the website for participating states). All online courses listed on the SREB site are reviewed by the SREB to ensure they meet the consortium's minimum requirements. If you live in one of the 16 participating states, you are guaranteed that the online courses listed on the electronic campus will transfer into your own degree program, even if the course is delivered by a campus two states away.

SREB's Electronic Campus is one of the best cross-state resources for locating online learning opportunities (as well as traditional learning opportunities). Go to the Electronic Campus (www.electroniccampus.org) home page and click the "I Am an Adult Learner" link, which takes you to a portal that assists adult learners in planning for college, exploring e-learning options, and even applying for courses or programs online.

You can locate thousands of courses and programs in any of the 16 SREB states. And if you can't find what you're looking for, SREB staff are available to help you find the right online degree program or course.

Cautionary Tales

Remember the old maps you'd see in your elementary school geography books—maps of what people thought the world looked like when it was believed to be flat? At the edge of the maps—at the edge of the world, as far as they were concerned—you'd always find the words, "Here there be dragons." When you begin to consider whether an online degree program is right for you, remember that there are modern-day dragons all over the Internet. You can easily fork over a lot of money and never see an academic credential come your way.

Choosing a Reputable School

Use the same caution when shopping for degree programs that you would when purchasing anything of value online. A sleek website isn't enough. You need to check multiple sources that provide evidence of an online college's reputation.

Extra Credit

Ask for a list of references or testimonials from former students or employers who have hired graduates from the online learning colleges you're researching.

You can't tell if an online college or degree program is reputable by simply looking for the ".edu" at the end of their website. Any operation can purchase a URL with a .edu ending and pose as a legitimate institution.

Accreditation

Read the fine print on the websites of the colleges or programs. Use the COOL website (www.nces.gov/ipeds/cool; for more on COOL, see Chapter 6) to check the accreditation status of the college you're considering, as well as if it is Title IV eligible.

For online universities, "accreditation" is key to determining whether or not the college meets certain standards of educational quality. You must do your homework to make sure that the college and program you select are reputable. Make the COOL site your "must" when searching for colleges of any kind.

Extra Credit

Accreditation is a seal of approval from an entity, saying that a particular college or university is performing up to par for the kind of college it is. The U.S. Department of Education accepts the seal of approval from a limited number of accrediting bodies for both traditional and online colleges. Licensing and accrediting aren't the same thing; note in the fine print when looking at online colleges who the accrediting body is and/or who licenses a particular school. Follow up with further research on those accrediting and licensing bodies.

Use Your State Officials

The best way to find out if an online college or university is reputable is to check with officials in your state who are responsible for higher education. Even if the state higher education agency doesn't have direct responsibility for accrediting an online college, the staff can help you do the necessary research on the college. State higher education officials also keep track of colleges and program offerings that are not consumer "best buys" and can help you avoid them.

State higher education staffers work for you. They are funded by their state government to help oversee higher education systems in that state, but they also fill the role of helping taxpayers in their states get the best higher education possible. They will help you avoid mistakes when selecting online learning opportunities. The state higher education agencies and websites are located in Appendix A. In some cases, the state agencies link to reputable online learning schools and programs, so check those sites out as well.

Cautionary Tales _____

The term *diploma mill* originally referred to correspondence schools that misled people into sending in money for what was essentially a worthless college diploma. The term applies to certain Internet-based companies that hide behind what sounds like legitimate online learning opportunities purely for the sake of making a profit. How do you distinguish a diploma mill from a legitimate online university? The first sign is that if it sounds too good to be true, it probably is. If a school promises you a degree in one short year when you've had no college before, it's probably too good to be true.

Most state agencies keep a list of diploma mills. If you have doubts about a program you're considering, your best bet is to check with your state higher education agency.

The Least You Need to Know

◆ Distance learning isn't for everyone, but for the right individual it might be the easiest and most efficient means of earning a college degree.

◆ Don't let fancy graphics and an official-looking website fool you into making a bad choice.

◆ Never provide personal or financial information to an online college until you've made sure that it is a legitimate operation.

◆ Always check with state officials to validate accreditation claims.

## Chapter 8

Selecting the Right Program

In This Chapter

- Choosing your courses
- Deciding on a major
- Considering a liberal studies degree
- Learning the value of fast-track programs
- Deciding on a full-time or part-time schedule

Adult students are often unsure about what degree or academic program will help them enter into, or advance within, their chosen career field. Choosing the right academic program before ever taking a class can save you time and money.

When adult students have previous college experience, many believe that their best choice is to finish the original degree program. But you're a different person than you were when you were in college the last time, and what you want today might be very different than before. Your interests may have changed. Your career plans may have changed. So don't think that you absolutely have to continue down the academic path you chose when you were 18.

Selecting the right program isn't just a question of what degree program you choose or what kind of college you attend. You can also decide how your academic program is structured. As colleges have become more focused on academic outcomes and less on how many hours students sit in their seats, more options have emerged. You have choices now that you didn't have even 10 years ago. And it's been adult students who have stimulated the recent variety in college programming.

Students, especially adult students, have been viewing colleges with a consumer's eye, and demand services for the money they pay. In addition, publicly funded college and university systems have found themselves competing for students in an environment where for-profit and not-for-profit accredited colleges have much to offer to adult students in the way of fast-track degree programs. Some of these nonpublic colleges and alternative programs cost more than traditional colleges, but researchers who study adult learners note that adults would rather pay more money for convenience.

The degree program you choose may dictate what options are available to you in terms of what college you attend, and vice versa. Keep in mind the different kinds of colleges you've learned about (see Chapter 6) as you think through your best options for selecting your degree program.

Special Programs for Returning Adults

Special programs for returning adults have grown in number as states have come to understand that college degrees have replaced the high school diploma as the minimum real standard of knowledge and skills needed for today's technologically advanced workforce. Many of the jobs that your parents could enter with a high school diploma are gone. Most well-paying jobs now require a college degree.

Programs for adults that had a technology focus grew in great numbers during the 1990s before the dot-com bust. In the 1990s, industries were practically waiting at the doors of the colleges on graduation day, snapping up new graduates, providing signing bonuses, and luring traditional and adult students into high-tech fields. Companies would approach colleges and say things such as, "We need 150 people with the skills to do our work within 60 days, can you deliver?"

The demand for technologically skilled employees outpaced traditional college programs. To meet the demand, colleges began to design programs especially for adult students, programs that could be completed at a quicker pace because demand was exceeding the number of graduates in certain high-tech areas.

You can benefit from these programs. You benefit by having more options to get your degree quickly and efficiently.

Bridge Programs

Some colleges offer bridge programs that help *cohorts* of students who have been out of college for some time re-adapt to the campus environment. Typically, bridge programs are held in the summer months, in advance of the fall semester or the fall return to college.

Bridge programs are meant to ease the transition from your family and work life to life as a student. You'll learn study skills and even go over basic academic content that will help you once school begins. Sometimes, enrollment in a bridge program is required if your credentials show you need a refresher in the basics. Take advantage of such programs if offered; you'll be more able to handle the rigors of the college classroom.

Bridge programs are usually shorter in duration than academic courses, but may be one-half to full-day courses and may last one week to a month. Ask the college about their bridge program offerings and consider whether any of them make sense for you. Although they may be time-intensive, their short duration makes bridge programs a pretty efficient means of getting back into the swing of school, and you'll start school with a group of people who are in the same boat that you are!

def•i•ni•tion

A **cohort** of students is a group of students who start a program at the same time. For instance, the students who entered Anytown College in the fall semester of 2006, who were 25 years of age or older, formed a cohort. Colleges collect data on different cohorts and measure their progress as they move through their years on campus.

Cautionary Tales

Check to make sure the bridge program you enroll in is specifically for adult students. Other bridge programs are geared toward younger students, especially for those on the cusp of college readiness; these bridge programs would not serve your needs.

Academic Programs for Working Adults Only

You already know that some colleges make it their primary mission to serve adult learners. Their programs are designed to meet adult learner schedules and academic needs. Programs such as this can actually cost a lot more money, but if the schools are accredited and eligible to provide federal financial aid, you may be able to reduce the impact of the increased cost by applying for financial aid.

Colleges that have made serving adult learners their primary mission are usually very convenient. However, many of them limit their degree program offerings to a small number of academic areas. If you want to get a degree in business or accounting, for example, such a college might work fine for you.

Liberal Studies Degrees

One of the choices you will need to make when deciding on your degree program is whether you want to focus your interests into a specific degree program where you are prepared to do one thing very well, or whether you want broad knowledge of many subjects so you can fit into a number of careers.

> **Extra Credit** _____
>
> Liberal studies has nothing to do with politics! The use of the word liberal merely means that you end up with a wide body of knowledge.
>
> If you have the time, you can work toward a specific degree and take some of the courses that liberal studies majors are taking as electives; if you do that, you will be one well-rounded graduate!

Liberal studies (sometimes also called liberal arts or liberal arts and sciences) programs produce graduates who have broad skill sets that they can apply to any number of careers. Liberal studies programs are really the most traditional type of college degrees available. In recent years, there has been a resurgence of liberal studies programs because they meet the needs of so many students who want a college degree but don't care whether their degree is in a specific area.

Although some employers and academics turn their noses up at liberal studies degrees, these degrees are compelling choices for adult learners. A liberal studies degree may not prepare you to be an organic chemist in a medical research facility, but it can prepare you for public service, for business and industry leadership, for human resources services, and for so many other career areas.

Talk to your advisor about whether a liberal studies degree will get you where you want to be, or whether your career plans require you to choose a specific academic degree program.

Fast-Track Degree Completion Programs

You've probably heard about fast-track degree programs on the radio or in television ads. Fast-track programs or *adult degree completion programs* are designed to help students who have previously built-up college credits go back to college and finish a degree in a much shorter time than if they returned to a traditional college.

Fast-track programs often use a cohort model—they enroll a certain number of students in the program and all the students take all their classes together and graduate at the same time.

Private colleges, in particular, have done a good job of creating fast-track programs because their campuses often have the flexibility to do so. Public colleges are gradually making their way to such programs as well. Many fast-track programs are specifically designed for liberal studies and a limited number of academic degree program areas. One of the reasons that the programs are "fast-track" is because they are only offered to students who have a certain number of credits completed toward a degree. Also, students who enter the programs go through a set curriculum, which is why many of the programs only produce liberal studies graduates.

def•i•ni•tion

Adult degree completion program is a term used to describe many fast-track degree attainment programs. Programs such as these generally work with students who have earned credit toward a degree but stopped attending college. The purpose of these special programs is to help adults obtain their degrees much more quickly than they could have in a traditional academic program.

When choosing an adult degree completion program, you may find that your degree choices are limited to a few degree program areas. This is because many academic programs cannot be completed adequately in a semester or two. A fast-track program might be right for you if you find one in an academic area that will help you change careers or move up in your job. Or if all you're looking for is a Bachelor's degree and aren't choosy about which academic area your degree is in, an adult degree completion program may also work great for you.

There are pros and cons to selecting a fast-track program. Pros include fast time-to-degree and convenience. Cons include the limited fields in which these degrees are offered.

Working Within Traditional Academic Programs

Having more choices for degree programs won't necessarily make your job easier. In fact, you'll probably feel overwhelmed when you see all the choices and begin weighing the pros and cons of one college versus another, costs of one college over another, and academic offerings at one school versus another. It's like a buffet dinner where everything on the table is your favorite food—it's all good, but you can't eat it all, so you have to choose.

Approach the decision process in small bites, digesting information a piece at a time, until you can put all the choices together into a decision—a decision that eventually becomes your plan. Keeping up with the buffet example, choose each meal course one at a time, making sure all the flavors will go together, to give you one fantastic meal—dessert included!

Extra Credit

Colleges offer course catalogs in both print and online forms. The catalogs explain all of the courses the college or university offers and describe the purposes of the class, as well as any prerequisites. The catalog, however, is not a list of courses offered each semester; it only outlines the course offerings the college has in its repertoire. To choose classes for a particular semester, you want to look for a *course schedule*. Usually available at the beginning of the previous term, the course schedule gives you specific classes that will be offered in the following term, including information on times, locations, and the names of faculty members teaching the classes. These are also available in print and online forms.

You don't have to make a decision the minute you walk into your advisor's office, so don't feel pressured to do so. However, colleges generally want you to declare a major before the beginning of your junior year, or halfway through, depending on how the college counts credit hours. Your personal circumstances will dictate not only when you declare a major, but also if you declare a major in a degree program that fits the aforementioned liberal studies option or a traditional academic program.

Time is usually the critical factor in the kind of program you choose. Should you declare a traditional academic major, your time-to-degree will be longer than if you choose an adult degree completion program. Frankly, this decision is so individualized it's hard to come up with a set of hard-and-fast steps to help you make that decision. Still, set aside all your individual circumstances and review the following reasons why you may wish to consider selecting a traditional academic program:

◆ Professional licensing and certification entities require traditional two-year or four-year academic degrees. These include accounting, radiologic technology, and nursing, to name a few.

◆ Many fields require traditional programs and expertise beyond a Bachelor's degree. These include psychology, library science, counseling, pharmacy, medicine, law, and other professional and graduate degrees.

♦ A specific academic degree conveys an understanding of specific knowledge, abilities, and skill sets for potential employers.

♦ If you begin a traditional academic program, your time-to-degree may be similar to fast-track programs if you have already completed all your general education courses.

♦ You will have more college options to choose from when selecting a traditional academic program.

♦ In addition to more college choices, you will have more varied courses to choose from in a traditional academic program.

> **Extra Credit** _____
>
> A good relationship with your academic advisor can go a long way in helping you sort through the academic, job-related, and personal considerations in choosing a degree program.

♦ Any form of teaching, whether for kindergarten through twelfth grade, community college, college, or university, requires traditional academic program completion at the undergraduate level, and some require study at the graduate level as well.

♦ If your career interests require graduate school of any form, a traditional academic program will allow you to avoid having to take *leveling* courses—courses you are already expected to have under your belt by the time you enter graduate school.

♦ You will interact with a more diverse group of students.

♦ You can complete your degree at your own pace, and go as slowly as one class a semester or as quickly as full-time.

On top of all these considerations are your family situation, your time constraints, your job situation, and other personal variables.

Keep in mind that traditional academic programs aren't more difficult than liberal studies or fast-track programs. And you may not feel as if you've fully "done college" unless you have completed a traditional academic degree program.

Part-Time Versus Full-Time Programs

Even though more than half of all the students in college today are adults (over the age of 25), few of them attend college full-time. Different colleges have different definitions of full-time, but the majority of schools on a semester system consider 12 credit hours (a financial aid definition; still, some colleges require 15 hours as full-time) of courses to be full-time. Most classes are 3 credit hours per semester, so a 12-credit-hour load would mean four classes.

Four classes in a single semester is a lot for an adult who works full-time and also manages a family. Having said that, some adults do manage to go to school full-time and work a full-time job, provided that their spouse helps out a lot and they have some time to study.

As you and your spouse and family talk through your plans for college, consider whether or not you can, for a short period of time, live on one income. If both husband and wife have been working and one wants to attend college, review your finances and see if your family can live through a short period of time on a tight budget. For instance, if you forgo your daily latté, pack a brown-bag lunch, and skip that European vacation this year, you just might be able to swing it.

Extra Credit _____

If you do find a way to enroll in college full-time, studies show that you're more likely to stay in college and complete your degree.

It might be difficult to even consider such sacrifices, but there are benefits to trying. If you do return full-time, you will complete your degree faster. The second income you can add to the household after you hold a Bachelor's degree can be as much as twice what you're earning now. So if you and your family can live on one income for a couple of years, there's a good chance that you can do college full-time.

For many adult students (such as single parents), however, the realities of today's economy make it impossible for them to return to college full-time. Look on the bright side: although it will take you longer to get your degree, the pace of part-time college work is likely to be less stressful. When going part-time, though, you have to keep motivating yourself to enroll and attend at least one class every semester.

Try to take summer classes as well, because you can make it through two summer classes in a short period of time; fall and spring semesters are longer, but your classes don't meet as often.

Taking more classes per semester might have financial benefits you never considered. If you attend half-time (6 hours), you may be able to receive financial aid. If you only take one class per semester, more often than not, you will have to foot your own bill.

> **Student Center**
>
> Jina has two children, is married, and has held a fairly good-paying job for more than 20 years. She'd reached the highest position she could hold in her company without a college degree, but the demands of life always kept her from going to college full-time. Persistently, consistently, Jina took a class each semester year after year. Not long ago, she walked across the stage and earned her Bachelor's degree. She's now been promoted to an executive position in her company and says that all the time and effort was worth it; she is one of the few in her company who has a college degree and longevity in her company. Her future is a bright one.

The Least You Need to Know

- You don't have to continue the same academic program you began the last time you were in college.

- You're in a good position to take advantage of recent adult-friendly changes in how academic programs are constructed.

- Some colleges offer programs just for adults.

- Fast-track programs can help you get your degree quickly.

- Some careers require that you take a traditional academic route.

- Whether you attend college full- or part-time, it's worth the effort to complete your degree and increase your earning potential.

Part 3

Paying for College

The good news is that going to college won't send you to the poorhouse. There are more ways to pay for college than ever before, in part because so many jobs require a college degree. Federal and state governments offer need-based financial aid and student loan programs. Campuses offer tuition waivers. And, each year, millions in private scholarship money go unused.

College probably does cost more now than when you last looked at the price tag. The costs will differ, though, depending on whether you choose a public school or a private college. Big research universities cost more than community colleges do. Your choice of degree program and college will also impact how much college will cost.

In this part, I help you fill out the Free Application for Federal Student Aid (FAFSA) and walk you through various need- and merit-based aid options out there. I also take the mystery out of student loan programs and even offer you some tips on negotiating a lower tuition bill.

How Much Will College Cost?

In This Chapter

- Comparing college costs
- Negotiating student fees
- Calculating the true cost of going to college
- Determining your financial aid eligibility

Survey after survey in the United States shows that people consistently overestimate how much it costs to go to college. Young and mature students alike often stay away from college because they mistakenly believe it is too expensive for them.

It's true that some colleges cost several thousand dollars a year, but these are few and far between. The expensive colleges are usually private colleges with international reputations. But even the cost of the highest-priced colleges can be made more reasonable by financial aid.

Myths abound when it comes to college costs. In this chapter, though, you'll read some straight talk about costs and what to look for as you're comparing colleges. There's no single answer to the question "How much will it cost to go to college?" There are, however, a series of questions you can pose when comparing colleges that will help you gauge the relative cost to *you* for each college you survey.

Looking Into the Cost of College

You have a wide range of choices when it comes to college. However, the phrase "you get what you pay for" doesn't apply to a college education, because sometimes the least expensive colleges have fabulous faculty and academic programs. Likewise, the most expensive colleges may not offer a better education than a less expensive college. A bunch—and I do mean a *bunch*—of factors contribute to a college's bottom line.

> **Extra Credit**
>
> The College Board publishes an annual listing of college costs called *Trends in College Pricing*. The publication can be accessed on the College Board's website at www.collegeboard.com/research/home.

Did you know that there is a difference in the published price of college and how much you will need to pay out of your pocket? Much like when you are buying a car, rarely do students have to pay the "sticker price" when going to college. Financial aid of all kinds—grants, scholarships, and student loans—reduce the financial impact of going to college.

Nearly two thirds of all full-time undergraduate students receive grant aid from the government or the college. Don't think that just because someone you know wasn't eligible for aid when he went to college that you won't be. A number of factors figure into your aid eligibility. The important thing to remember is that, no matter the price of going to college, odds are you can qualify for some kind of aid to help reduce your college bills.

> **Cautionary Tales**
>
> As you read reports on college costs and on financial aid, note that many reports use national averages. Within those averages, there is a great deal of variability in cost. Trends are good for gauging how things have progressed over a period of time, and it's good for you to see what has happened to college costs since you were last in school. But don't read about national averages and think you're done. Do local research as well—you might live in a state where college costs are higher or lower than the national average.

Here are some things to keep in mind as you begin looking at the financial impact of going to college:

◆ A college's *published price* is the price of attending college at a particular institution for a single academic year or semester before financial aid is factored into the cost. This is the amount you are likely to see listed on college websites. Think of the published price as being equivalent to the "sticker price" of a new car.

◆ A college's *net price* is the average price of attending college after federal, state, institutional, and private financial aid are taken into consideration. On average, this more accurately indicates how affordable a college is to a particular student or family. *This is the average amount that you will pay out of your pocket.* Students with a high financial aid need (and who therefore receive more aid) may have a net price of zero; students with more personal resources will be expected to pay more of their own college expenses. You will not find the net price on college websites; you need to go through the financial aid application process before you know precisely how much it will cost *you* to attend the college of your choice.

Many people make the mistake of looking only at a college's published price and therefore think that college is outside their financial means. Until you actually go through the financial aid process, you won't know what your bottom-line cost is.

Extra Credit _____

Many colleges publish their financial aid in terms of total aid awarded. At first glance, it might look like the college provides a large number of scholarships and grants. However, financial aid disclosures also include student loans awarded as part of the college's financial aid estimates. You will get a better estimate of a campus's commitment to free, nonloan aid if you ask for nonloan aid *and* loan-based aid as separate figures—just to make sure that their financial aid picture isn't being skewed by a large student loan volume.

To get a better idea of how much your college costs are, on average, check to see the ratio of a college's published price with its net price. College officials can provide this information for you, even if it's as simple as giving you the average amount of financial aid that students receive. Once you know the average amount of financial aid, subtract that amount from the published price (making sure that you're comparing semester price with semester financial aid average or annual price with annual financial aid average). You won't have an exact price at this point, but you will have a better idea of the net price of the college and, therefore, a better idea of what it might cost *you* to attend a particular college.

If you obtain the net price of each college you are considering, you'll be more closely comparing apples to apples.

Too often, students look only at the published tuition price for a college. However, tuition is merely the cost associated with delivering classes. Several other costs should also be considered when pricing colleges.

What the Word "Tuition" Really Means

Most campuses have a "per credit hour" price for tuition that varies greatly from school to school. Keep in mind that a per credit hour cost is usually not the same as the cost of a single class. To find out how much a class costs, you must multiply the number of credit hours for the course by the per credit hour price.

For example, let's say a college charges $60 per credit hour. You want to take an English Composition class that is worth three credit hours. To calculate the tuition for this class, multiply the three credit hours by the $60 credit hour price to get a total cost of $180 (3 × $60 = $180).

Repeat this calculation for each class you want to take, and you will get the total cost of tuition for the semester.

Extra Credit

Some colleges charge different rates per credit hour depending on the type of class being offered. For example, it usually costs less for a college to deliver an English class than it does to deliver an engineering or chemistry course. In some cases, campuses will assign a higher per credit hour fee to more expensive classes.

A few colleges have simplified the matter by having students pay a set tuition amount if a student is attending full-time (anywhere from the minimum full-time requirement of 12 credit hours per semester to 18 credit hours). In addition to making tuition a simpler amount to calculate, colleges do this in order to encourage students to take more hours per semester. If you can take 18 hours for the same price as 12 hours, you're getting 6 hours—as much as two classes—free. Eighteen credit hours is a big commitment, however, so take care not to sign up for more classes than you can reasonably fit into your life just because the price is right.

Ask for Truth in Tuition

You've probably seen or heard news stories about the large increases in tuition over the past several years. These stories make it sound as if the costs are skyrocketing out of a regular person's ability to pay. Too many people (reporters included) think that a college's published tuition price is actually the full cost of going to college. By now, though, *you* know that it is not.

It is true, however, that colleges have been raising tuition. Many states have passed tax cuts that have reduced the amount of tax dollars that are available to help pay for college. When this happens, it means that students must pay a greater proportion of the cost of college. Colleges have fixed costs (keeping the lights on, hiring good faculty, providing student services) and when taxes are cut, tuition rates generally increase. In many cases, these tax cuts mean that you're paying less in state tax dollars. And for most people, the tax cuts even out any increase in tuition.

Also keep in mind that if you are attending a public college or university, you're not really paying the full cost of your education. In fact, your "net price" is generally around one third of the total cost. The state in which you live provides tax dollars to help pay for the remaining two thirds of the actual cost.

Also, when tuition rises, you aren't bearing the cost alone because the increases in tuition are likely going to be mitigated by an increase in the financial aid you're awarded.

def•i•ni•tion

Although tuition costs are talked about incessantly, what do those figures *really* mean? **Truth in tuition** means that a campus lets you know what proportion of the total cost tuition really is. Tuition, though important, is but a small part of the overall cost of attending college.

What about private colleges? Private colleges, rather than being supported by the state, are often supported by donor contributions. Tuition rates at private colleges are, indeed, generally much higher than you find at public colleges because, no matter how fabulous a donor base a private college has, it's rarely as much as state support for public colleges.

Keep in mind that as long as the private college is Title IV eligible (meaning students can receive federal financial aid made available to them through the Title IV financial aid provisions in the Higher Education Act), you can receive federal financial aid. Remember, too, that federal financial aid (including loans) is calculated on the college's cost of attendance. In many cases, because of financial aid availability, the net price of attending a private college can still be competitive with a public college.

There are caps, or limits, on how much financial aid any one person can receive in a single year, however, so you don't expect

Extra Credit

Private colleges also offer federal student aid. There are a few colleges in the United States that have chosen to take no federal dollars, even for student scholarships, because it frees them from having to meet certain federal guidelines. If you attend a private college and receive federal financial aid, that college must abide by all applicable federal laws, including civil rights laws.

100 percent of your cost of attendance at an expensive private college to be covered by federal financial aid. Private colleges work to make up the difference with institutional aid and private scholarships.

Paying Fees on Top of Tuition Costs

Colleges and universities also apply fees to your account over and above any tuition that you pay. These fees, plus your tuition, are the cost of taking that one English Composition course.

Not all classes have the same fees associated with them. Some classes involve additional fees because you are using more college resources. These can include science and engineering courses, where you will pay for the use of a laboratory and/or materials. They can also include art and architecture courses where standard supplies are provided for every student. These courses can even include music classes, particularly if you need to use a university-provided instrument. The course description in the course catalog generally indicates if additional fees are required.

Not all fees are related to the cost of delivering the course. Other fees are assessed for areas of the campus that provide services. Some colleges will waive some of these fees for commuting adult students.

For some campuses, a select number of fees might not even be assessed to your account because you are classified as a commuter student. Obviously, of course, you wouldn't be assigned fees for room and board in a dormitory, because you don't live on campus. You're probably also not selecting a meal plan on campus, as resident students do, so those fees aren't likely to show up. But some fees are assessed automatically for services on campus that you *know* you will never use.

Extra Credit _____

You don't have to be a dorm-living, full-time student to purchase a meal plan on most campuses. Sometimes it can be cost-efficient for you to purchase a small meal plan even when you're a commuter student. Campus food is often less expensive than the nearest restaurant or fast-food establishment, and most college campuses feature major food vendors offering quite good food. Buying a small meal plan card can save you money and time while also helping make sure you eat and stay on top of your academic game on those very busy days when you have school and work.

Some of the fees that may be negotiable for nonresident and/or adult students on some campuses include the following:

- **Infirmary fees.** Nearly every campus with residential students has an infirmary on-site. The fees that support the infirmary are rarely budget-breaking; however, if you know that you will never be using the infirmary's services because of your own health-care coverage through work, this fee can be negotiated. Keep in mind, though, that if your coverage at work is minimal, college infirmaries are often very convenient and inexpensive. Before you negotiate this fee away, consider its potential benefits.

- **Technology fees.** Campuses often assess a technology fee to support computer labs on campus. You may be able to negotiate a reduction in part of this fee, but do so only if you don't plan on taking advantage of a campus e-mail address or computer lab.

- **Student activity fees.** Before you try to get this fee waived, find out exactly what student activities are supported through these dollars. If the fees help operate a tutoring center, it's worth your while to pay it. However, if it's there to support activities that will primarily be used by younger students who live on campus, you might be in a position to negotiate its removal from your account.

- **Campus newspaper fees.** If you're coming in and out of a campus, or taking a class or two online and will never be picking up a student newspaper, you'd be in a position to negotiate such a fee. However, be fair about this one. If you like to pick up the paper on the way to your class, or if you access the newspaper online, be a good sport and pay this fee.

- **Fitness center/pool fees.** Larger campuses often have high-quality gyms, fitness centers, and/or swimming pools for student use. If you're a regular member of a gym and don't need these facilities, you can often negotiate this fee. However, do some price shopping. Check out the campus facilities as well as noncredit aerobic classes, weight training classes, and so on. Campus gyms and fitness centers are often much less expensive than private gym fees. Another benefit to campus gyms is that they are often open longer hours.

One of the reasons to take a close look at the fees being assessed on student accounts is that campuses sometimes increase fees as a way to avoid raising tuition. Fees are determined at the university level, whereas tuition costs usually involve the input of a governing board or a coordinating board. In some states, tuition may even be governed by state legislatures.

Books and Instructional Materials

Books and materials will also contribute to the cost of going to college. Some classes, especially those that have laboratory sections, may also require that you buy supplies, chemicals, and/or other consumable materials that you will use during the course of the semester.

Extra Credit _____

One thing may come as a pleasant surprise to you if you've been out of college for a while. Textbooks now tend to come with ancillary study aids in the form of CDs and DVDs. These often contain chapter summaries, sample tests, and review questions.

Less Obvious College Costs

Tuition and fees, together, offer the best side-by-side comparison when looking at college costs. However, many students, especially returning adults who haven't considered these elements in some time, forget that there are costs associated with college that fly below the radar screen. Sure, you're going to have to eat whether you're in college or not. But have you thought about increased transportation costs associated with traveling to class? What about how much it might cost you to buy a new laptop? Basic living costs do figure into the cost of attending college, so think about the number of classes you're taking, the interruption to your daily transportation schedule, and the food you won't be eating at home.

Cost of Attendance

Cost of attendance (_COA_) is a federal term, and is determined using rules that were established by federal law. COA is the upper limit of financial aid that you can receive (loan and nonloan aid alike) on a particular college campus. COA will be higher for some colleges than others. The following items are included in the federal COA definition of eligible costs for full-time, undergraduate students:

- Tuition and fees
- On-campus room and board or housing and food for students who live off-campus
- Books
- Supplies
- Transportation

- Loan fees
- Child care or dependent care, if applicable
- Miscellaneous expenses, such as the cost of a computer

- Costs related to student disability, with amounts based on the kind of disability and type of equipment or services needed
- Reasonable costs for eligible study-abroad programs

The calculations for COA are different for students who are attending less than half-time (six credit hours is considered half-time for an undergraduate student, as defined by law). For half-time students, COA does not include living expenses, only tuition and fees, books, supplies, transportation, and dependent care expenses.

The best way to see the full range of eligible costs for you is to talk directly with a financial aid official at one or more of the colleges you are considering. Although COA is defined in law, if you have unusual circumstances and needs and are attending less than half-time, you may be able to get additional assistance.

How Cost of Attendance Affects Financial Aid

You can never receive more in financial aid than 100 percent of COA as determined for you at a particular institution. Lower-cost institutions in areas of the country with lower living expenses will have a lower COA calculated than high-cost institutions in areas of the country with higher costs of living.

Your aid, including your student loan aid, will be capped each semester by your official COA. There are also national caps for loan aid—caps which haven't been raised sufficiently to meet the past decade's increases in costs.

The Least You Need to Know

- Look beyond tuition to find the cost of returning to college.
- How your state funds higher education will impact how much you, the student, pays.
- Federal laws dictate how the cost of attendance (COA) is calculated for each campus.
- COA is calculated differently if you return to college less than half-time.
- Fees that are assessed on top of tuition can increase your college costs but may also be negotiated.

## Chapter 10

Affording College: Free Financial Aid

In This Chapter

- ◆ Filling out the Free Application for Federal Student Aid (FAFSA)
- ◆ Learning about the different kinds of financial aid available
- ◆ Qualifying for federal and state grants
- ◆ Applying for merit-based scholarships
- ◆ Getting free financial aid advice

It's a widely held belief that adult students have enough money to pay their own way through college. That belief, however, is wrong more often than not. In many states, one half to two thirds of adults older than age 25 who are returning to college meet the low-income criteria that make them eligible for free federal aid.

Unfortunately, many state and federal free financial aid policies place a greater emphasis on paying for students to attend college directly out of high school. All too often adult students are treated as an afterthought. Still, free financial aid can be yours for the taking, provided you meet certain need-based criteria. If you don't qualify for free financial aid, you can still take advantage of low-interest student loans (See Chapter 11).

On the one hand, it's a good thing that funds are available so that young students (including, perhaps, your own children) have the chance to go to college right out of high school. In fact, national data tells us that students who go directly to college after high school are more likely to stay in college and obtain their degrees.

As good as that sounds, though, adults need financial aid, too. Just as with younger students, studies show that when adults receive the aid they need they are more likely to finish college and get their degrees.

Don't worry: there's plenty of aid to go around—it's just a matter of what *kind* of aid you qualify for.

Federal Financial Aid: An Overview

The federal government makes available three kinds of federal student aid:

- **Grants**—financial aid that doesn't have to be repaid.
- **Work-study**—allows you to earn money for your education.
- **Loans**—allow you to borrow money for school. You must repay your loans, with interest.

FEDERAL STUDENT AID SUMMARY CHART

Federal Student Aid Program	Type of Aid	Program Details	Annual Award Limits
Federal Pell Grant	Grant: does not have to be repaid	Available almost exclusively to undergraduates; all eligible students will receive the Federal Pell Grant amount they qualify for	$400 to $4,050 for 2006-07
Federal Supplemental Educational Opportunity Grant (FSEOG)	Grant: does not have to be repaid	For undergraduates with exceptional financial need; priority is given to Federal Pell Grant recipients; funds depend on availability at school	$100 to $4,000
Federal Work-Study	Money is earned while attending school; does not have to be repaid	For undergraduate and graduate students; jobs can be on campus or off campus; students are paid at least federal minimum wage	No annual minimum or maximum award amounts
Federal Perkins Loan	Loan: must be repaid	Interest charged on this loan is 5 percent for both undergraduate and graduate students; payment is owed to the school that made the loan	$4,000 maximum for undergraduate students; $6,000 maximum for graduate and professional students; no minimum award amount
Subsidized Direct or FFEL Stafford Loan	Loan: must be repaid	Subsidized: U.S. Department of Education pays interest while borrower is in school and during grace and deferment periods; you must be at least a half-time* student	$2,625 to $8,500, depending on grade level
Unsubsidized Direct or FFEL Stafford Loan	Loan: must be repaid	Unsubsidized: Borrower is responsible for interest during life of the loan; you must be at least a half-time* student; financial need is not a requirement	$2,625 to $18,500, depending on grade level (includes any subsidized amounts received for the same period)
Direct or FFEL PLUS Loan	Loan: must be repaid	Available to parents of dependent undergraduate students who are enrolled at least half-time*	Maximum amount is cost of attendance* minus any other financial aid the student receives; no minimum award amount

Source: U.S. Department of Education, Federal Student Aid, Students Channel, Funding Education Beyond High School: The Guide to Federal Student Aid, *Washington, D.C., 2006.*

This chapter explains federal grant aid and other forms of financial aid that you don't have to pay back, such as state grant aid and scholarships. Chapter 11 tackles federal work-study and federal student loans. These broad categories of financial aid can be broken down into various types of grants and loans. The previous figure provides a quick overview of all the major federal financial aid programs available to adult students.

How Adult Students Access Grant Aid

Students of all ages must fill out a *Free Application for Federal Student Aid* (*FAFSA*) form to qualify for federal *grant aid*, most forms of state grant aid, and most campus-based grant aid as well. You can pick up a paper copy of the FAFSA at any financial aid office on campus or even at a high school counselor's office.

def•i•ni•tion

FAFSA (pronounced FAF-suh), which stands for **Free Application for Federal Student Aid,** is one of the most important acronyms you'll learn as you return to college. If you want any form of financial aid, you must fill out this form to see what kind of aid you qualify for. You should fill out a FAFSA no matter what your financial situation is. You might be surprised what aid is available to you! You will need to fill out the FAFSA each academic year that you are attending college.

Grant aid is financial aid that is free, meaning that you don't have to pay back any grant money given to you (unless, of course, you withdraw from school and owe a refund).

Filling Out the FAFSA

With the paper form, you fill out a number of pages of personal information and data. Then you submit it to the federal government via snail mail and wait for a Student Aid Report (SAR) to be sent back to you and to the campuses that you indicate on your FAFSA. The SAR is a report generated out of the data that you input; it indicates what aid you are eligible for at the federal level. See Appendix B for sample copies of the FAFSA and SAR. The following figure illustrates the financial aid process.

The paper form of the FAFSA is rapidly being replaced by the online version. If you go to www.fafsa.ed.gov, you can fill out the FAFSA online and submit the form over the Internet. To do so, you'll need to sign up for a Personal Identification Number (PIN) to ensure the security of your data. You'll need this PIN for subsequent access to your FAFSA records; keep it in a safe location so others don't have access to information about your identity.

HOW DO I APPLY FOR FEDERAL STUDENT AID?

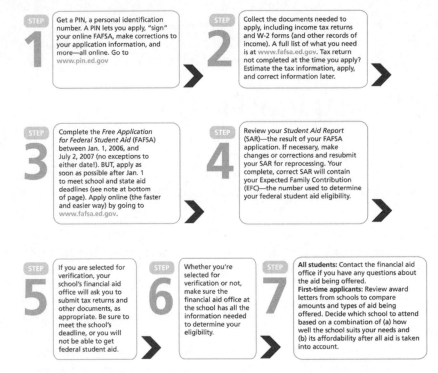

STEP 1 Get a PIN, a personal identification number. A PIN lets you apply, "sign" your online FAFSA, make corrections to your application information, and more—all online. Go to www.pin.ed.gov

STEP 2 Collect the documents needed to apply, including income tax returns and W-2 forms (and other records of income). A full list of what you need is at www.fafsa.ed.gov. Tax return not completed at the time you apply? Estimate the tax information, apply, and correct information later.

STEP 3 Complete the *Free Application for Federal Student Aid* (FAFSA) between Jan. 1, 2006, and July 2, 2007 (no exceptions to either date!). BUT, apply as soon as possible after Jan. 1 to meet school and state aid deadlines (see note at bottom of page). Apply online (the faster and easier way) by going to www.fafsa.ed.gov.

STEP 4 Review your *Student Aid Report* (SAR)—the result of your FAFSA application. If necessary, make changes or corrections and resubmit your SAR for reprocessing. Your complete, correct SAR will contain your Expected Family Contribution (EFC)—the number used to determine your federal student aid eligibility.

STEP 5 If you are selected for verification, your school's financial aid office will ask you to submit tax returns and other documents, as appropriate. Be sure to meet the school's deadline, or you will not be able to get federal student aid.

STEP 6 Whether you're selected for verification or not, make sure the financial aid office at the school has all the information needed to determine your eligibility.

STEP 7 **All students:** Contact the financial aid office if you have any questions about the aid being offered. **First-time applicants:** Review award letters from schools to compare amounts and types of aid being offered. Decide which school to attend based on a combination of (a) how well the school suits your needs and (b) its affordability after all aid is taken into account.

Note:
Y ou also might be able to get financial aid from your state government, your school or a private scholarship. Research nonfederal aid early (ideally, start in the spring of your junior year of high school). Be sure to meet all application deadlines!

Source: U.S. Department of Education, Federal Student Aid, Students Channel, Funding Education Beyond High School: The Guide to Federal Student Aid, *Washington, D.C., 2006.*

The FAFSA's online site uses highly sophisticated security, so you should feel comfortable inputting your information into this federal government form.

Whether you are using the paper or online version, it's going to take some time to fill out the form. Over the past decade, the government has made the FAFSA an easier document to complete (the feds call it "reducing the paperwork burden"), but it's still an onerous form to fill out. It's not quite as bad as filling out your taxes, but it can still be taxing to complete!

If you're using the online version, after you input a piece of data that is used in multiple parts of the form, that particular piece of data automatically "pre-populates" other data fields. For example, if you input your name and Social Security number on page one of the online form and it's also needed on page five, you won't have to fill it out again. This nifty feature will save you time over the paper version of the FAFSA.

Extra Credit _____

You can save time and effort using the online version of the FAFSA. In addition to the efficiency of using the online format, you will receive reports and communications from the federal government, as well as the campuses you send your data to, via e-mail. You will receive your SAR and other information much sooner than students who use the paper version.

Your best bet is to set aside some time to make sure you have with you all the pertinent information you'll need to complete the form. Some of the information you will need includes the following:

◆ **Demographic information:** Name, birth date, gender, race, contact information, and so on.

◆ **Earnings information:** Your most recent W-2 forms and/or tax forms submitted to the Internal Revenue Service. If you're attending college in the fall, then you will need the data from the tax forms for the same calendar year as the fall semester when you go to college.

◆ **Academic information:** Your academic history as well as a list of which colleges you want your SAR report sent to for scholarship, grant, and loan information.

These are just a few of the documents that you will need to have on hand to fill out the FAFSA. The U.S. Department of Education provides a worksheet you can print out in advance of completing the online application, so you'll have all of the information you need before you get started.

The step-by-step directions for filling out the FAFSA are easy to follow and not only explain what information is required in each part of the form but also, when needed, how and where to locate the information. For instance, when you need information from your tax forms, the FAFSA directions indicate what line of your tax form the information appears on.

Even if you are only seeking state or campus-based aid, you'll probably have to fill out the FAFSA. Most state and campus-based agencies use the uniform FAFSA form when determining financial aid eligibility. You might as well come to terms with the fact that you'll need to fill out the FAFSA.

You can also get assistance filling out the FAFSA by making an appointment with an official in a college financial aid office. Your best bet for getting help is to complete as much of the FAFSA as possible on your own and then get help with the parts that you are having trouble with. If the financial aid office is staffed well, you may also be able to get help over the phone.

Extra Credit _____

Many states have College Goal Sunday programs through which you can get free help in filling out the FAFSA. You can search the Internet for College Goal Sunday programs and see if your state has one. Even though not all states have College Goal Sunday programs, most campuses have some form of financial aid help day. Make use of these free forums; they are there to help you!

Some states even provide financial aid counselors in a telethon-based format on the public television station. Through these televised events, sponsors share information about financial aid while trained financial aid experts answer any questions you might have.

The U.S. Department of Education's website (www.fafsa.ed.gov) tries to make filling out the FAFSA as easy as possible, but don't worry if you run into a snag. Whether you pick up the phone for help or seek help in person from a financial aid official, you will be able to find all the help you need.

Qualifying for Financial Aid

To be eligible for federal student aid, you must meet the following basic eligibility requirements as outlined by the Office of Federal Student Aid:

◆ Demonstrate financial need (except for certain loans; see Chapter 11).

◆ Be a U.S. citizen or eligible noncitizen with a valid Social Security number. If you are not a U.S. citizen, contact the Office of Federal Student Aid at 1-800-4-FED-AID (1-800-433-3243) or www.federalstudentaid.ed.gov to see whether you qualify.

◆ Be working toward a degree or certificate in an _eligible program_.

def•i•ni•tion _____

According to the Office of Federal Student Aid, an **eligible program** is a program of organized instruction or study that leads to an academic, professional, or vocational degree or certificate, or other recognized educational credential. Certain exceptions exist for teachers enrolled in programs to obtain a professional credential or certification required by their state or students who must take certain course work to qualify for admission into an eligible program.

◆ Show, by one of the following means, that you're qualified to obtain a post-secondary education:

  ◆ Have a high school diploma or its equivalent.

  ◆ Pass an approved ability-to-benefit (ATB) test (if you don't have a diploma or GED, a school can administer a test to determine whether you can benefit from the education offered at that school).

  ◆ Meet other federally-approved standards.

  ◆ Complete a high school education in a home school setting approved under state law.

◆ Register with the Selective Service, if you're a male between the ages of 18 and 25.

◆ Maintain satisfactory academic progress once in school.

Cautionary Tales _____

Question 31 on the FAFSA asks, "Have you ever been convicted of possessing or selling illegal drugs?" Leaving this question blank automatically makes you ineligible for federal student aid. If you have been convicted of selling or possessing illegal drugs, fill out a "Drug Worksheet" (available online at www.fafsa.ed.gov, in the "Worksheets" section of the site) to find out if you are eligible to receive student aid. Even if you are ineligible for federal aid because of a drug conviction, you might still qualify for state or school-based aid.

Federal and State Grants

The federal government offers two kinds of grants:

◆ Federal Pell Grants

◆ Federal Supplemental Educational Opportunity Grants (FSEOG)

In addition, states make financial aid available to their residents. The following sections explain each of these grant types.

The Federal Pell Grant

The most predominant form of federal grant aid for students attending college is the Pell Grant, which is available to low-income students. Unlike student loans, you do not have to pay this grant back. You can only receive a Pell Grant as an undergraduate student; it's not available to students working on graduate degrees.

To determine whether you are eligible for a Pell Grant, the government considers your *Estimated Family Contribution (EFC)*. EFC is the part of the cost of attending college you are expected to provide to support your own college experience. It is based on your income and the cost of the college you are planning to attend. EFC is a sort of sliding scale, based on income, so that the lowest-income students receive the largest grants. For example, a student with an EFC of zero would be eligible for the maximum amount of Pell aid.

def•i•ni•tion

Estimated Family Contribution, or EFC, is the part of the cost of attending college you are expected to provide to support your own college experience.

The maximum Pell Grant is currently $4,050 per year. Increases in the Pell Grant have not kept pace with recent increases in tuition, so its buying power has declined. The buying power of the grant is also lower at higher-priced institutions. But for lower-priced schools such as community colleges, the Pell Grant takes care of the total cost of attendance for many students. At more expensive institutions the Pell Grant can be combined with state grant aid and/or student loans to pay for the cost of attendance.

If you received Pell Grants during a previous stint in college, let your financial aid office know. Your status may have changed since the last time you received a Pell Grant. Regardless, your federal aid will be determined by your current financial situation as determined by your FAFSA.

The Federal Supplemental Educational Opportunity Grant (FSEOG)

FSEOGs are available to undergraduates with exceptional financial need—those with the lowest EFC numbers. It is particularly important to apply early if you want to be considered for an FSEOG Grant, because funds are limited, and not everyone who qualifies for the grant might get one.

FSEOGs differ from the Pell Grant in that not all schools participate in the FSEOG program. And unlike Pell Grants, the amount of other student aid you receive can affect the amount of your FSEOG award.

Federal Pell Grant recipients receive priority for FSEOG awards, which range from $100 to $4,000.

State Grants

States primarily invest in need-based grants or grants that combine need and merit as qualifications.

The federal government has special programs that provide matching funds for states that invest state tax dollars in need-based aid. Each state's aid program differs in how it's administered, but the states base "need" on your FAFSA results, just as the federal government does.

Other state aid (grants and/or scholarships) is provided out of lottery proceeds and other large-scale state forms of revenue. Most states with lottery-based scholarships limit applicants to the students who are just exiting high school. However, check with your state's higher education agency (see Appendix A) to see if adult students can qualify for the lottery scholarship, if your state has one.

If your state's lottery scholarship does provide funding for adult students, ascertain whether the funds are available based on need only (which, again, is likely to be based on the FAFSA or some other state-developed income verification process), or if merit is also a factor.

After you learn about your eligibility, ask the officials at your state higher education agency how to apply. Some states require an application form separate from the FAFSA. Other states have campus officials notify them of students who are eligible based on FAFSA results or FAFSA results combined with academic history. In the case of state-based scholarships, with the exception of those tied to federal matching funds, there's no single way to apply. States may be similar in how they operate state scholarship programs, but the actual process happens 50 different ways—one for each state!

Scholarships for Adult Students

Even though adult students make up more than half the student body on many campuses, scholarships that are "for adults only" are still fairly rare. Talk to the financial aid officers at your campus of choice and try to get your name in the hat for local scholarships created for adults. You're more likely to find campus-managed scholarships that are open to students of all ages. These are your best bets for finding scholarships that fit you.

Not all scholarships available to you are managed by the campuses. Local civic organizations and foundations also sponsor scholarships, and many of them handle the management of the scholarships themselves. Rarely are these scholarships limited only to traditional students.

Money Based on Academic Merit

There many different definitions of merit. Merit doesn't always mean that you had a 4.0 GPA in high school or graduated at the top of your class. In some cases, merit means that, as a student, you overcame life obstacles or participated in community service. Many states and campuses have redefined merit to go beyond mere academic performance. One reason that merit has been defined more broadly is the recognition that you can be a straight-A student but still not be able to communicate well or otherwise be the kind of well-rounded student that colleges seek.

Extra Credit

There are a number of ways that states define merit, and you need to check with your individual state and/or college to determine if you qualify for the merit-based grants and scholarships particular to your state. You could be more meritorious than you thought you were!

Colleges and financial aid programs also look at the kind of courses prospective financial aid recipients took when they were last in college or when they were in high school. For example, it's not hard to get straight As if you went through life taking the easiest classes you could take. A better student might be the one who was brave enough to take calculus and made a "B" or "C" than someone who took the proverbial basket-weaving course and made an "A." Today's colleges are considering much more than grades when defining merit.

Funding Based on Financial Need

Most states have a system in place through which your selected campus, after it receives information from your FAFSA, identifies whether you qualify for need-based, state-based aid. Unfortunately, there are usually more applicants than there are dollars available, so states grant this aid on a first-come, first-qualified, first-served basis. You will have a better chance of receiving need-based state aid if you submit your FAFSA early.

Try to finish your FAFSA during the month of February. If you do, you'll be in the running, in most cases, to receive need-based aid in the upcoming fall semester.

Cautionary Tales

The FAFSA must be completed and submitted to the U.S. Department of Education by the end of June each year. In some cases, the Department will extend the deadline to the first business day in July. No FAFSA will be accepted after this deadline and, should you miss this absolute deadline, you won't be eligible for federal aid for the upcoming academic year.

Special Campus-Based Scholarships

Campus-based scholarships are available only to students planning to attend that particular school. The sources of campus scholarships can come from investments the campus makes through a campus foundation, local campus fund-raising, and alumni who donate funds to their favorite college.

Your FAFSA information, in most cases, will put you in the running for campus scholarships. Other scholarships on campus are more directed (usually at the behest of a donor) and will require an additional application. Go to your financial aid office and see if there are campus scholarships you must apply for, over and above those you can receive through your FAFSA information.

Employers Paying for College

Good for you if you're fortunate enough to work for a company that provides tuition assistance!

If your company will pay your tuition, take advantage of it! Employers usually reimburse students for the cost of their classes *after* the class has been completed. Some companies might reimburse at lesser rates depending on the grades you make.

Cautionary Tales

Check your company's policies closely, as many will only support academic pursuits completely aligned with your current or potential job.

Some adults simply cannot afford to pay for classes and wait 4 months for the reimbursement from their employer. If you find yourself in this situation, you may have to do some negotiating. Some campuses make low-interest bridge loans that will cover the cost of tuition until the employer reimburses you. You will likely have to fill out forms that designate the reimbursement amount to be paid from your employer directly to the college.

Another option is to work with your employer to see if your tuition can be paid at the time it's due. There's safety in numbers, though, if you need this kind of help from your employer. It will be an easier thing to accomplish at work if 10 of you need this kind of consideration than if only you need it. It *has* been done, however, and different solutions come from employees simply asking. Maybe the employer will provide 50 percent up front and the rest later. You never know until you ask!

Community Organization and Foundation Scholarships

Your public library is a great place to find lists of local foundations and civic organizations that sponsor scholarships. Many of the scholarships these organizations sponsor are fairly small—typically ranging from a couple of hundred dollars to a couple of thousand dollars—so don't count on getting 4 years of college paid from one organization. There is, however, a nice bit of prestige that comes from being a recipient of a scholarship from a civic organization or foundation. And every little bit of aid helps.

Student Center

Leslie, now a professional psychologist, was the recipient of a $400 per-semester scholarship one year, awarded to her by a Business and Professional Women's local chapter. The scholarship was awarded to her at the annual meeting of the chapter and Leslie was asked to speak at the meeting. Today, Leslie not only has her college degree but also enjoys the friendship of many of the women in that organization, as she's now a member.

The only downside to searching for scholarships from organizations outside the campus is that you're probably going to have to do more paperwork. Each organization will have its own application form. One might want a one-page essay on why you feel you deserve the scholarship, while another may want you to prepare a paper on a social issue. If you look through the names and ages of past recipients, you may see a litany of recent high school graduates; it may just be because they had the time to complete all the applications necessary.

Cautionary Tales

Some scholarships are taxable and/or have strings attached to them. As with any other document you sign pertaining to college, read through the fine print of any scholarship you are offered before accepting it.

Some scholarships, depending on how they are awarded and funded, may be taxable. Check with your accountant or local tax expert to see if any scholarships offered to you have tax implications.

Also, you must report any noncampus scholarships to your financial aid office; in no case can you be awarded more than 100 percent of the campus-approved cost of attendance. Outside scholarships count against that total as well. However, outside scholarships can reduce how much you might need to take out in student loans, so it's worth trying to win them.

When Financial Aid "Assistance" Is Misleading

As you look for financial aid, you will run into people who, for a fee, will help you fill out your FAFSA. Think about this for a minute. If you take them up on that offer, you are out money that you didn't have to pay, as you can fill out the FAFSA on your own or with free assistance from college staff. In addition, you will be giving someone access to your private financial information as well as your Social Security number. Given that, is it a good idea to pay someone to help you fill out your FAFSA? Probably not.

That doesn't mean that there aren't some reputable companies out there who do provide a reasonable service for a reasonable fee. The best litmus test is this—are you being offered a service that a college or university will provide for you at no cost?

> **Cautionary Tales**
>
> The most important thing to remember when someone offers you help in finding grants or scholarships is this: if it sounds too good to be true, it probably is.

Spotting a Financial Aid Scam

You've probably seen news stories about people who paid a thousand dollars or more for "guaranteed" scholarships, only to end up with nothing but more debt.

Before working with a company to help you find money for school, call your state's higher education agency listed in Appendix A. Find out if they know about the company or service you are considering. Ask if the services you are thinking of paying for are available for free, either through the state itself or through college departments. "Scam" is a loaded word, and the company might not be scamming you per se, but you might be paying for something you don't need.

There are some things you can look for when considering a company or a service that offers scholarship or financial aid assistance:

◆ Do they guarantee you scholarships? If so, read the fine print; they might actually be guaranteeing you a *list* of scholarships.

◆ Do you have to pay a fee up front for the service? If the fee is due up front and not contingent on the company's ability to locate scholarships for you, consider the amount of the fee. Is it really worth your giving someone a check for a thousand dollars for scholarships that may not even cover that cost? Be careful!

◆ Do they provide a service that anyone can provide if they just type in the word "scholarships" in a good Internet search engine?

    ◆ Do they have a list of references you can contact?

    ◆ Do they have a list of previous clients who received scholarships that you can
        contact?

Yes, there are some companies that do a good job helping students access financial
aid. They typically won't require a big sum up front and will ask you to pay based on
results.

Be careful, be diligent, and do your homework. If you do, you won't see your own
face on the local news, upset about spending money for nothing.

Financial Aid Advice Is Free

Qualified financial aid experts on college campuses and in state agencies provide you
with the most up-to-date advice on accessing financial aid for free.

It's free to you when you ask, but state tax dollars or the operating expenses on college
campuses support the salaries of the professionals that you will work with. You will
find that the people who work in financial aid offices in colleges are very customer
service-oriented. They are very good at breaking down all the confusing federal and
state legalese and jargon and making the process of getting financial aid a much easier
endeavor.

You will get better, and more personal, attention at a campus or state financial aid
office if you seek help early. In other words, don't put off your questions until the last
minute. Many scholarships and grants require that FAFSAs be turned in by certain
deadlines in April each year. If you show up the day before deadline, expect to wait in
a long line and not get the staff's undivided attention. Ask for help early in February,
if you can, and you will have a better chance of getting some individual attention.

Find out if your school has personnel specifically assigned to help adult students navigate all the steps in the financial aid process. These staff members may not be located
in the financial aid office; instead, they might be a part of the student services staff or
working within a nontraditional student association. Ask each campus you are working with if they have staff or counselors assigned specifically for working with adult
students on financial aid issues.

No one at any level of assistance on a college campus or in a state agency will ask you
for money. Their assistance is free and there for the taking. If you seek help and don't
feel you work well with the first person you talk to, keep looking. You will find any
number of enthusiastic, student-focused personnel ready to help you afford college.

The Least You Need to Know

- Filling out the FAFSA is the most important step to getting financial aid.

- Scholarships based on merit aren't just for academic merit.

- Use employer-provided tuition assistance if it's available and makes sense given your career plans.

- Civic and community organization scholarships take time, but may be worth the effort.

- Let the buyer beware if you decide to pay someone to help you find financial aid. The best advice is most often free.

## Chapter 11

Other Ways to Pay for School

In This Chapter

- ◆ Making sense of student loan programs
- ◆ Repaying student loans
- ◆ Considering state savings programs
- ◆ Identifying federal tax benefits for education expenses

The kinds of free financial aid covered in Chapter 10 won't help everyone pay for college. For instance, if you're taking one class at a time, grants and scholarships probably won't be available to you. If you're attending school part-time, you may be able to secure some free financial aid, but not nearly enough to cover your expenses. And even if you're attending college full-time, you'll likely find that free financial aid doesn't cover all your expenses unless you're attending a low-price college or university.

For everyone else who relies on financial aid, the gap between scholarships and grants and the total price of attending college is often filled with student loans. College prices have increased at greater rates than the cost of living, and student loan dollars are filling that gap.

Student loans are low-interest loans that you can receive through your campus. You can elect to accept federally guaranteed student loans or go to your personal banker for a student loan. Student loans can mean the difference between attending college and not attending college for many adult students. They can be a true help when you don't have the private means to pay for college.

If student loans didn't exist, many people would never be able to go to college. The price of college, even when publicly subsidized, is out of reach for most people, especially those taking more than one class per semester. A student loan can give you the peace of mind to go ahead and make the decision to return to college.

Using Private Money to Pay for College

Adult learners with children of their own often find themselves in a dilemma when it comes to using their savings to pay their tuition. They wonder whether they should spend the money on their tuition or save it to pay for their children's college expenses.

You can do both, especially if you're taking one class at a time. One class per semester isn't likely to break you, no matter what college you choose, and you can assuage your conscience about your children by depositing an equal amount into a savings account or other money management tool for your children.

Right now, though, college is about you and your future. If you can get a degree and generate more earnings for your family, then it's worth it to spend the money now on yourself. The increased earnings that come about as a result of your college degree can go farther in helping your children's college fund than if you remained in a lower-paying job, setting aside a few dollars here and there for your kids. Also, there are simply more financial aid resources available for first-time, full-time freshmen coming straight out of high school, which will help pay your children's college bills.

It's a hard choice, there's no doubt about it, but having faith in your own abilities to learn and improve your life is a gift that you can give yourself and your children now, all the while knowing that you'll be able to provide for them when the time comes.

Should You Pay for College with a Credit Card?

Normally, putting your college bills on a credit card isn't a good idea. However, there are times when doing so might be appropriate. If you're waiting for your employer to reimburse you at the end of a semester for classes that you're taking, then you can put your college bill on a credit card and apply the employer's reimbursement check to pay off the credit card.

Just be sure that you actually use the reimbursement check to pay off the credit card. Otherwise, your credit card debt might become unmanageable.

Take time to think about the pros and cons of putting your college expenses on a credit card. If you do decide to pay for your college expenses this way, make a payback plan and stick to it. You don't want to end up with a new degree and an accompanying pay raise, only to have to send all extra money to the credit card company.

Cautionary Tales

Only you know if your family situation is such that using a credit card to pay for your college classes and fees is a good idea. As a rule, it's only a good idea as a short-term solution.

Federal Work-Study

Federal Work-Study provides part-time employment for students enrolled in school who demonstrate financial need. The money earned through the program is intended to help pay educational expenses. Work-Study is available to undergraduate and graduate students attending school full-time and part-time. The program is administered by schools participating in the Federal Work-Study Program.

Don't think that Work-Study jobs are only for the younger students, either; adult students can qualify as well. Rather than taking out a student loan to help pay for college costs, consider inquiring about Work-Study opportunities on campus. Not all Federal Work-Study jobs have to be on campus. You can also work for private nonprofit organizations or a public agency, as long as the work is in the public interest. In addition, some schools have arrangements with private sector for-profit employers for Federal Work-Study jobs. Discuss your options with your school's financial aid office.

The pay depends on the job, but must meet the federal minimum wage. The total amount you earn must not exceed your total Federal Work-Study award.

Federal Student Loan Programs

Federal student loan programs are complicated, and to describe all their ins and outs I'd need an entire book. Instead, I offer an overview of how student loans work, how they are managed, how you qualify for them, and how you pay them back.

Student loans have grown so much in the past two decades that lawmakers and policy makers are concerned about how much debt students of all ages are building up. The average student loan for an undergraduate student is in the tens of thousands now. For doctors and lawyers and other professional degrees, it's not uncommon for them to leave school with student loan debt in excess of $100,000.

Extra Credit _____

Using student loans to help pay for college can help you finish your degree earlier. If you can go to college full-time and work only part-time (or not at all), student loans can help cover your living expenses. If you want to get your degree as quickly as possible, taking out low-interest student loans can be your ticket.

People who take out student loans to complete college (especially if they go on to graduate school) pretty much get used to the fact that they will be making payments on their student loans for a long, long time. Without government-backed student loans, though, few of us could really afford to go to college.

The first item of business in obtaining a student loan is filling out the Free Application for Federal Student Aid (FAFSA). (See Chapter 10 for a complete description of this form and the application process.) In addition to using the FAFSA for the purpose of grants and scholarships, college financial aid personnel also use the FAFSA results for the purpose of awarding student loans and campus-based financial aid.

For families who demonstrate financial need, subsidized loans are available to help reduce the eventual cost of obtaining a college degree. A subsidized loan is a loan in which interest doesn't accrue while you're in college. The government makes your interest payments while you're in school. Interest begins to accrue on the loan after you leave college, whether from dropping out of school or obtaining your degree. An unsubsidized loan is one in which the interest accrues while you're in college.

Extra Credit _____

When you fill out the FAFSA, your income information is used to determine if you qualify for subsidized loans (loans in which interest does not accrue while you're in school) or unsubsidized loans (loans in which interest accrues while you're in school). This determination is income-sensitive and is re-evaluated annually when you complete your FAFSA.

There are many different kinds of federal student loans, and different colleges choose which kind of student loan arrangement they wish to operate under. Rarely is that important to you as you prepare for college, but you can ask your financial aid officer to describe the student loan arrangement that the campus works under. Some direct student loans are backed by the federal government while others make loans that are serviced by state guaranty agencies.

The following table lists the kinds of federal student loans and their characteristics.

STUDENT LOAN COMPARISON CHART

Loan Program	Eligibility	Award Amounts	Interest Rate	Lender/Length of Repayment
Federal Perkins Loans	Undergraduate and graduate students; do not have to be enrolled at least half-time*	Undergraduate—up to $4,000 a year (maximum of $20,000 as an undergraduate) Graduate—up to $6,000 a year (maximum of $40,000, including undergraduate loans) Amount actually received depends on financial need, amount of other aid, availability of funds at school	5 percent	Lender is your school Repay your school or its agent Up to 10 years to repay, depending on amount owed
FFEL Stafford Loans	Undergraduate and graduate students; must be enrolled at least half-time*	Depends on grade level in school and dependency status Financial need not necessary	Changes yearly; for 2005-06 was 5.3 percent for loans in repayment For those with financial need, government pays interest during school and certain other periods	Lender is a bank, credit union, or other participating private lender Repay the loan holder or its agent Between 10 and 25 years to repay, depending on amount owed and type of repayment plan selected
Direct Stafford Loans	Same as above	Same as above	Same as above	Lender is the U.S. Department of Education; repay Department Between 10 and 30 years to repay, depending on amount owed and type of repayment plan selected

Source: U.S. Department of Education, Federal Student Aid, Students Channel, Funding Education Beyond High School: The Guide to Federal Student Aid, *Washington, D.C., 2006.*

Although you always have the option of paying loan payments while you're in college, all student loan payments can be deferred until you leave school or graduate. Students receiving unsubsidized loans can elect to pay the interest while they are in school to reduce their long-term debt load.

Many students take out a combination of subsidized and unsubsidized loans, particularly if they are attending college full-time, because the cap on the amount of subsidized loans is lower than it is for unsubsidized loans.

Student loans can fill the estimated family contribution (EFC) gap for you (see Chapter 10). For instance, if your EFC after considering grant aid is $2,000, you can take out a student loan in the amount of $2,000. In fact, you can accept student loans up to 100 percent of the cost of attendance at the college or university you choose to attend. Remember that cost of attendance includes living expenses as well as tuition and books.

Extra Credit

If you return to college while you have active student loans that you are repaying, you can arrange to stop paying on your loans as long as you are in college and meeting the requirements of your loan program.

The following table lists the maximum annual loan limits on federal loans for 2006, though at the time this book went to press legislation was pending in Congress that would make them obsolete.

MAXIMUM ANNUAL LOAN LIMITS CHART—SUBSIDIZED AND
UNSUBSIDIZED DIRECT AND FFEL (FEDERAL) STAFFORD LOANS

	Independent Undergraduate Student	Graduate/Professional Student
1st Year	$6,625—No more than $2,625 of this amount may be in subsidized loans.	
2nd Year	$7,500—No more than $3,500 of this amount may be in subsidized loans.	$18,500—No more than $8,500 of this amount may be in subsidized loans.
3rd and 4th Years (each)	$10,500—No more than $5,500 of this amount may be in subsidized loans.	
Maximum Total Debt from Stafford Loans When You Graduate	$46,000—No more than $23,000 of this amount may be in subsidized loans.	$138,500—No more than $65,500 of this amount may be in subsidized loans. The graduate debt limit includes Stafford Loans received for undergraduate study.

NOTE: For periods of study shorter than an academic year, the amounts you can borrow will be less than those listed. Remember, you might receive less if you receive other financial aid that's used to cover a portion of your cost of attendance.

Your school can refuse to certify your loan application or can certify a loan for an amount less than you would otherwise be eligible for if the school documents the reason for its action and explains the reason to you in writing. The school's decision is final and cannot be appealed to the U.S. Department of Education.

Source: U.S. Department of Education, Federal Student Aid, Students Channel, Funding Education Beyond High School: The Guide to Federal Student Aid, *Washington, D.C., 2006.*

The paperwork associated with taking out student loans can be daunting, and although the government has tried to make the process simpler over the years, it still takes some effort to make sense of all the provisions of whatever student loan you choose to take out.

Cautionary Tales

Always use accurate information when completing any federal form associated with financial aid. As with all federal forms, you are signing that your information is accurate under penalty of perjury if the data is incorrect. Treat your financial aid forms as you would your tax return: be scrupulously honest.

After you graduate from or stop attending college, you must complete exit interview paperwork attached to your student loans. You'll need to sign a form acknowledging that your loans must be paid back, even if you are not satisfied with the quality of your education.

You can arrange to repay your loans in different ways. For example, if you get a job that doesn't pay very much, you can set up your repayment program so that you make lower payments early in the loan repayment process and increase those payments over time.

The following tables show examples of loan repayment amounts. Keep in mind that these are just examples and will vary depending on the interest rate, the amount of the loan, and the term of the loan.

EXAMPLES OF TYPICAL DIRECT AND FFEL STAFFORD LOAN REPAYMENTS[a] CHART
Monthly Payments and Total Amounts
Repaid Under Different Repayment Plans

Total Debt When Borrower Enters Repayment	Standard [b]		Extended [c] (20 years used as example)		Graduated (20 years used as example)		For Direct Loans Only: Income Contingent [d] (Income = $25,000)			
							Single		Married/HOH [e]	
	Per Month	Total Repaid	Per Month	Total Repaid	Per Month	Total Repaid	Per Month	Total Repaid	Per Month	Total Repaid
$2,500	$50	$3,074	$50	$3,074	$25	$4,029	$21	$4,788	$20	$5,106
$5,000	$61	$7,359	$55	$7,893	$35	$8,649	$43	$9,576	$40	$10,212
$7,500	$92	$11,039	$82	$11,840	$53	$12,970	$64	$14,364	$60	$15,318
$10,000	$123	$14,718	$97	$17,463	$69	$19,175	$85	$19,152	$80	$20,424
$15,000	$184	$22,077	$146	$26,194	$103	$28,762	$128	$28,727	$121	$30,636
$31,000	$380	$45,627	$264	$63,394	$213	$68,854	$264	$59,370	$215	$66,087

[a] Payments are calculated using the maximum interest rate of 8.25 percent for student borrowers. For July 1, 2005, to June 30, 2006, the interest rate for loans obtained on or after July 1, 1998, and in repayment is 5.30 percent. Interest rates are adjusted each year on July 1.

[b] Equal and fixed monthly payments ($50 minimum).
[c] Loan amounts below $31,000 apply only to Direct Loans.
[d] Assumes a 5 percent annual income growth (Census Bureau).
[e] HOH is Head of Household. Assumes a family size of two.

Source: U.S. Department of Education, Federal Student Aid, Students Channel, Funding Education Beyond High School: The Guide to Federal Student Aid, *Washington, D.C., 2006.*

EXAMPLES OF TYPICAL PERKINS LOAN REPAYMENTS CHART

Total Loan Amount	Number of Payments	Approximate Monthly Payment	Total Interest Charges	Total Repaid
$4,000	120	$42.43	$1,091.01	$5,091.01
$5,000	120	$53.03	$1,364.03	$6,364.03
$15,000	120	$159.10	$4,091.73	$19,091.73

Source: U.S. Department of Education, Federal Student Aid, Students Channel, Funding Education Beyond High School: The Guide to Federal Student Aid, *Washington, D.C., 2006.*

After you graduate from school, you get an immediate *deferment* on your student loan for six months. This deferment is intended to give you plenty of time to secure a new job and settle down in a new place should you need to. It's difficult to be granted a deferment after the first six months. Refer to the following table for a summary of deferment conditions.

def•i•ni•tion

During a **deferment** on your student loan, interest doesn't accrue and you don't have to make payments on your loan.

LOAN DEFERMENT SUMMARY CHART

Deferment Condition	Stafford Loans		Perkins Loans
	Direct Loans[a,b]	FFEL Loans[a,c]	
At least half-time* study at a postsecondary school	YES	YES	YES
Study in an approved graduate fellowship program or in an approved rehabilitation training program for the disabled	YES	YES	YES
Unable to find full-time employment (only on pre-July 1, 1993, loans)	Up to 3 Years	Up to 3 Years	Up to 3 Years
Economic hardship	Up to 3 Years [d]	Up to 3 Years [d]	Up to 3 Years [d]
Engages in service listed under discharge/cancellation conditions	NO	NO	YES [e]

[a] For PLUS Loans and unsubsidized Stafford Loans, only principal is deferred. Interest continues to accrue.

[b] A Direct Loan borrower who has an outstanding balance on a FFEL disbursed before July 1, 1993, might be eligible for additional deferments provided the outstanding FFEL balance existed when the borrower received his or her first Direct Loan.

[c] Applies to loans first disbursed on or after July 1, 1993, to a borrower who has no outstanding FFEL or Federal

Supplemental Loans for Students (Federal SLS) loan on the date he or she signed the promissory note.* (Note that the Federal SLS Program was repealed beginning with the 1994-95 award year.)

[d] Many Peace Corps volunteers, for example, will qualify for a deferment based on economic hardship.

[e] More information on teaching service deferments and cancellations can be found online at www.studentaid.ed.gov. At the site, click on the "Repaying" tab, and then click on "Cancellation and Deferment Options for Teachers."

Source: U.S. Department of Education, Federal Student Aid, Students Channel, Funding Education Beyond High School: The Guide to Federal Student Aid, Washington, D.C., 2006.

If, during your student loan repayment cycle, you have a short-term setback such as unemployment or illness and you can't repay your loan(s), you can apply for forbearance. During forbearance, you won't have to make your student loan payments. However, interest does accrue and is added to your total student loan amount due. Although it's easier to get forbearance after you begin paying your loans, you should reserve forbearance requests for when you really need them because the interest will increase the amount you ultimately must pay back.

Cautionary Tales

When I was an undergraduate student in the early 1980s, I had a professor who gloated that he had never paid back a dime of his student loans. Unfortunately, the feds can't show up at his door and demand their money because the laws governing repayment of student loans were different when he went to college. It's because of people like my freeloading professor—people who never paid their loans—that the laws *did* change.

Managing Your Loans Long-Term

While you are repaying your student loan, your lender may change over time. This is because packages of student loans are "sold" on the secondary market, similar to how home mortgages are sold. Don't be surprised if you have to change who you write your checks to several times over the life of your loan.

Also, many vendors will consolidate your loans so that you only have to make one payment and you can lock in your interest rate. Be very careful in selecting an entity to consolidate your loans. Also, ask if the vendor will actually be consolidating your loans, or only your payments. Many students who are consolidating their loans now find that their loans are still listed separately on their credit bureau file; only their payments were consolidated at the lower interest rate. This can become important when you want to buy a home or a car, as it may affect your credit score.

The best advice for you, if you're considering using student loans as a way to help pay for college, is to make an appointment with a financial aid professional at your college campus and have them explain how all the different loans work.

Getting Your Loans Cancelled

There is some good news buried amidst all this financial data: it is possible to be released from all obligations to repay your student loans. This is called a loan discharge, and the federal government discharges loans if you meet certain criteria outlined in the following two tables. Before you get your hopes up, though, keep in mind that the federal government is *very* strict about rules pertaining to loan discharges, so be sure to consult with a financial aid officer about the possibilities of getting out from under your loan obligations.

PERKINS LOAN DISCHARGE (CANCELLATION) SUMMARY CHART

Cancellation Conditions [a]	Amount Forgiven
Bankruptcy (in rare cases—cancellation is possible only if the bankruptcy court rules that repayment would cause undue hardship)	100 percent
Closed school (before student could complete program of study)—applies to loans received on or after Jan. 1, 1986	100 percent
Borrower's total and permanent disability [b] or death	100 percent
Full-time teacher in a designated elementary or secondary school serving students from low-income families [c]	Up to 100 percent
Full-time special education teacher (includes teaching children with disabilities in a public or other nonprofit elementary or secondary school) [c]	Up to 100 percent
Full-time qualified professional provider of early intervention services for the disabled	Up to 100 percent
Full-time teacher of math, science, foreign languages, bilingual education, or other fields designated as teacher shortage areas	Up to 100 percent
Full-time employee of a public or nonprofit child- or family-services agency providing services to high-risk children and their families from low-income communities	Up to 100 percent
Full-time nurse or medical technician	Up to 100 percent
Full-time law enforcement or corrections officer	Up to 100 percent
Full-time staff member in the education component of a Head Start Program	Up to 100 percent
Vista or Peace Corps volunteer	Up to 70 percent
Service in the U.S. Armed Forces	Up to 50 percent in areas of hostilities or imminent danger

[a] As of Oct. 7, 1998, all Perkins Loan borrowers are eligible for all cancellation benefits regardless of when the loan was made or the terms of the borrower's promissory note. * However, this benefit is not retroactive to services performed before Oct. 7, 1998.

[b] Total and permanent disability is defined as the inability to work and earn money because of an illness or injury that is expected to continue indefinitely or to result in death. If you are determined to be totally and permanently disabled based on a physician's certification, your loan will be conditionally discharged for up to three years. This conditional discharge period begins on the date you became totally and permanently disabled, as certified by your physician. During this conditional discharge period, you do not have to make payments on your loan(s). To qualify for a final discharge due to total and permanent disability, you must meet the following requirements during the conditional dis - charge period: (1) your earnings from employment must not exceed the poverty line amount for a family of two; and (2) you

must not receive any additional loans under the FFEL, Direct Loan or Perkins Loan programs. If you do not continue to meet these requirements at any time during or at the end of the conditional discharge period, your loan(s) will be taken out of conditional discharge status and you must resume making payments on your loans. You cannot qualify for loan discharge based on a condition that existed before the loan was made, unless a doctor certifies that your condition substantially dete riorated after you obtained the loan. For more information on qualifying for this discharge, review your promissory note* and Borrower's Rights and Responsibilities Statement or contact your loan holder.

[c] Detailed information on teaching service cancellation/deferment options can be found at www.studentaid.ed.gov. At the site, click on the "Repaying" tab, then on "Cancellation and Deferment Options for Teachers."

Source: U.S. Department of Education, Federal Student Aid, Students Channel, Funding Education Beyond High School: The Guide to Federal Student Aid, *Washington, D.C., 2006.*

DIRECT/FFEL STAFFORD LOAN DISCHARGE (CANCELLATION) SUMMARY CHART

Discharge/Forgiveness Conditions	Amount Discharged/Forgiven	Notes
Borrower's total and permanent disability or death [a]	100 percent	For a PLUS Loan, includes the death, but not disability, of the student for whom the parents borrowed.
Full-time teacher for five consecutive years in a designated elementary or secondary school serving students from low-income families	Up to $5,000 (up to $17,500 for teachers in certain specialties) of the total loan amount outstanding after completion of the fifth year of teaching. Under the Direct and FFEL Consolidation Loan programs, only the portion of the consolida - tion loan used to repay eligible Direct Loans or FFEL Loans qualifies for loan forgiveness.	For Direct and FFEL Stafford Loans received on or after Oct. 1, 1998, by a borrower with no outstanding loan balance as of that date. At least one of the five consecutive years of teaching must occur after the 1997-98 academic year. To find out whether your school is considered a low-income school, go to www.studentaid.ed.gov. Click on the "Repaying" tab, then click on "Cancellation and Deferment Options for Teachers." Or, call 1-800-4-FED-AID (1-800-433-3243).
Bankruptcy (in rare cases)	100 percent	Cancellation is possible only if the bankruptcy court rules that repayment would cause undue hardship.
Closed school (before student could complete program of study) or false loan certification	100 percent	For loans received on or after Jan. 1, 1986
School does not make required return of loan funds to the lender	Up to the amount that the school was required to return	For loans received on or after Jan. 1, 1986

[a] Total and permanent disability is defined as the inability to work and earn money because of an illness or injury that is expected to continue indefinitely or to result in death. If you are determined to be totally and permanently disabled based on a physician's certification, your loan will be conditionally discharged for up to three years. This conditional discharge period begins on the date you became totally and permanently disabled, as certified by your physician. During this conditional discharge period, you do not have to make payments on your loan(s). To qualify for a final discharge due to total and perma - nent disability, you must meet the following requirements during the conditional discharge period: (1) your earnings from employ - ment must not exceed the poverty line amount for a family of

two; and (2) you must not receive any additional loans under the FFEL, Direct Loan or Perkins Loan programs. If you do not continue to meet these requirements at any time during or at the end of the conditional discharge period, your loan(s) will be taken out of conditional discharge status and you must resume making payments on your loans. You cannot qualify for loan discharge based on a condition that existed before the loan was made, unless a doctor certifies that your condition substantially deteriorated after you obtained the loan. For more information on qualifying for this discharge, review your promissory note* and Borrower's Rights and Responsibilities Statement or contact your loan holder.

Source: U.S. Department of Education, Federal Student Aid, Students Channel, Funding Education Beyond High School: The Guide to Federal Student Aid, *Washington, D.C., 2006.*

Private Student Loans

If you have a good relationship with a bank or other lender, you can take advantage of short-term private student loans. These are far less common than the government-backed student loans, but are an option for people with a good credit history with a particular lending institution. Keep in mind that, unlike the government-backed loans, these nonsecured types of loans may require that you begin paying them back immediately.

You might need to seek private student loans if you plan to attend a high-priced institution full-time. The federal government has a cap on the amount of loans that a student can take out each year. At very high-priced institutions, the total cost of attendance can actually exceed the federal loan limits. In the absence of personal resources to cover the additional amount, private student loans are an option you can use to help pay for the balance.

You may even decide to try a finance company or take advantage of an offer for money in the mail. If you do, take the time to scrutinize the terms of the loan. Find out if you have to pay all the interest calculated on the entire loan's term even if you pay it off early. Are there other prepayment penalties? Do interest rates increase if you miss a payment?

When it comes to taking out any kind of loan, just make sure that you've read all the fine print before signing a financing agreement.

Extra Credit

Even if you do have a good relationship with your bank, your best bet for student loans is to accept all federally backed subsidized and/or unsubsidized loans before seeking private financing of your college education. The interest rates are lower, on average, and you will have much more flexible repayment options.

Saving for College: It Doesn't Take a Lifetime

Most people think of college savings as something you start up when there's a new baby in the family or a fund you begin for your children. But college savings aren't just for children and young adults. You can create a savings plan to help you pay for college, no matter your age.

Extra Credit

If you plan to attend college within the next year, set aside some money to help you make it through the first semester. How? Try going out to eat less often and put the savings aside.

State College Savings Programs

States have created special savings accounts to help parents save for their children's college. These college savings programs are often referred to as "529 savings programs," so named because of the law that allows for such programs.

These savings programs vary from state to state and are managed by different agencies in each state. If you're unsure which entity manages your state's college savings program, ask officials with your state higher education agency (listed in Appendix A) to put you in contact with the correct agency or entity. You can also learn more detailed information about your state's college savings program at the College Savings Network's website, www.collegesavings.org.

Although the savings programs are designed to save money over the long term for young students, you can also make deposits to the accounts in your name or your husband's or wife's name and treat them as short-term investments. You won't earn the kind of interest that the savings program will generate when you're saving over a 17- or 18-year period for children, but there are other benefits to using your state's college savings program.

State Tax Benefits of College Savings Programs

If you use the state college savings program as an account for your college expenses, you can reap some state tax benefits for doing so. The rules differ from state to state, but generally, when you deposit an amount into the account, states allow you to deduct that amount from your overall income for state tax purposes. For example, if your taxable income is $35,000 and you set aside $1,000 for college, your taxable income would be reduced to $34,000.

Suppose, for example, that you have $5,000 in a state savings account. When you withdraw the money to pay for college, you pay taxes based on your income at the time you use the funds for college, not the income at the time you made the deposit. This isn't all that important for adult students in terms of tax savings unless you save money in the plan for a couple of years and then decide to leave the workforce while attending college. If you do so, then your taxes on the money you deposited into a state savings account would be much lower.

You can see how the benefits of these savings programs increase as time goes by, but you can still use these programs to save money and get tax benefits now and when you go to school.

Federal Tax Implications for Education Expenses

In addition to benefits within your state for college savings, some relatively new federal tax benefits reduce your taxable income if you pay for higher education expenses. These include two major programs, the Hope tax credit and the Lifelong Learning tax credit.

The instructions and worksheets for calculating whether you qualify for these and other federal tax incentives for higher education expenses can be found online at www.irs.gov.

Income caps limit who can make use of the federal tax benefits, so consult a tax professional and read through all instructions to see if you qualify.

Reducing Your Bottom Line

I talked about reducing college bills by negotiating lower student fees in Chapter 9. You can also reduce how much you pay for college *and* shorten your time to degree by petitioning for credit for some courses.

If you can document proficiency in certain academic areas through work-based or union-based certifications or credentials, the college may have a means to grant you course credit for your knowledge and skills. The way colleges evaluate learning that takes place outside the college environment is specific to the institution, so you may have to work with your advisor to take advantage of these special options.

Getting Credit for Classes You Have Already Taken

Here's some good news: it's possible to get college credit for life and/or work experience. For example, if you've been doing payroll and accounts payable/receivable and you think you can bypass an entry-level accounting class, provide your best evidence and see if the college will accept your prior learning experience for credit. Not all colleges offer such credit, and on those campuses that do, you'll need to apply for it.

Most colleges will require you to create a portfolio that showcases your knowledge and skills. It should include any credentials you've earned through work, evidence of expertise in certain academic areas that you've gained through life experience, as well as any letters of recommendation, certificates of completion, and anything else that you believe demonstrates your proficiency.

Cautionary Tales

Rarely will a college dictate the format in which the portfolio for prior learning experience is presented, and they will be more interested in what is in your portfolio than how pretty the cover is. A pretty cover won't fool anyone into thinking you have experience if you don't.

On most campuses you must pay a fee to have your prior learning experience portfolio evaluated. Keep in mind that the fee is almost always much less than the cost of a class.

Almost all colleges are comfortable issuing standardized tests that yield a simple yes-or-no answer about course credit earned outside the classroom. Fewer colleges have professionals in academic areas who've been trained to assess prior learning experience portfolios. Policies for how portfolios are assessed can differ greatly from campus to campus. Be prepared for the assessment to take some time, and be patient with the process. If the campus asks you to redo your information and put it into a different format so they can more easily assess your work, do it. It's worth the short time investment now to be able to avoid classes covering content you already know very well.

Earning Credit by Testing Out of Classes

You can also reduce your tuition bill by "testing out" of some classes. Students usually test out of entry-level courses, but it's also possible to test out of upper-level courses depending on your experience and the content area. For example, if your degree program requires two years of a foreign language and you speak Spanish fluently, you can take a test or series of tests to see if you can bypass some or all the foreign language requirements.

Just as you must pay for the services of campus professionals who examine your portfolio for credit for prior learning, the assessments that campuses use to determine whether you can test out of classes also require a fee. The fees are much less than the course(s) you are working to earn credit for, and if you do test out of certain classes, you will be able to earn your degree much faster.

Not All Classes Will Count

Colleges have minimum requirements for how many hours of classes must be taken at their college. Most often called "residency requirements" (not to be confused with your state residency status), the minimum requirements are how colleges control the quality and reputation of their college degrees.

If you've earned a lot of college credit through testing or through prior learning experience, you may not be allowed to count all the classes toward your core degree courses.

You may also be allowed to use your prior learning or skills assessed through testing as electives, but not as core courses.

Colleges are not required to grant you course credit for prior learning, and they are allowed to limit the number of credits from other institutions or for life experiences. However, if you can apply these credits to your degree program, take advantage of them; you can save money by doing so.

The Least You Need to Know

- ◆ Think twice before you use your credit card to pay your college expenses.
- ◆ Student loans are low-interest loans that can help you pay for college; most have generous repayment options.
- ◆ You can earn college credit by testing out of certain subjects.
- ◆ You can save money by earning credit for life and work experiences.

Part 4

On-Campus Survival Skills

Oddly enough, the issue that college students complain about most often has nothing to do with their coursework: it's the campus parking situation. This part helps you make your return to college as painless as possible by encouraging you to scout out your campus well in advance of your first day of classes. That way, when the first day rolls around, you'll know where your classes are, the location of important campus offices, the best spot to grab a good lunch, and of course, the best place to park.

Enrollment itself can be daunting if you haven't gone through it in a while. Fortunately, most campuses now have online enrollment options. Choosing classes that best suit your degree program can seem overwhelming, but campus advisors are there to help you through the process.

This part also offers tips on how to attend class, do homework, and interact with faculty.

## Chapter 12

Navigating the Enrollment Maze

In This Chapter

- ◆ Finding a good advisor
- ◆ Deciding on the best time of day to take a class
- ◆ Enrolling online and in person
- ◆ Paying your tuition and fees

The once-daunting process of enrolling for college has become a lot easier in recent years thanks to technological advances that enable students to enroll in and pay for classes via the Internet.

Not all campuses are fully operational for online enrollment yet. Some allow you to sign up for classes online, but still require that payment be made the old-fashioned way. And a few technologically challenged schools still require that you enroll in person.

No matter what kind of enrollment system a college uses, successful enrollment depends on good advisement. But you have to do your part, too. Do your homework ahead of time, using many of the strategies you've already read about. Then, when you meet with your advisor, you'll be organized and ready to ask questions.

Getting Good Campus Advisement

Different colleges use different structures for academic advising. On some campuses, each student is assigned a faculty advisor, particularly after a major is declared. Before students declare majors, however, it's most likely that a pool of academic advisors will work with students until an academic major is declared.

If you have some idea what broad area you are interested in, your advisor may be assigned based on the potential *college* on campus you are likely to continue your studies. A pool of academic advisors serves the college; these advisors do nothing but advise students. They don't teach classes or do other academic activities—their sole job is to advise students.

def•i•ni•tion

Within a campus structure, a **college** is a means of dividing the campus up, organization-ally, into broad categories. For example, you may see a "college of arts and sciences," a "college of education," or, for graduate studies, a "graduate college."

On other campuses, students benefit from the exper-tise of both professional advisors and faculty members.

No matter what advisement structure your college has, as you progress through your program of study, it's likely that you will find one faculty member who is not only your best teacher, but also someone who will enjoy a collegial relationship with you. In that case, faculty members play a sort of de facto advisor role, even if you must have your paperwork signed by an official campus advisor.

Adult Learner Advisors

Recognizing that adult students face different life and work issues from younger stu-dents, some colleges have advisors who specialize in working with adult students.

 Extra Credit

Remember, you might be called a nontraditional student by your school even though the majority of today's students don't fit the traditional student mode. A recent study funded by the U.S. Department of Education shows that almost three quarters of all students on campus today have traits more in common with adult students than with traditional, recently graduated high school students.

Even if your advisor doesn't specialize in working with adult students, he or she is there to help you with everything you need on campus. Your primary advisor should give you his or her phone number and e-mail address so you can contact them at any time. To an advisor, no question is a stupid question. Your advisor can help you nego-tiate the red tape you might encounter during enrollment or help you appeal a grade. He or she can direct you to tutoring or mentoring resources and assist you with study skills. If you don't have a computer, your advisor can direct you to campus technology centers. Advisors keep day-care resource information handy and can also help you if transportation is a problem for you. Even if you just need a good ear or an advocate on campus, a good advisor will be there for you.

Cautionary Tales

Don't be surprised if your academic advisor, like some of your teachers, is younger than you. Keep in mind that, no matter their age, they are highly trained and deserve to be treated with courtesy and respect. That doesn't mean you shouldn't feel free to ask questions or assert your opinion with your advisor.

Degree Program Advisor and Academic Planning

In addition to helping you navigate campus bureaucracy, your advisor is also in charge of making sure that you meet all the campus requirements for general education courses and for courses that are required for your degree program.

But you should never blindly rely on your advisor to tell you what to do and when. It's ultimately your responsibility to read and adhere to the requirements for your degree program.

No advisor is perfect, and no one is mistake-free. You can save yourself from taking a class you don't need if you are familiar with your degree requirements when you meet with your advisor. You also can save yourself from needing one more class when you thought you were done and ready to walk across the stage to get your diploma.

Advisors can be your best advocates on campus, and most will go above and beyond just helping you fill out your academic plan and semester schedules each year. Take advantage of all that they have to offer.

Choosing Classes Around Life and Work

If you're working full-time and adding college to your life, you might find it frustrat-ing that some of the courses you need are offered when it's least convenient for you.

You're less likely to encounter this problem when you're taking general education classes, because these are often offered in the evenings. As you get further into your degree program, however, you will probably find that more and more courses are offered at inconvenient times. In some academic programs, you might even need a course that is only taught by a single faculty member, and it may only be offered once every year, or even once every two years. Your advisor can usually give you a heads-up about courses that will fall into this category, so you're likely to have some time to plan for it.

What can you do when this happens? Here are some suggestions for handling this situation:

- Talk to your employer about changing your work schedule for a semester. Have a plan thought out when you meet with your employer. If you're going to require time off during the workday to take a class, present a plan that either allows you to use leave time or an alternate work schedule.

Extra Credit

You might consider asking a colleague to cover for you while you're gone. Find someone at work with whom your "trade-offs" in work time could be mutually beneficial. For example, if you have to be gone for two hours a day, three days a week for a semester, you might be able to take some weekend time for your colleague so she can spend more time with her family.

- Check to see if your college will honor a similar course taught on an alternate campus at a time that's convenient for you. This strategy will require a little research and maybe even some negotiating, particularly if your "home college" doesn't already have an academic exchange agreement with the alternate college. Your advisor can be very helpful to you here.

- Seek a policy exception, one that would allow you to substitute a similar course for the one that is required. You will need to show that the courses are equivalent in difficulty and that outcomes will be close enough, academically, to reasonably substitute for the required class.

- Ask the faculty member who teaches the course whether you can learn the content through an independent study course. In some cases, faculty members will be happy to do so; in other cases, the academic content of the class will be so critical to the degree that you must actually take the course. An independent study version of a course may also require a policy exception, because it will likely have a different course number. You'll need the assistance of an advisor to make this work.

Even with the academic alternatives identified above, your best bet academically is to arrange your work life in such a way that will allow you to actually take the required course. The sequence of courses that add up to a particular degree are carefully designed by faculty and academic communities.

Extra Credit

College courses that begin with a zero are non-credit-bearing developmental courses and earn zero credit. Courses that begin with a "one" are freshman level courses. Sophomore level courses begin with a two, junior level course numbers begin with a three, and senior level course numbers begin with a four. Graduate course numbers begin with five and continue upward, depending on how many years the graduate degree requires.

Daytime Classes

Courses on campus can begin as early as 6 A.M. If your college offers early morning classes and you work regular office hours, you can take a class or two before work—it'll be just like going to the gym before work, except you'll be getting a mental workout instead.

While evening classes generally pack a week's worth of work into a single, three-hour evening, daytime courses are scheduled differently. A three-hour daytime course meets for three hours during the week. Sometimes this is one hour at a time, three times a week; other times, you will meet twice a week, with classes an hour-and-a-half in duration. Classes that are longer than three credit hours are generally those that have labs or applied study in addition to classroom lecture. If you take a class with a lab, you will be able to choose from several laboratory times in most cases.

Cautionary Tales

Keep in mind that even if a college offers early morning courses, they might end up canceling the class due to low enrollment numbers. You can usually find out how many other students are enrolled by going online or by calling the enrollment office. If it looks like the class won't meet minimum enrollment requirements, have an alternate section of the course in mind that you can take.

Most college classes take place from 9 A.M. to 5 P.M. These are the hours when you'll be most likely to find the faculty in their offices, the administrators on campus, and the student and academic services in full operation.

def•i•ni•tion

An **enrollment period** is a period of time during which students can enroll for classes for the following semester. Students who are already taking classes are often allowed to enroll for next semester's courses before new students.

Certain times and certain classes will fill up early during the *enrollment periods*.

Popular daytime classes are those that begin mid-morning and go through early afternoon. These classes fill up quickly, so enroll early if you need to schedule classes during your lunchtime.

Late afternoon classes don't fill up as quickly, generally, so if you can go to work early and get off early, late afternoon classes may not pose a problem for your scheduling challenges.

Extra Credit

Daytime classes are more likely to be filled with younger traditional students. Being in a class with younger students can be a fun experience for adult learners, and indeed, many adults in college say that being around younger students actually keeps them young! You must decide if your learning style is one that allows you to mix well with a largely younger student population.

Evening and Weekend Classes

As more adult students are enrolling in college courses, colleges have added more evening and weekend classes. At very innovative campuses, classes are offered all through the night for the benefit of shift workers.

Young and adult students alike find that they actually like evening classes. And you can get a lot of credit hours under your belt if you're smart about how you schedule your evening and weekend classes.

Many evening classes are held on a single night of the week. The traditional length of most college courses is three credit hours, or three hours a week (science courses and those with labs are usually more hours per week). Don't be afraid of signing up for a class that's held for three hours, one night a week. Those three hours will absolutely zoom by each week! This schedule is also more efficient, as you only need to go to campus once a week for a single course. If you're able to find more than one course offered this way, you can go to school two nights a week and earn six credit hours, part-time, during a semester.

Faculty members generally like teaching three-hour evening classes because it gives them more opportunities to use different teaching and learning strategies. Faculty can use group activities and more interactive styles of teaching in a three-hour night class and still have time to "teach from the podium."

Students who take courses one night a week for three hours at a time also find that they develop better study relationships with their fellow students.

Both faculty and students like the depth of interaction weekend courses allow. The design of weekend courses depends on the college, but some are three, six, or even eight hours long. A weekend course in which the class time is longer can really help earn college hours quickly.

> **Cautionary Tales**
>
> When you take a night or weekend class, you can't easily fool your professor into thinking you've read the material when you haven't. There's enough time in class, and enough interaction between students and faculty, that you really need to know your material. Taking an evening or weekend class is a commitment to read the material and contribute in class.

There is a big downside to these evening and longer weekend courses: If you miss one night class, you're missing the equivalent of an entire week of class. If you miss a weekend class, you can be two to three weeks behind your colleagues. So sign up for these kinds of classes when you know that you can show up to every class.

Online or Television Courses

Online and/or televised courses require that you be a very self-directed learner. Many of the classes offered online are considered open-entry and open-exit. This means that you start your class at any time during the academic year and, within reason, you pace your learning until you can show you've met all the learning objectives for the class. You need to be technologically literate (not necessarily an expert) to take an online course.

You've probably run into a television class or two on public television when flipping channels. These courses generally require a specific textbook. Tests are given at certain times, usually at the sponsoring college itself, or other places in the community where telecourse students can meet and take an exam.

An upside to a telecourse is that you can record the class and watch it at midnight if you need to. You can rewind and watch a part of the class over and over again if you're having difficulty with a particular concept.

Some online courses are better than others. You know your learning style and whether you have the discipline to take a self-directed course. If you're the kind of student who learns better when you're in a room full of people, with ideas flying around the room at the speed of sound, then telecourses or online courses may not be your best choice.

However, if you're living a busy life with work and family and you're adding college to that mix, a few online or telecourses over the whole course of your degree program will help you earn the credits you need in an efficient way. Talk with your advisor if you're at all concerned about your ability to learn in a nonclassroom situation.

Enrolling in the Classes You've Chosen

The process of actually enrolling in courses can be frustrating and maddening if you're not ready for it. Enrollment always seems to have a "Murphy's Law" component, especially when you do it for the first time. It seems like something always goes wrong.

Extra Credit

Many campuses allow existing students to "pre-enroll" before new students get the chance.

Cautionary Tales

Don't wait until the last possible day and the last possible moment to enroll. The earlier in the enrollment process you register for classes, the more likely you are to get into your preferred classes and times.

You can minimize the chances that something will go wrong by completing the following steps:

1. Visit with your advisor and have all forms signed by the appropriate people on campus.

2. Select the courses you want to take as well as some alternate sections of those courses and/or substitute courses, in case the ones you want to take are full.

3. Do a practice run by observing a friend or colleague go through the enrollment process, especially if you're enrolling online. Your advisor should be able to help you with this.

4. Complete your financial aid paperwork and make sure it is already entered into the system; or have your method of payment in hand.

Online Enrollment

Campuses with online enrollment options make the enrollment process easy. You can enroll in classes while in your pajamas in front of your laptop while your favorite show is on TV!

The systems that colleges and universities use for enrollment are mostly meant to be user-friendly and, for lack of a better term, "idiot-proof"! Don't be afraid to enroll online; nothing you can do, no key you can punch, will erase the university's entire enrollment database. You can't make a mistake on most systems. Each step in the online enrollment process is designed for you to sequentially enter in information about yourself, then choose your courses and their times and section numbers.

The enrollment systems are also usually designed to match your entered information against the financial aid portion of the university's enrollment system.

Extra Credit

If you don't feel completely comfortable doing an online enrollment for the first time, most campuses set up computer labs where you can enroll with the assistance of enrollment experts, student workers, or academic advisors.

Traditional Enrollment

Traditional enrollment is becoming less and less common, but it's still used on some campuses.

You meet with your advisor and select courses, also likely making a list of alternative courses or sections if the ones you want to enroll in are full. The advisor usually signs your initial schedule. You must then wait in line for either a computer terminal to use for enrollment, or else wait for an enrollment professional to enter your data and assist you with any problems, questions, or course substitutions you may need to make.

Then you pay your bill at the campus finance office or show that you have enrolled so the financial staff can match your information with the financial aid database.

Finally, you get a confirmation of your schedule and bill, and are sometimes even given a photo identification card at that time.

Even this is a streamlined traditional enrollment process; as recently as 20 years ago, some colleges' computer systems were still using punch cards! Yet another reason why now is a great time to return to school.

Billing and Payment Options

Rarely will you encounter a college that wants a check or credit card on the day you register for classes. If, however, you do not have financial aid coming to you, the more advanced online enrollment systems will allow you to enter in a credit card number or a routing and account number from your checking account to pay for classes.

If you have financial aid coming to you, the tuition, fees, any books that you have purchased at the school's bookstore, and any other charges on your account will be taken from your gross financial aid award. If, after your financial aid is applied, you have a credit balance, your school will either directly deposit that credit to your checking account or issue you a check by mail. The credit balance from financial aid is to be used to pay for college expenses, such as food, living expenses, or even the purchase of a computer.

Managing Employer-Paid Classes

What if you're taking a class and your employer is paying for your school? Many employers wait until the semester ends to reimburse employees for their courses. However, many adult students don't have the resources to pay their tuition and then wait for reimbursement.

Schools and employers have been more flexible in recent years. You can negotiate with your employer to see if the college benefit can be paid at the time of enrollment (these are usually accompanied by a promise to pay back via payroll deduction if you don't actually complete the class). Or you can work with the college to carry your balance until the end of the semester when your employer pays for your school. This latter scenario is more common, and colleges can do this in a couple of ways. The university can carry your balance forward until the end, or provide some sort of "bridge" funding to pay for the class until your employer's reimbursement arrives. In some cases, you have to pay interest on this bridge funding. Just as with your employer, you are responsible for paying the college back when they provide bridge funding for your classes—that is, if you drop your class or don't finish the class.

Dropping or Adding Classes

It's very common for students to drop and add classes. Students make these changes for a variety of reasons—their schedule changes, they've found a better section to take, they don't like the instructor, and so on. During the first couple of weeks of school, if you drop a class, you may be eligible for at least partial tuition reimbursement. It is unlikely, however, that you will receive the full amount of tuition because, even if you went to the class only twice, you did use college resources for that class. The amount of reimbursement decreases the later in the semester that you drop your class. After a certain period of time, you'll have no reimbursement coming your way. If you drop a class and immediately add another class to take its place, you are unlikely to see any additional tuition.

The best advice, short of not dropping at all, is to drop and add classes as close to the first day of school as possible. In addition to the financial ramifications if you don't take another class, you want to add a substitute class as quickly as possible so that you don't fall behind, academically. Faculty members grow particularly peeved if you show up on Monday of the third week of class and ask, "So, what have I missed?"

This drop-and-add period at the beginning of the semester is purely for the purpose of shifting things around to better suit your schedule. Around midterms, you will find that there is an additional drop date. This drop date is the last day that you can drop a class without receiving a grade. Dropping in midsemester may be a good decision if you are failing a class (check with your advisor), but you won't receive any of your tuition or fees back at that time.

The Least You Need to Know

- ◆ Colleges are doing a good job, for the most part, in meeting adult learners' needs for advisement.

- ◆ Look for and utilize an adult learner advisor, if one is available on campus.

- ◆ Do your homework and choose classes that work for your schedule and your learning style.

- ◆ Enrollment will be a smooth process if you have all your pre-enrollment work complete.

- ◆ Online and traditional enrollment need not be a nightmare.

- ◆ Paying for college happens differently if you are receiving financial aid, paying for your own, or receiving employer reimbursement.

## Chapter 13

Before Classes Begin

In This Chapter

- ◆ Meeting your professors
- ◆ Getting the best deal on textbooks
- ◆ Joining an adult student association
- ◆ Exploring campus

Now that you've registered for classes and have made the first payment on your tuition bill, it's time to sit back and relax until school starts, right? Wrong! Now's the time to do some prep work to ensure that your first day of class—and your first semester of school—goes by without a hitch.

Don't worry—you'll still have plenty of time to enjoy those final days of freedom from homework *after* you follow the suggestions in this chapter. And you can relish those lazy days all the more because you'll know you've done everything within your power to prepare for a successful college career.

Meeting Your Professors and Instructors

The men and women who stand at the helm of college classrooms have a wide variety of teaching styles. Some will amaze you with their brilliance;

others will challenge your patience *and* your ability to stay awake in class. No matter how bright or dull your professors turn out to be, you will have a more positive experience with them if you make an effort to meet with them individually before classes begin or during the first week of class.

The week before and after the semester starts is a busy one for faculty and students alike. However, a brief meeting with your professor can benefit you in several ways. The most obvious benefit is that your professor will know you. It also demonstrates to your professor that you are truly interested in the class.

Call ahead and make a specific appointment; don't just show up at the instructor's office. Ask for a meeting of no more than 15 minutes. During the meeting try to convey two or three points about yourself that might make you memorable to the professor. Tell the professor why you chose his or her class and what you hope to learn. Let your professor know if you are interested in his or her field as a major. Ask for any advice or additional readings that might help you do well in class.

Extra Credit

Just as students have a course load, faculty members have a teaching load, which varies depending on their seniority, administrative duties, and the amount of research they are expected to do. In community colleges and smaller colleges, which usually place more of an emphasis on teaching than on research, your profs might teach four to five classes a week. This is considered a pretty heavy teaching load for a professor because of the other demands on his or her time.

Keep this first meeting brief and adopt a formal tone. If your instructor has a Ph.D., call him or her "Doctor." Never call your professor by his or her first name unless specifically invited to do so.

Extra Credit

You'll usually find your professors working in their offices during the week before classes begin. Do your best to visit with one or more of them that week. Many faces pass in front of the faculty each semester; make yours a friendly and memorable one.

Faculty usually post their office hours for each semester on their office door, on their syllabus, and also on their personal web page if they have one. Office hours are times when faculty will be in their offices and available to meet with students. It can be difficult for adult students who work full-time to meet with faculty because office hours are often set in the daytime, during traditional work hours. Faculty will, however, make appointments to meet at other times during the day if you ask them to do so. In addition, most professors are happy to answer questions via e-mail or phone.

If you want to guarantee time with your professor, go ahead and make an appointment, even during office hours. If you have an appointment, your professor will give you the undivided attention you asked for by making the appointment.

Learning from Teachers Who Are Younger Than You

Get used to this fact: you're probably going to take classes from faculty members who are younger than you. A freshly minted professor straight out of graduate school can be as young as 26 or 27 years old. Just as your age shouldn't figure into your ability to learn, your professor's age shouldn't affect her ability to teach.

Office Hours

When Tina began her work as an assistant professor at a large research university, she was a bit nervous about teaching students old enough to be her mother or father. Although a few older students in her classes made her youth an issue, for the most part, the adult students were her best. "The older students want to be there, want to learn, and want to do well. They don't want something handed to them like some younger students do. Because of that, they were a pleasure to teach and, after a while, I didn't even think about age."

Making Sense of the Academic Caste System

College professors are part of an academic caste system of sorts, and it's a system laden with all sorts of pros and cons. Although a professor's ranking shouldn't affect your experience with him or her, it's worth knowing a little bit about the system.

Faculty members' rankings within the college are a function of how long they've been on the faculty and the quality of their research, service, and teaching. Here's a rundown of the types of professorships and what they mean:

◆ **Teaching assistants (TA)** are graduate students who are earning money by teaching classes in their academic area of expertise. These students are also gaining experience, so you might encounter a TA who is teaching his or her very first class. TAs generally teach entry-level courses.

◆ **Graduate assistants (GA)** are usually focused on the research side of the academic discipline. You are most likely to be taught by a GA in a laboratory section.

◆ **Adjunct faculty** are instructors who are hired on a part-time basis to teach a class or two in a content area in which they have expertise. Adjuncts often end up teaching classes during times when full-time faculty don't want to, including

Cautionary Tales

The academic culture on campus doesn't always fully appreciate the role of adjunct faculty, and adjuncts rarely make much money for their teaching. Most of them love to teach and love what they're teaching. Don't shy away from a class being taught by a part-time faculty member; you may learn more than you ever dreamed.

evening classes and weekend classes. Most of the time, adjunct faculty members work full-time at another job and teach classes simply because they like teaching. Adult students often find much in common with adjunct faculty members—many adjuncts work all day and teach a class in the evening; many adult students work all day and *take* a class in the evening.

One of the plusses to taking a class taught by an adjunct is that they're likely to understand and apply theoretical concepts to real-world situations, because they're applying those concepts in their own work on a daily basis.

♦ **Assistant professor** is the entry-level rank for professors after obtaining their doctorate. In larger colleges and universities, assistant profs are under tremendous pressure to perform research, find research funding, and serve on committees. What does that mean for you? It usually means that these are some pretty busy people; they'll hold to their office hours and you should take advantage of them. You may not be able to find them in their office at other times.

Extra Credit

Regardless of your professor's rank, it's appropriate to address her as "Doctor." Some professors will ask their students to call them by their first name; don't do so unless your teacher asks you to.

Assistant professors are at the beginnings of their careers and excited about their field. Don't assume that, just because faculty members are new or young, they can't also be the best teachers you ever had.

♦ **Associate professors** are a step above the assistant professor ranking. The title is awarded after the professor completes required criteria. The associate professor level is generally where a faculty member's career either takes off or levels off.

♦ **Full professors** with *tenure* are the most esteemed among their colleagues. Faculty members who achieve full professor status have usually completed a strong body of research, have been successful in bringing grant funding to the campus, and have excellent teaching skills.

Word-of-mouth is another good way to find out about your professors. You can also ask on-campus departments about the general evaluation of professors by previous students. You won't be able to see individual teacher evaluations, but you may be able to get some general feedback.

Many universities post the teaching and research credentials of their faculty members online so you can survey the options for different courses. Nontraditional or adult student associations can also help match you and your learning style with faculty members whose teaching styles will fit you best.

def•i•ni•tion

Tenure is supposed to mean complete job security for faculty members, and it's granted after professors have undergone years of work, research, teaching, and community service. Even though tenure gives faculty a lot of teaching and research freedom, it doesn't mean that a professor can do anything she wants. On most campuses, faculty can be fired for cause, even if tenured.

Extra Credit

You can find out about your professors in advance of registering for their class. There are websites devoted to evaluating professors by students. Keep in mind, though, that these evaluations are most often completed by students who feel very strongly about their professors, one way or another. Check websites, but don't base all your decision-making on what you read.

Buying Books and Instructional Materials

After you've selected your courses, you can purchase your books and other materials for your classes in advance of the first day of class. In addition to college campus bookstores, you can order books through many online stores. The introduction of online bookstores has brought a healthy competition to the textbook market; you can save a lot of money if you purchase textbooks online.

Extra Credit

To find used textbook sellers, do an Internet search for the textbook name and/or author, or simply the words "college textbooks." You will find reputable sellers online with easily recognizable names (such as Amazon.com and Half.ebay.com). Make sure your online bookseller has a secure means of accepting payment, and weigh the pros and cons of more expensive campus store purchases against shipping and handling costs when you buy online.

Some professors post the required books and required materials on the college website; others post lists in the campus bookstore.

Don't wait until the last minute to buy your books. The sooner you do it, the more likely you are to secure used or less-expensive editions of books in the campus bookstore or online. If you wait until you attend the first day of class (a habit of younger students who like to see just "how important" the textbook will really be), you're going to either find the bookstore shelves sparse or be too late to get a good bargain online.

Paying for Your Books with Financial Aid

If you qualify for financial aid and are relying on that aid to help you purchase your textbooks, you might not be able to buy your books until your financial aid *disbursement* date. Financial aid typically disburses within the first couple of weeks of each new semester.

def•i•ni•tion

Disbursement is the process in which your financial aid is moved into your campus account. After all costs in your account are paid, you will either be issued an overage check or the balance of your financial aid will be directly deposited into your bank account for off-campus college costs.

Many campus bookstores allow you to charge your books to your university account in advance of the semester's start. Keep in mind, though, that you'll be paying premium bookstore prices unless you shop early enough to pick up used books.

College bookstores also sell school-related materials such as notebooks, lab equipment, graph paper, and even computers. You can charge these to your college account as well, but expect to pay higher prices for the convenience.

Finding the Best Prices on Textbooks

Major online booksellers, such as Amazon.com, Half.ebay.com, and others, have textbooks available in their warehouses and through third-party booksellers. Be careful, as you research your textbook needs, to note which edition of a particular textbook you need; it's very easy to see a textbook title and accidentally purchase a previous edition that won't work for your class.

If you don't have to rely on financial aid to buy your books, and you start early, you can save 50 percent or more on textbook costs if you do your online homework. Saving money on your textbooks is yet another reason that taking your time to plan ahead can help you ease back into the role of student—easing the impact on your wallet at the same time.

Joining an Adult Student Association

Even if you work full-time and/or are a busy mom or dad with a load of off-campus commitments, you can benefit by joining an adult student association on-campus. Do this before the semester begins and you can get in on all beginning-of-the-semester activities. Many adult student associations are kid-friendly and even provide daycare arrangements when meetings or events are taking place.

These student associations go by a number of different names, and even though adult students are the majority on a lot of campuses, the most prevalent name for these associations remains the nontraditional student's association.

The makeup and services for the associations differ from campus to campus, but in general, you can count on finding the following services and activities:

- ◆ A voice for adult students in the student government

- ◆ Tutoring and mentoring services and referrals

- ◆ Advice and assistance with daycare

- ◆ Help with study skills and career planning

- ◆ Advocates for you who can help you through a tough patch with a professor or help intervene with campus administration problems

- ◆ Other adult members who attend social functions together

- ◆ Adult student advisors who are accustomed to helping students balance work, family, and school

- ◆ Someone to listen to you; often the hardest thing to find when you need it

Walking Through Your Class Schedule

If you're taking classes on a traditional college campus, and if you're taking more than one class at a time, it's a good idea to walk through your class schedule ahead of time. Get a campus map and locate your classrooms. Open the doors if they're empty and look around the room. Scope out where you'd like to sit.

This walk-through is particularly important if you're returning to college full-time, if you haven't been on the campus before, or if you're the kind of person who likes to dot your i's and cross your t's ahead of time. Knowing where you're going and when can help instill confidence on the first day of class. There's no point in wasting your worries on whether you can find your classroom (a recurring nightmare for students of all ages, oddly enough).

While you're on campus walking through your schedule, go ahead and locate the other places you'll likely need to visit while you're attending school, such as:

- Tutoring centers
- Cafeterias and snack bars
- Student activities offices
- Bursar or financial offices
- Testing centers
- Career centers

- Places to get student newspapers
- Stores that sell college merchandise
- Check-cashing or banking facilities
- Athletic ticket offices
- Police or emergency responder offices

Examining the Parking Arrangements

Most adult students are on a tight timeline. Whether you're hauling it to class after work or trying to squeeze in a course over your lunch hour, you need to check out the parking arrangements on campus and plot out your parking plans. You might have to park and dash into class with seconds to spare, so you want to be prepared.

Parking is a perennial problem for commuting students, especially on older college campuses. Many older campuses were built for residential students, with little thought given to the needs of commuters because there were so few adult students—or even nonresidential students—on campus when they were built. Many of these older campuses have since built parking garages to meet the needs of their commuting students, but even then, the garages are often a good 15-minute walk from class.

Cautionary Tales

Nothing will stress you out like not being able to find a parking place, and at the last minute, you might tempt fate and park in a lot reserved for faculty and staff. Keep in mind, however, that campuses have people who patrol parking lots and who ticket vehicles that don't have the proper parking permits or that are parked at expired meters.

Larger campuses, especially those that have had to use "out parcels" of land for commuter parking, have invested in bus or trolley systems to get students to class and minimize traffic jams on campus streets. Most of these systems are free to students boarding or unloading at specified stops on and near campus. The downside to these bus and trolley systems is that you're at the mercy of the driver and the number of stops in between you and your classroom. If you know you have plenty of time, however, a good transport system will allow you to park in less-expensive parking lots and will also help keep you out of the elements. If you do wish to use a campus bus or trolley system, this is one more aspect of college that you can "dry-run" through before classes begin.

If you go to school in a city, public transportation can be the best option for getting to class with a minimum of fuss. Busses and/or subway systems have stops near or on college campuses in most cities. If the subway or bus stop is unfamiliar to you, go ahead and ride the line before you need to begin class.

The Least You Need to Know

- There's plenty of work for you to do before the semester even begins.
- Faculty rank and status can dictate their availability to students.
- Part-time faculty can be a bonus for adult learners.
- Save money on textbooks by purchasing them online or through used booksellers.
- Familiarize yourself with the campus, class location, and parking arrangements in advance of your first day of class.

## Chapter 14

Succeeding in the Campus Culture

In This Chapter

◆ Adjusting to different classroom environments

◆ Making sense of the syllabus

◆ Teaming up with note-taking buddies

◆ Knowing when to ask for help

A good friend of mine used to keep a small poster in his office that said, "To live well, one must remain unseen." There may be a little bit of truth to that sentiment, but when it comes to the college campus, remaining completely unseen just isn't an option if you want to succeed.

You also don't want to be too visible. What is "too visible"? It's hard to quantify, but you don't want to be so visible that you make a nuisance of yourself! There's a fine line between being pleasantly noticed and being a problem student—a line that you just have to figure out on your own. And that line, that careful balance, can be different from classroom to classroom, a function of your professors and their personality, as well as a function of the peers in your classes.

Of course, you can take online courses or telecourses if you really do desire to remain completely unseen. But if you'll be in a regular classroom, there are social and professional rules of conduct that apply. Some rules are obvious; others are subtle. No one is likely to tell you what those subtle rules are; you have to feel them out for yourself. This chapter arms you with some of these "subtle skills" you'll need to read, adapt to, and succeed in the campus culture.

In the Classroom

When you walk into your classroom for the first time, keep an eye out for clues to the type of class it's going to be.

The first thing you should do is "read the room." Look around at the other students in class. Pay attention to the ratio of older students to younger students. Do the older students all seem to gather in one area of the classroom?

Listen to some of the conversations that students are having before the professor walks in. Introduce yourself to the person in front of you and beside you. Try to gauge their comfort level in the classroom; shake their hands as you introduce yourself.

Look at how the chairs are arranged. The chair arrangement will tell you a lot about how the professor plans to teach the class. If you're in a classroom with stadium-style seating and the room holds upward of 75 to 80 people, you're probably going to have a professor who teaches from the podium, uses an overhead projector with PowerPoint on occasion and, with such a large class, probably gives multiple choice or true-or-false tests. The room just isn't amenable to group work or less formal means of teaching; the sheer size of the class makes it impractical for the professor to give essay tests, and the entire experience will likely be less personal.

Extra Credit

Just because you're in a large classroom doesn't mean you won't have any interaction with your professor. Even in a large lecture hall, your professor might ask questions during class.

If you walk into a room and see tables joined together to form a "circle" of sorts, with chairs all around, then you're going to be in a class that will be more interactive and the teaching is likely to be more give-and-take in nature. You will probably be expected to participate in class, and so the pressure to be prepared each day will be higher. It will be harder to "hide" if you haven't done your reading or assignments. Start off on the right foot by introducing yourself to the people on each side of you.

On the first day of class, watch what happens when it's time for class to begin and the professor walks in. The professor will always take roll on the first day; it's important to know if he or she will do so consistently and if your presence or absence can affect your grade.

Watch to see if the students all quiet down when the professor walks in, or if the room must be brought to attention. See if you can spot students who don't settle down easily. If you're sitting close to a group of students like this, don't sit near them the next time you come to class. You don't have to put up with students who interfere with your education, so move if you need to.

These techniques for "reading" the classroom are all probably things you've used in the context of your work, in social situations, or in church. Learn to adapt these skills to the classroom and you will be more than ready to compete with those "professional students" who go to class all day.

By the end of your first day in class, you will have enough clues in front of you to be able to make an educated guess as to how the entire semester will proceed.

The Syllabus Rules All

If there's one thing that professors lament over and over again, it's that their students don't read the *syllabus*. Everything you need to know about your class is on that syllabus. From the book(s) you will need, to the units you're covering, to test dates, the syllabus is your one-stop source of information.

def•i•ni•tion

The word **syllabus** has Latin roots and means an outline of the primary points of a lecture, class, or course of study. In addition to the main points of the class, a syllabus usually contains information pertinent to test schedules, classroom policies and practices, and contact information for the professor.

Keep your syllabus with your materials for the course and refer to it often. If you lose it, ask for another one. You might also check to see if your professor posts the syllabus online.

Review the syllabus for possible conflicts right away, and if you spot any, address them as early in the semester as possible. For example, suppose you notice that a test will be held on a date that you know you'll be out of town for work. Talk with your professor during the first week of class to see if you can take the test on a different date. The same holds true if you see a test on a date when you know your son or daughter will be in the Thanksgiving play at school. Make alternative arrangements early; most professors will be accommodating.

Remember, when it comes to conflicts you see on a syllabus, solving them earlier is better.

> **Cautionary Tales**
>
> Professors report that adult students often wait until it's too late for them to make accommodations for the conflicts that arise. If you wait too late in the semester, you'll be putting your professor in a difficult situation; you'll be asking her to grant you considerations that other students don't have.

A Contract for Teaching and Learning

The syllabus is more than just a schedule. It also outlines the material to be covered and, more often than not, the time frame for each subject or unit.

Think of the syllabus as a contract of sorts. The professor agrees to teach you a certain amount of information and skills within a certain period of time. The professor lays out his or her expectations for what you should read and write and prepare for. Test dates are clear. You and your professor, through the syllabus, have a "deal." The professor agrees to teach. You agree to learn.

Read the Fine Print

Always, always, always, read the "fine print" in a syllabus. Now, the fine print is rarely actually written in a smaller font, and really isn't fine print at all. It is, however, the set of rules that the professor outlines for the class.

Here you'll see the absence policies and roll-taking policies. You'll run into professors who don't take roll at all. These professors take the perspective that you're the consumer, and if you don't care enough to show up, you'll get the grades you deserve come test time. However, you will also come across professors who are strict about attendance. Some are even strict about tardiness. I know of one professor who, if you are tardy, marks you absent that day. Such professors know that there is no way you can learn what they are teaching if you don't come to class.

Another piece of fine print to pay attention to is make-up policies. Some professors allow no make-up tests whatsoever. Others have limited make-up policies. Almost all, however, will work with you in advance to allow you to take a test early for a date on which you will have a conflict.

If you're taking more than one class, you'll encounter different policies in different classrooms. Keep up with them. The professors are completely in charge of the classroom. Work with them, abide by the syllabus and classroom rules, and you will be prepared to succeed!

Other Students

You're not going to be learning in a vacuum; the students around you in the classroom are going to be part of your learning environment. Sometimes other students can be helpful in understanding difficult concepts. And sometimes other students can be a real nuisance.

There's a certain category of students that you're probably going to see in each classroom. What's important is how you handle each of them:

- **The know-it-all:** This student usually sits in the front row and raises her hand for every question posed to the class. She knows the answers to all the professor's questions and even asks questions designed to test what the professor knows!

    Handling the know-it-all: Raise your own hand when the professor asks a question. The professor will be pleased to call on someone else. Know also that this kind of student is usually just looking for affirmation. He's not any smarter than you!

- **The note stealer:** This type of student rarely shows up for class, spots someone they know attends class regularly and is not above asking "Hey, can I have your notes for the past two weeks?"

    Handling the note stealer: You'll be tempted to share notes, because a habitual note stealer can be quite friendly and disarming. It's how they've made it through life! Politely refuse and never give your notes out to a note stealer. You may never get them back! Also suggest that they ask the professor for material covered while they were absent. Truthfully, they probably won't do it, but will instead try to find another student who can't resist their charming selves.

◆ **The laptop kid:** Laptop kids are more and more prevalent. They're students who take all their notes during class on a laptop. If you have three or four of them near you, you may find yourself distracted by the clicking sound of their fingers hitting the keys.

Handling the laptop kid: The best thing you can do with a laptop kid is move to another part of the classroom where you can be closer to students who take notes on paper. No, you're not a dinosaur if you take notes by hand.

These are just three of the student "types" you're likely to encounter as you return to the classroom. It's actually fun to look around and see the diversity of people you're learning with in the same classroom. You're one of them!

Build a Buddy System in Each Class

A good buddy in each class is as good as gold! But you've got to build your buddy system early in the semester. During the first week of class listen to students, paying attention to how they talk to others and how they answer questions in class. Make the acquaintance of students who sit in front of you, behind you, and beside you.

Befriend people in your class(es) who can be relied on to take good notes and share them if you happen to miss a class. This isn't the same as being a "note stealer," but rather a friendly agreement between or among a small group of students in the same class.

You should have more than one buddy in each class, just in case two of you miss class on the same day. Look at how each of you takes notes; try to understand each other's "system" of note-taking. And, above all, get a buddy whose handwriting is legible (or else find a buddy who also doubles as a laptop kid)!

Your buddy who provides you with notes when you're gone may or may not be a member of your study group. Getting a good group of people together to study takes a little more scrutiny, a better sense of study styles, and oral communication ability. So don't feel like you have to study with your note-taking buddies.

Give and Take

A college classroom can be one of the most exciting places on the planet! Rarely can you go anywhere else and find such a free, focused, and even passionate exchange of ideas. Treasure what happens in a college classroom, because it's really unique. You won't find the same dynamic in staff meetings at work or during dinner conversations. The give and take you will experience in a college classroom requires that you participate and that you respect (even if you don't agree) the opinions of others.

Extra Credit _____

Remember the adage about not talking about politics or religion? That might work for parties, but not in a college classroom. Be prepared to encounter people who, politically and religiously, have very different beliefs than you do. To have your beliefs respected, avoid confronting others or putting others down who don't believe as you do. There's a time and a place for that kind of dialogue, and unless you're in a class designed for debate, a college classroom is not that place!

That's not to say that academic arguments don't get heated. They do! They can be even more fun if the students on each side of an argument feel passionately about their position. Maybe, at the end of a great debate in class, you come away with a complete change of mind, so persuasive were your classmates. Perhaps you solidify a position that you weren't sure about, so rich was the information discussed.

Give and take really is what college is all about. You've probably been in situations in the work world where your creativity was diminished because what matters is the bottom line. Maybe you're venturing into college after taking care of young children for a while. Well, get ready for a ride—one that's intellectual, emotional, and even physical at times.

Your First Report Card

You won't get your report card until the end of the semester (or trimester, or quarter, depending on how your school's academic year is structured). However, you will have a good sense of what your grade or grades are before your report card lands in your mailbox. That's because the class syllabus will have clued you in as to what percentage tests and assignments contribute to your final grade. Don't wait around until the end of the semester to wonder how you've been doing.

You know your test grades and what grades you've been getting on papers and assignments. Not every student will make an "A" on everything. Adult students, however, are more likely to seek out help if their grades aren't as high as they expect out of themselves.

Extra Credit

Midterm grades are often posted a few days before the final class drop date for the semester. The posting of midterms will help you decide whether you should drop a course for that semester and try again at a later time.

If you were a "B" average student in high school, you have likely set yourself up to think of yourself as a "B" average student in college. That's fine, but even students who are making "B's" may want some help to give them a chance at making higher grades.

How and where you seek help will be a function of where you are, grade wise, and where you want to go. If you're trying to keep your head above water and avoid failing classes, you will need a different strategy than if you're simply trying to improve your grades (and/or increase what you are learning).

Getting Help if Your Grades Aren't Great

On-campus help is available for any academic problem you have. Campuses often have tutoring centers staffed by upper-division or graduate students who are ready to assist students with anything from algebra or trigonometry to microeconomics, history, or biology. General tutoring centers are a good choice for you if you're having trouble grasping a particular concept and just need some additional help.

Many campuses have created tutoring and resource centers focused on mathematics of all kinds. If math is your problem subject, and your campus has a math resource center, you can do homework at math centers and get help with problems.

Office Hours

John, a community college professor, notes that students in community colleges aren't afraid to ask for help, but they also are less certain of themselves as students and don't think they are capable of getting higher degrees. Women in particular, John says, don't think toward upper degrees or graduate school, when many are talented and should go further.

Because so many students need help with writing, many campuses also have writing centers, with staff who can assist in everything from literary prose to technical writing.

If you need more one-on-one help with a subject, you can hire a tutor. Check the student center or department office of the class you're having trouble with. Both of these locations on campus, in addition to any tutoring centers, will have the names of qualified tutors.

Professors are also good sources for tutors and can often guide you to graduate students or upper-division students in their departments who can assist you with topics you are finding troublesome. If you ask your professor for recommendations, you're not only showing how serious you are about doing well in class, you're also more likely to be referred to a tutor who knows the professor's expectations.

Extra Credit

Don't know what the going rate is for paying a personal tutor? Check with the campus tutoring center and find out what they're paying their tutors on an hourly basis.

Your best bet with any tutor is to meet in a public location, such as a study carrel in your campus library, or a campus coffee shop or cafeteria. Tutors who are endorsed by the campus are generally highly trustworthy; however, it still makes sense to meet them in a public location.

You can engage the tutor for any length of time that suits your needs. If it's a difficult subject, you might want to hire the tutor for the entire semester. If you're just having trouble getting through one particularly tough chapter, then you can hire the tutor just long enough to get through the difficult material.

When you engage a tutor, use campus resources to choose your tutor. It's the best way to ensure you get a tutor whose skills will enhance your own.

Working with Your Professor or Instructor

As noted in Chapter 13, your professor or instructor will hold office hours to help students. If your professor's office hours are at an inconvenient time for you, you can always make an appointment to meet with him at a different time.

You'll be sharing office hours with other students who will also be popping by to see your professor. So if you think you'll need more than 15 minutes or so, it's best to set an appointment.

Your professor's teaching and research schedule may be quite full and they may be teaching large classes. Don't take it personally if your teacher suggests that you engage a tutor; it will be a genuine indication that your professor believes you need more help outside of class than he or she can give you.

Cautionary Tales

Your professors are not tutors; they have done their part during class time. If you need more help than a good 15-minute review, seek the help of a tutoring center or a tutor.

Staying in Good Academic Standing

Every college defines what it means to remain in good academic standing. It's important to stay in good standing not just for your eligibility to take classes, but also to continue receiving financial aid.

If you attend all your classes, do your homework, and study regularly, the standards shouldn't be difficult to maintain. So why not raise the bar for yourself, and set your own standard of good academic standing? For instance, if you must achieve a 2.0 grade point average (GPA) to remain in good academic standing, why not set your own personal standard of good academic standing at 3.0?

You may go back into college knowing that you will never make straight As. So what? You know what your best is, so make a promise to yourself to do your best. You might surprise yourself and find that, this time around, you're a pretty good student after all!

Grades Matter for Financial Aid Eligibility

Grades may not matter much for you when it comes to your sense of personal worth, but they do matter when it comes to financial aid.

Any scholarships you've received that are based on merit likely contain minimum grade requirements. You can lose a scholarship if you don't make the grades expected of you.

For most free financial aid, maintaining good academic standing is the benchmark for continuing financial aid. Many campuses have adapted 2.0 GPA as their academic standing benchmark because the same GPA is used in maintaining federal aid eligibility.

If at the end of spring semester you risk losing your scholarship or other financial aid, talk to your advisor about taking summer classes to raise your grades. Depending on your GPA and how well you do in the summer class, you might be able to bring your GPA up a couple of tenths of a point.

Don't wait until the end of the spring semester to address poor grades. You will know well before the end of the school year if you're having problems. You might have to drop a class that you're failing in order to save your financial aid. You can always go back to that class at a later date. Work with your advisor to understand the academic and financial implications of your choices.

Attendance Matters for Good Grades

Even if some of your professors don't have attendance policies, you're not free of the responsibility to go to class. Professors who don't have attendance policies are those who, for the most part, leave it up to the students—all of whom are actual adults and are paying for the classes—to care enough to be there.

Adult students rarely simply skip class because they don't feel like going; adults most often miss class for family or work reasons. Still, if you have to miss more than one class for even a very good reason, you can jeopardize your good grades.

A class missed here and there won't hurt you, especially if you have developed a good buddy system in your classes. But don't skip class on a regular basis and expect to do well. Even if you do have buddies providing you with notes, and even if you've read the text, you're missing out on a lot of subtleties in class. The subtleties can make all the difference in understanding the content or not. In college, it's really hard to fake your way through.

You might have already learned this lesson when you went to college right out of high school. In fact, high schools are so easy for so many young students now that students experience culture shock when they get to college and see how much more stringent the expectations are.

The Least You Need to Know

- Be noticed in class for all the right reasons.
- Read the classroom dynamics and work to adapt to the teaching-learning situation in each one.
- Brace yourself for annoyances during class and learn how to cope with them.
- Make good note-taking buddies in each class you take.
- Don't wait until it's too late to ask for help if you aren't doing well.
- Poor grades can have real consequences.

## Chapter 15

Student Services and Campus Opportunities

In This Chapter

- Making the most of student services
- Participating in student government or scheduling committees
- Using tutoring services on campus
- Making college and your job work together
- Taking advantage of the campus career office

Is there really going to be a social structure on campus that you'll feel a part of? Sure there is, and it doesn't matter if you're planning to attend a small community college or a sprawling university.

What draws people together on a college campus often has little to do with age or stage. It's that you have something in common. In no other social situation will you probably have an opportunity to befriend a 19-year-old girl who's fresh out of high school. Sure, you might be old enough to be her mother, but when you're taking a class together, you are peers. You'll be surprised how quickly these relationships take shape.

But there will be times when you do want to be with people your age, if only to express concerns about college that your 19-year-old classmate can't begin to grasp. Relax, there are plenty of opportunities to interact with other adults. And the best place to start is in the student services area of the college.

Student services (sometimes also called student affairs) is there to help all students. Whether you want to be active in student government, need help with a class, or want a campus job, student services officials are there to help you.

Adult Situations

One of my favorite *Calvin and Hobbes* comic strips shows Calvin reading the newspaper's movie and TV listings. He comes across a TV movie that has "adult situations." Curious, Calvin asks Hobbes what "adult situations" means.

Guilelessly, Hobbes allows that adult situations are "probably things like going to work, paying bills, taking responsibilities." Calvin is repulsed by the thought and says "they don't kid around when they say 'for mature audiences.'" Hobbes, philosophical, ponders how these "adult situation movies manage to make any money."

If you can remember reading *Calvin and Hobbes* comic strips when they were fresh in the newspaper, you're probably an adult student. But seriously, there really *are* unique needs you will have in college that younger students won't have and, like Calvin, the younger students won't even understand what your needs are, why you have these needs, or even really care about them.

Don't be put off by that! The younger students just haven't lived as much life as you have. Their view of the world is much narrower than yours. You might be great pals when it comes to studying Kate Chopin's *The Awakening* in a literature class, but you're not likely to share a lot of time together outside of your studies.

Instead, find ways and places where you can express your "adultness." Join organizations on campus where you and other moms and dads can tell funny stories about your children. Participate in social activities where you and other adult students can bring your spouses and/or your children. Join groups that help make college a better place for adults. Even if you're working yourself to the bone while trying to get your college degree, a few hours on a couple of weekends during the semester might be all it takes for college to feel like a second home to you.

Adult Student Organizations

Almost every campus has an organization for adult students. Still, almost every campus that has an organization such as this continues to call it a nontraditional student association. This term is used almost universally, even on campuses where adult students are the majority!

Adult student associations have officers, members, and sometimes even paid staff who operate the office and manage services and activities that adults need. Join your adult student association before classes begin so that you are able to take advantage of their opportunities early in the semester.

Another option for interacting with adult students is to use the Internet. One good site is www.adultstudentcenter.com, an online student center that contains message boards, online mentoring resources, real student stories, and support structures for adult students.

There are other online students available on the Internet. Your own college may even have pages devoted to adult student interaction. If your college doesn't have such a service, then suggest that they add one at your first adult student association meeting!

Student Government

Student government is serious business on college campuses. Not only is student government an important resumé booster, but there are serious responsibilities associated with the offices.

Student government is the elected voice of the student body when it comes to important campus policies and procedures. College presidents listen to the formal resolutions passed by student governments, pay attention to the items that are on the student government agendas, and do their best to implement what students say they need. Campus student government representatives also populate state-level student advisory boards in order to let state officials know what student concerns are. For example, representatives of state and campus student governments may testify at public hearings on tuition increases.

Extra Credit

In some states, student government members not only advise campus administrators but advise state board members as well. These student advisory boards can have an impact on adult higher education statewide.

Student governments, in most cases, reserve one or more seats in their governance structures for adult student members. Often, the seats for adult students are given to officers of the adult student association.

Student governments have a variety of responsibilities, in some cases helping to mediate student-faculty disagreements, grievances, and other problems. They represent the entire student body in different venues, including meeting with alumni, representing their college with the state's legislature and members of Congress, and advising campus administration on student issues. On some campuses, student governments are responsible for managing programs and services that are supported by student fees, such as the student center, recreational facilities, and so on. Student government members who participate in these activities gain valuable management experience.

> ### Student Center
>
> Michael joined his adult student organization on campus and, though he considered himself a shy person, also took a seat on the student government. He worked part-time during college and had his mind set on getting a degree in accounting. Student government, though, changed him. He became politically astute through his work with student government and became a vocal advocate for student issues. Within a year, Michael changed his major, and eventually went to Washington, D.C., to complete an internship on Capitol Hill.

Consider what would happen if there were no adult student voices in student government. You could find yourself on a college campus that has more adult students than traditional ones with only traditional students operating the student government, advising the administration about what the campus needs.

Without adult student membership, you would never have a voice. You may not feel that you're the type who can sit on a student government. You may simply not have the time. But you can join the adult student organization and present your needs to the adults who *do* represent you on campus.

Adults who have served in student government have been responsible for many of the innovations on campuses that accommodate adult students' unique needs.

Tutoring and Mentoring

The student services office at your school can guide you to the kind of tutoring and mentoring services you need. Although you can also work directly with an academic department for the subject you're having trouble with, adult student services might be in a better position to match you with a tutor closer to your own age. Some adults don't mind having tutors who are young enough to be their children or grandchildren, while others can't get accustomed to such an age difference in a tutoring relationship.

Even if you aren't a member of your campus's adult student organization, the organization's staff or members will still help match you with tutors or mentors who are also adult students.

If you have expertise in a particular subject area, you might be able to become a tutor. Not only will you earn some money, you will share your knowledge with another adult student and help them make it through college. Whether you're on the giving end of a tutoring relationship or the receiving end, you can gain social benefits that don't come with a price attached to them.

> **Office Hours**
>
> Karen is an academic advisor at a large university. She has a number of adult students in her group of advisees and says that adults are best at knowing when they need a tutor. They're not afraid to ask for help.

Scheduling Committees

It's a complex feat, creating schedules of courses and matching them to faculty members in every department on campus. Administrators on campus prepare enrollment projections to anticipate how many sections of particular classes will be needed, which are the best times to offer the classes, and then match faculty members to those classes.

Campuses often have scheduling committees on which students can serve. Consider becoming a part of a scheduling committee. Adult students, especially if working through their formal organization, can help make sure that more night sections of required courses are offered. Weekend courses might show up more on the schedule if the adults on campus want them. For some adults, 6 A.M. class offerings make all the difference in being able to take one or two classes a semester.

> **Extra Credit**
>
> Friendships among faculty and students are common in graduate school, but as more adult students attend college as undergraduates, it's becoming more common for faculty and undergraduate adult students to strike up friendships as well. If you befriend a faculty member, don't expect them to compromise their academic integrity to give you special treatment in class or on assignments.

You can help make sure future semesters have the courses you need, when you need them, by participating in the scheduling process.

Blending College and Work

You're a step ahead of others if you're pursuing a degree in an academic area in which you already work. Maybe you've gone as far up in your company as possible and now need your degree to move into a management position. No matter what your situation, find ways to make your work and your academic life help each other.

When doing assignments for class, think about projects that you have going on at work. Are there ways you can combine your work with school? Can you write a paper about a project you're working on at your job? Can you try a new innovation at work that you've thought about while learning new concepts in class?

You don't have to wait until you get your degree to try something new at the office. Surprise your boss with something new that helps the company. Surprise your professor by bringing a real-life project into the classroom.

Internships

Internships are like apprenticeships where you work in a real job environment related to your academic field. You can earn academic credit for internships, be paid, or a combination of both. Some fields, particularly in the graduate levels, require internships and/or observation hours. Internships are a great way to take what you learn in the classroom and apply it in the real work world. As an intern, you also interact with professionals who have experience and can show you the ropes.

Depending on the academic discipline, internships can last from one week to a year, or even longer for graduate school and medical school.

> ### Student Center
>
> Rich was working on two Bachelor's degrees—one in political science and one in journalism—when he was given the chance to work as a public affairs intern for a member of Congress. A major corporation sponsored his internship. He earned a small stipend each month, academic credit, and was provided living accommodations. The semester-long internship allowed Rich to learn all aspects of managing public affairs activities in a Congressional office. The internship also helped Rich decide upon journalism as his primary career, though he's been able to apply his experience in Congress to his journalism career in many ways.

As you advance toward your degree, you may have the option to do internships. Many companies have ongoing internship programs with local colleges. For instance, many newspaper companies take interns of all ages who are majoring in journalism, marketing, and public relations. The interns are assigned to beat reporters, copy writers, and editors. For the company, supporting internships provides a good future pool of full-time employees, and some of the interns get hired on even before they finish college.

If you're married, a parent, and you're fitting college into your already busy life, you need to consider whether you have the time to do an unpaid internship. However, if you plan ahead you should be able to fit an internship into your college experience.

Extra Credit

You might be able to negotiate an internship with your current employer. You probably won't get internship credit for merely going to work and doing the same job you do every day. However, if you talk to your supervisor, you might be able to negotiate a short-term position in a different department, one where you're learning a different aspect of the company. Try and negotiate a mutually beneficial internship; it's just one more way that you can blend college and work and not have to lose money in the process.

Campus Employment

You don't have to be 18 and living in a dorm to work on campus. Campus jobs are plentiful and they enable students to earn money while getting valuable work experience.

In many campus jobs, you can study during "down times," and your employer isn't going to mind (provided that your work is done).

If you have computer skills, you might be able to get a job proctoring a computer lab to earn money as a student employee. Or you might consider serving as a campus tutor or a paid mentor. Earning money on campus with campus employment pays you more than money; it pays you experience.

Extra Credit

One great place to work while in school is in the library. The campus library usually has a lot of openings for student employees, and if you work in the library, you end up getting more out of your job than just a paycheck: after a few weeks in a library, you will gain skills in locating resources and information that will pay huge dividends in your own academic work.

College and Career Services

As you move closer and closer to your graduation date, you should take advantage of the career services center. College staff who operate career centers always wish that students would make use of their resources far earlier in their college careers than they typically do. Too many students wait until the final semester, when they're looking for a new job, to consult with career services staff.

If you wait until the end of your college career, you're throwing away free resources that can help you all through college. Deciding on a career and a major is more than just selecting a degree program that sounds interesting. It's far better to match a degree program to your interests, skills, and abilities.

Career Exploration

In high school, you probably took tests to identify your interests and abilities. Mine told me that I should work with automotives, and I got a lot of teasing because of that. Just because I know a lot about cars doesn't mean that I want to build a career around them. High school is a time when students should be exploring careers, not making a complete, lifelong decision.

If you've come back to college because you've been working in dead-end jobs, you're still in a career exploration phase. Go to the campus career center before you declare a major. Take assessments that tell you about your values and interests. The results will be different from those you got in high school because you're older, you've had more life experiences, and you probably have a better idea where you want to go with your life.

Campus career centers have multiple assessments you can take to help you determine what kind of career might fit your interests and skills. Learn from these and talk to the counselors who work in the center about your results. Use the resources of the career center to figure out who you are and what you like to do.

Also explore the job outlook for certain majors. Career counselors can help you find out which jobs are expected to grow over the next decade and which jobs will be the highest paying. Remember, though, all the jobs you consider should also be viewed with an eye to the results of your career exploration tests. Your values and your life interests will tell you where you need to go. Don't choose a major that you loathe just because the field is expected to grow and pay good money!

Job Assistance and Placement

Even if you're obtaining a degree to move up in the company where you already work, consider making use of the job assistance and placement services on campus. It costs you nothing to look.

Counselors in career offices will help you update your resumé. They can teach you how to create different forms of resumés, such as functional (which focuses on what you do and have done) or chronological (which characterizes your work and college life in a sequential fashion).

Career counselors can also provide you with literature or help improve your interview skills.

During the spring semester, most college career offices have job fairs or arrange one-on-one meetings between employers and students. Career fairs are generally information-oriented and don't allow in-depth interaction, but in some cases, you can complete a first interview right at a company's booth!

When employers make arrangements to come to campus for one-on-one interviews, most often you will need to get your name on a list to meet with them. Though they are usually only on campus for a short period of time, if you keep your eye on announcements in the campus career office and/or work with a career counselor who will e-mail you when employers are coming to campus, you can make sure you get a chance at an interview.

Do Employers Care About Your Grades?

Adult students and young students alike wonder if employers care about grades. Do they only care if you got a degree, or do they care what your class rank is?

It depends. Some employers will want to see your grades and others won't. It also depends on the kind of job you're looking for. If potential employers request your transcript as part of your application package, they probably care about your grades. Even then, however, employers may care more about the courses you took within your major than your grades in your nonmajor courses.

Employer Views on Grades and "Hard Skills"

Grades in core academic classes, those junior and senior level courses in your specified academic major, can be important to employers. Think about it: if they need an employee to whom they're going to entrust high-dollar equipment, and you made Ds in your core classes, you're probably not going to be first on the employer's list.

Employers care about what you know and can do. They care if you can come to work for them with a minimum of additional training and get the job done. Sometimes they look to your grades as an indication of whether you can do these things, especially in classes that directly relate to your job.

"Soft Skills" Matter to Employers, Too

A futurist I heard speak recently said that "employees are hired for their hard skills and fired for their soft skills." What are soft skills? They are really nothing more than work etiquette. They include …

- Showing up to work on time
- Working well on a team project
- Being willing to put in extra time on a deadline project
- Honesty
- Oral and written communication skills
- Initiative and creative problem-solving
- Flexibility and adaptability

These are not all the soft skills that you'll be required to demonstrate in the workplace. If you communicate almost wholly by computer in an organization, there's even a set of e-mail etiquette rules for how you communicate with other staff or supervisors.

You can be one heck of a great engineer, a guy who made great grades in college and did some fabulous solitary experiments to earn good grades in college. But if you can't function well in a working environment, your engineering skills alone won't help you. The employer will find another great engineer who also "works well with others."

The Least You Need to Know

- Joining an adult student organization can really make you feel like you're a part of the college.
- Serve in campus government or on scheduling committees to ensure that adult student issues are addressed.

◆ Seek projects that will help you with work and school at the same time.

◆ Make continuous use of career services on campus—they're free!

Part 5

Managing College, Work, and Family

How do you manage to work and be a mom or dad and be a college student *and* keep all those parts of your life balanced? This can be the hardest part about returning to college.

From not having a babysitter on a test date to squeezing in study time around your kids' schedule to negotiating with your employer to use computer facilities for schoolwork, these variables require more planning and thinking-through than any other.

You can choose a career or degree plan in one day and follow that very predictable path until you get a degree. But your family and work can bring added challenges to your college experience, and you must prepare for these challenges if you want to succeed. This part involves the hardest work, but also the greatest benefits. You'll be setting an example for your kids, moving to a greater earning potential, and building a much more secure life for you and your family.

## Chapter 16

Marriage and Relationships

In This Chapter

- ◆ Learning about common relationship problems when one spouse returns to college

- ◆ Identifying communication strategies to prevent misunderstandings at home

- ◆ Integrating your new college friends into your existing social life

- ◆ Avoiding the negative aspects of college degree disparity

When adult students and their spouses begin talking about a return to college, they typically discuss the financial impact of paying for college, potential schedule problems, and even whether they can still manage to learn in a classroom environment. One potential problem usually remains unspoken, however: the impact going to college will have on their relationship. Nothing will sneak up on you faster when you return to college than unresolved relationship problems.

Husbands and wives can sit around the dinner table late at night, pore over a college catalog or class schedule, and believe that they are doing all they can do to prepare for the experience of returning to college. The financial planning is done, the academic planning is done. But their relationship is about to undergo new challenges.

The Biggest Test of Them All

Going back to college isn't merely an academic exercise; it's a social exercise, one that can negatively affect your marriage or primary relationship unless you're prepared to address the issues that your trek back to college will bring into your home.

Rarely is anyone on campus prepared to help you with relationship issues brought about by a return to college. You won't typically find brochures on this issue sitting around college admissions offices. College websites don't usually devote space to this topic. In fact, hardly anyone even talks about the pressures on marriage and family that happen when an adult in the household returns to college.

And yet, the return to college by one adult in the household can be the impetus for discord, anger, lack of understanding, jealousy, and even divorce in situations where the warning signs are ignored or noticed too late.

Cautionary Tales

Just because you're going back to college doesn't mean that you are somehow better or superior to your spouse who doesn't have a degree. It's too easy to begin thinking of yourself as more "cultured" or more "worldly" simply because you can talk about abstract theories or new computer programs. Have confidence in yourself, but remember who you live with and why you got together in the first place.

Don't let this chapter scare you. It's here to make sure that you don't become a statistic. You can take steps to make sure that none of these problems happen to you and your spouse. You can deal with the problems when they arise and not let issues fester. It's as important to your college planning to focus on your primary relationship as it is to choose the right degree program.

To keep things simple, I've used the words "spouse" or "husband" and "wife" throughout this chapter; you can substitute any other name for your significant other—boyfriend, girlfriend, partner, and so on. The issues apply to all significant relationships. After you read this chapter, give it to your spouse to read. Both of you will benefit from talking through the issues in this chapter.

Preparing Your Spouse for Changes

Researchers who study marriage and family know that most people marry or form a significant bond because of their commonalities. You and your spouse share similar interests, similar backgrounds, or complement each other in important ways that "complete" each other. You likely share common educational backgrounds, have matching faith interests, and share common core values.

The minute that one of you makes the decision to return to college, you start down a path that changes the relationship dynamic.

You're changing the unspoken balance of similarities and differences that was in place when you said "I do," and you have to acknowledge those changes, deal with them, and integrate them into your relationship. If you don't, you can end up with a double-barreled problem: your academic pursuits can harm your relationship, and your relationship problems can harm your academic progress.

Common Problems When One Spouse Goes Back to School

When one spouse returns to college, changes in the relationship are usually subtle and may not even come up during the very first semester of school. During your first semester back, your husband or wife is likely very involved in your education, supporting your stepping out into something new. You anchor your sense of self-worth and who you are with your spouse, a familiar and comfortable person who validates you and supports you completely.

Couples who end up having problems, however, fail to see early warning signs—small chasms in the relationship that grow larger in barely noticeable ways. These small problems go unresolved between couples, and the small things become bigger over time and can add up to the dreaded "irreconcilable differences."

The following scenarios represent the most common problems that creep up in marriages and significant relationships when a spouse returns to college. As you read them, think about warning signs, think about ways to see problems early, and think about how you would react in similar situations. Consider possible solutions and how likely or unlikely such scenarios are for you and your spouse.

They Like Me, They Really Like Me!

College might be the first time in your adult life that adult peers other than your spouse give you praise that makes you feel smart and successful. These are the kind of affirmations that you're not going to get anywhere else.

More often than people care to admit, adult students take grades as a direct indication of how much a professor likes them. In reality, grades are just a measure of knowledge and skills. The same thing can happen with younger students; however, because most professors are older than they are, the impact of peer evaluation doesn't usually create the same sort of social misconceptions. Adult students are more at risk for these sorts of issues because they are closer in age to most professors.

At home no one grades you for what you do. Your wife doesn't thank you for doing the laundry by giving you an A- and a written "attaboy" for your work. Your husband doesn't give you a grade for helping out in the yard with a written appraisal of your work and a note placed in your "permanent record." So here is where adults get into trouble with the "they like me" problem—they think that their spouses don't like or understand them nearly as much as their professors do simply because the validation isn't as concrete.

Cautionary Tales

Consider what it's like to get a paper back from a professor; one that compliments you on your writing, on the argument you made, or on your overall contribution to the class. Professors *grade* you, and this act of grading gives you a sort of gauge on "how smart" you are. You might internalize this "grading scale" as an indication of your value as a person. You wouldn't be the first to do so; students of all ages tend to misattribute a teacher's grading of their work as some form of personal compliment or criticism. It's all too easy to treat a professor's evaluation of your work as an evaluation of you.

This scenario might sound silly upon first reading, but it happens every day to students returning to college. Keep in mind that marriage and relationships aren't on an A to F grading scale. And professors don't tell you how much they like or don't like you through the grades they give you.

You Don't Understand Me Anymore!

You come bursting through the front door after class, eager to tell your spouse about this fantastic new science concept you learned, only to find a fairly lukewarm response. You're vulnerable at this point. You're wearing your love and enthusiasm for school on your sleeve, and if you don't see an equivalent level of enthusiasm from your spouse, you can easily feel rejected. Don't fall into this trap.

When you return to college, you're choosing an academic path that interests *you*, not one that interests your spouse. So why should you care if your spouse doesn't express a lot of interest in what you're learning? However, a surprising number of adult students misinterpret their spouse's disinterest in their education as a negative evaluation of *them*.

For one thing, your spouse doesn't have any frame of reference for actually appreciating what you've learned. He doesn't have the context of your class through which to see what you've learned. She doesn't know the content area like you do. It's too easy to view a blank stare negatively, especially if you've got a nice group of pals in class who are high-fiving you for a great paper, or a professor who singles you out in class for a compliment. You simply cannot compare the two reactions.

Another reason that your spouse might not enthusiastically pat you on the back for your amazing new discovery is how you tell your story. Are you sharing and perhaps even teaching your husband or wife the concept? Or are you trying to draw attention to the fact that you know more than your spouse?

It's unrealistic to expect your husband or wife to be as jazzed about what you're learning as you are.

Name-Dropping and the Study-Group Phenomenon

Adult learners, tread very, very carefully here. The problem I'm about to describe can spell big trouble for marriages and relationships. You really have to guard against this particular problem creeping into your home.

This big marriage problem doesn't usually show up unless the previous problem scenarios have already taken place. Perhaps you already feel like you're not getting the affirmations at home that you get in school. Perhaps you perceive your spouse's lack of enthusiasm for your degree problem as a slight. If you've not corrected your behavior and/or any misperceptions you and your spouse might have by now, your relationship is primed for the name-dropping and study-group problems.

This problem can begin subtly. You come home from class and start mentioning your study partner with some frequency. Ah, your study partner just happens to be the opposite sex. You might be doing your name-dropping innocently enough, and you may indeed be impressed with how well you study with your partner; good study partners can help each other be very successful when they click. But think about how this constant name-dropping sounds to your spouse.

Extra Credit

Include your spouse in your studies by holding study sessions at your own home; make it a dinner and study session. Introduce your husband or wife to your study partners or classmates. Expand your spouse's circle of friends while you expand your own circle.

Such references are often really more than name-dropping; they are a very subtle way of asking your spouse to be as interested in your academic pursuits as your study partner is. Neither you nor your spouse are going to realize this unless you see this behavior and call it for what it is. Recognize it, if you are doing it. Catch yourself and correct your behavior.

> **Cautionary Tales** _____
>
> No one can be expected to return to college and never have a member of the opposite sex in a study group. But remember that there is safety in numbers. A study group with four people in it will likely help you learn more and be better for the name-dropping problem potential than if you study with one other person of the opposite sex.

Avoiding Problems Through Communication

Communication is the key to preventing all the problems I just described from arising in the first place. You must communicate with your spouse even if you're typically a person of few words. As the student in the relationship, it's your responsibility to make sure that problems don't arise. And yes, it takes work.

> **Extra Credit** _____
>
> To communicate successfully, you must accept that women and men do communicate differently. You can buy books that tell you all about the science of communication, but you just need to use common sense in communicating with your partner.

What should you communicate and when? The commonsense answer is to apply the "golden rule"—talk about issues that you'd want to know about if you were on the other side of the equation. Above all, make your partner feel secure in your relationship.

Second, never, ever lie. Even small lies when communicating with your spouse about college and its demands and activities can pile up and become unwieldy. Even if you think that your husband or wife might sigh heavily or complain about school activities or the time it takes away from the home, meet this head-on and tell the truth.

Can you communicate too much? Yes, you can communicate too much, especially if you're trying to apply a communication style to your relationship that you've never used before. Don't use research on communication as a means to completely reshape how you talk to your spouse about your college experiences. Changing your style can come across as false or even as yet another means of saying to your partner, "I know more than you do—even about communication!"

The responsibility falls to the student in the family to keep lines of communication open. You must always be willing to say where you were or why you're late coming home from class or why you didn't call first, and address any number of small communication issues that can fester and grow into serious problems.

Cautionary Tales _____

Communication means more than just talking. The spouse who is not in college can begin to feel left out of your life if you spend so much time on school that you neglect little things in your relationship. Talk often and purposefully work to keep doing the little things that mean a lot to your spouse.

Being Realistic About Time Commitments

Students and their spouses alike are often surprised by how much time college takes. A rule of thumb is that one credit hour of class equals one hour of study outside of class. So, even one three-hour class taken per week is likely to require three additional hours of reading, studying, and/or test preparation.

You and your spouse need to be realistic about how much time college is going to take up, and what this means for the nonstudent in the relationship. It can mean that the nonstudent in the house bears more responsibility around the home. It can mean that the student is no longer free to pick the kids up after work.

Your return to college will require that you and your spouse sit down ahead of time and map out what changes to the home will take place. Decide ahead of time how to cope with problems that might emerge—for example, if the kids are sick or if your nonstudent spouse is traveling for work and his plane is delayed.

Be honest with your spouse about the time you will need to study and make sure that she is devoted to helping you through your studies by taking on the additional responsibilities in the home. Anticipate as many "unusual" situations as you can and plan for them.

Even if you don't have any children at home or if you're retired and going back to college, there will be a change in routine between you and your spouse. Talk about the time disruptions and how to manage them together.

New Experiences, New Friends

You'll probably begin to meet a lot of new friends in college. Where else can you find a whole room full of people who get excited about environmental science or calculus or architecture?

Being part of a group of people who like the same things that you like, who read the same books, who probably watch the same shows on TV or work in similar jobs to yours, can be quite intoxicating. You and your fellow students will feed off each others' enthusiasm, and you'll learn from each other in ways that no professor could ever teach you. You'll feel validated by others who share your interests. In academic arenas, this is called *collegiality*. It can seem to you, though, like a brand-new world.

def•i•ni•tion

Collegiality refers to the academic give and take that takes place among academic colleagues. In this case, collegiality among students means that, quite often, what you can accomplish together, as colleagues, is far greater than what you could accomplish academically on your own.

Temper the intoxicating aspects of collegiality with the reality that a classroom is just a *temporary* homogenization of people from diverse backgrounds and you'll be able to enjoy true collegiality among your new friends and colleagues.

Don't Neglect Your Family and Old Friends

Getting a college degree is important, but not so important that you should abandon old friends in the process. Most of the scenarios in this chapter describe problems that can arise within the family, but the same caution should be used when you're thinking about your current circle of friends, work colleagues, or neighbors.

If you've been going hunting with a group of guys every year, make a point of continuing that practice, even if you're feeling pressured by your studies. Just as you make time for your reading and homework, you should make time to keep the basics of who you are in place.

If you regularly join a group of women or men at church to do special activities together, continue doing so. Keep longstanding commitments with friends as much as possible.

Preventing Jealousies

You will be responsible for making sure that jealousies don't occur. The name-dropping scenario I described earlier in the chapter gives you just a glimpse of the kind of jealousies that can arise if you are careless in how you go about talking about your school experiences.

Jealousies aren't just about fears of other people intruding on your marriage or relationship. You're in the process of improving yourself; your spouse might come to view that as a slight if you aren't careful.

Jealousies can arise purely out of fear of the unknown as well. It doesn't take a big event for jealousy to begin; what you need to remember is that jealousies *are* all about fear—fear of change, of losing you to another person, or even the fear of you becoming someone different because of your college degree. Your job is to show that, no matter how many college degrees you get, you're the same person your spouse married.

Dealing with Degree Disparity

Degree disparity means that one spouse or member of a significant relationship has either a higher-level college degree than the other or that one member has a college degree while the other does not.

def•i•ni•tion

> **Degree disparity** refers to any situation in which one person has a higher level of education than another. In this case, the disparity is framed in the context of a marriage or significant relationship and therefore describes the disparity between spouses or significant others. Degree disparity can, but doesn't have to, affect relationships negatively in both social and financial ways.

Degree disparity is a significant measure of similarities and differences in one important way: earning potential. Because you can earn more money with higher levels of education, on average, if your spouse has a lower college degree—or no degree at all—you might earn more money than your spouse. The following table demonstrates the interaction between degree disparity and risk for relationship problems that, if unaddressed, may cause serious problems.

The degree disparity matrix shows not only that there exists diminishing disparity as level of education increases for both spouses, but also that the greatest disparity occurs when one spouse has only a high school education and the other spouse has one or more degrees. The greatest risk in relationships will happen when one spouse has no frame of reference at all for the educational experiences of the other spouse.

Degree disparity isn't necessarily a death sentence for marriage and relationships, however. Again, the adult student working on a higher degree, especially when the spouse is a high school graduate, bears responsibility for making sure that degree disparity doesn't affect the relationship negatively.

College Degree Disparity and Risk Potential by Level of Education

	Spouse 1			
	High School	**Bachelor's**	**Master's**	**Doctoral**
Spouse 2				
High School	Low	High	High	High
Bachelor's	High	Low	Moderate	Moderate
Master's	High	Moderate	Low	Low
Doctoral	High	Moderate	Low	Low

Source: "Degree Disparity and Relationship Risk Potential," by the author, previously unpublished.

When You Have a Degree and Your Spouse Doesn't

When you have or are working toward a college degree and your spouse doesn't have one, you must make sure your spouse understands that your degree will not affect how you feel about him. Someone who works hard but only has a high school education can feel intimidated by the spouse who takes up the challenge of college as an adult. Simply the act of planning for college can make your spouse feel left out if you aren't careful how you handle the process.

Not every spouse even realizes that he is or will be insecure about his mate's journey toward a college degree; and the symptoms of insecurity might be subtle. So, as you return to college, you should help your spouse feel secure about your return. He needs to know that gaining education will not change how you feel about him. Treat him as a partner in your education. If you do this, then he will feel like a part of your college experience even if he has never set foot on a campus. If you have children, include your spouse in all activities designed to help your children adapt to Mom or Dad going to college (see Chapter 17).

Making Your Spouse Your Biggest Fan

There are a number of ways that you can make your spouse your greatest supporter. One way is to take turns with college. One of you works while the other obtains a degree, and then you switch roles. Many couples earn their degrees using this strategy.

If your family situation allows it, take a class together, even if your spouse isn't looking to get the same degree as you (or any degree at all). Take a class that you are both interested in, even if it's just an elective course.

Give as much as you take. Your spouse is going to take on more of the day-to-day responsibilities, especially when you have a big test coming up or a paper due. Thank him for the extra help. Plan a special weekend together or get a babysitter and plan a fun evening out at least once a month.

Thank your spouse often, and mean it when you do. Find ways to attribute your success to your spouse; for example, thank her in the introduction of a paper you've written.

Ask your spouse to read papers you write and weigh in on them. Take suggestions seriously, and avoid any temptation to get defensive about your writing. Lose the ego when it comes to what you write; you never know, your spouse might just have a wonderful idea to strengthen what you've done.

Bottom line: you and your spouse must keep in mind that your journey back to college is something you're doing not only for yourself, but for the long-term benefit of your family. You may be the person who gets the diploma when it's all said and done, but you will have earned that diploma with the help of an unsung hero in your home … your spouse.

The Least You Need to Know

- ◆ Your marriage or relationship will be affected by your return to college.
- ◆ Avoid common relationship problems with communication.
- ◆ Don't walk into traps that make your spouse feel left out of your daily life.
- ◆ Thank your spouse frequently.
- ◆ Include your spouse in your college work in a way that fits both of your needs.

College Makes Parents into Students

In This Chapter

◆ Managing work, school, and parenting

◆ Finding facilities on or near campus for childcare and summer programs

◆ Talking to your kids about college

Parents often delay their return to college because of their children. Some believe that going to college might detract from their ability to adequately parent their children. Others believe that their demands as a parent will prevent them from succeeding in college. However, it's possible to succeed as a college student *and* as a parent at the same time.

Most college-going moms and dads find the changes less stressful for their children than for the spouse in the house (see Chapter 16). However, *how* you introduce this new college experience to your family can make all the difference in how your children react and adapt to the situation.

Children Are Affected by Change

Preparing your family for change and managing time well is the key to having high-quality family and college lives.

Extra Credit

In some college towns, the local YMCA or another nonprofit organization or church holds special "lock-ins" or extended care opportunities during finals week. Lock-ins and extended care facilities like these provide a safe and fun environment while allowing parents maximum study time for finals.

Your first semester back to college may not go as smoothly as you would like; as a dad, you may be relying on your wife to pick up the kids after work when it used to be your job to do so. Changes in schedules might also mean that, as a mom, you rely on your husband to help the kids with homework while you're at a night class.

Some colleges have on-campus daycare facilities for students' children. If campuses don't have their own daycare facility, they often form partnerships with nearby off-campus daycare facilities to help students place younger children in a high-quality daycare environment, even during night classes.

Preschool Children

Younger children are the most sensitive to changes in daily family routines. As a parent, you need to pay close attention to what your children look for in terms of stability. What might seem like a simple routine to an adult can feel like a cornerstone of stability to a young child. Make sure you prepare your children for change, no matter how insignificant the change seems to you. With good planning, children not only will adapt to the short-term life changes but will also benefit from the process.

Student Center

Donna, who returned to college when her daughter entered kindergarten, relates the following experience: "I found that my kindergartener was accustomed to a set routine during my first semester back at college. The first few weeks of the fall semester were going fine. Then it became time to turn the clocks back to standard time. The following day, my daughter met me at the door when I picked her up at daycare, angry and declaring, 'You're late! It's after dark!' Although it was amusing that the source of her angst was just the act of turning back the clock, I had to reassure her that I was not late, I didn't stay at school longer than normal, and in the end, she learned about time changes the hard way. It just got dark earlier than it had when she was at daycare the previous Friday!"

When talking to your children about college, keep things simple and concrete. For example, a young child won't necessarily understand what a college degree is, because it's a fairly abstract concept. A young child will understand, however, the concept of school and learning new things. The younger the child, the more concrete your dialogue about college should be.

School-Aged Children

You'll need to prepare your school-aged children, especially those in elementary school, for changes as well. Even older children, as self-sufficient as they may seem, will need you to talk to them. Tell them about your decision to go to college and how life will be different for a while. Children in high school will likely watch you closely as you go through college, because they'll be making their own college decisions soon.

How you talk with your children as you prepare for and attend college will depend on your children's ages and personalities. As a parent, you know best how to read your children's reactions to your new role as a college student.

Familiarity Breeds Content Kids

Draw comparisons between your school experience and your children's. For example, if you are taking a college algebra class, tell your children how algebra is just a fancy word for math—like the math they do in school, but more difficult. Tell them how their field trip to a local factory is like what you will be doing in a science lab. Show them the campus library and compare it to their school library.

> **Extra Credit**
>
> Children have one frame of reference for education and school—their own experiences. College buildings and how college classes are structured are very different from grades K–12. You need to provide a new frame of reference for what college is like.

Take Children on a Tour of Your Campus

Just as children like to be able to picture you at work, they will also want to be able to picture you at college. Take them. Let them see where you will be when you are in this mysterious new place called "college."

Colleges don't roll up the sidewalks at the close of the normal business day, so you've got plenty of opportunities in advance of your first day of class to help your children get comfortable with your new role as a student.

When you take your younger children to see the college campus, you can personalize the experience for them with some simple activities:

◆ Take pictures. Give each child a disposable camera to take photos during your campus tour.

◆ Eat together. Treat your children to lunch or eat a snack at your campus cafeteria, food court, or snack bar.

◆ Buy a book. Purchase a spiral notebook for your children in the campus bookstore, preferably with a campus logo on it. Now they'll have a college notebook just like Mom or Dad.

◆ Tell a story, draw a picture. After the campus tour, have your children write a story about their trip in their special college notebooks and/or draw pictures about their visit.

Older children will also enjoy seeing the campus and grabbing a snack at the campus food court. As a matter of fact, high school children can benefit doubly from a campus tour because they will be making college decisions soon. In addition to showing them where your classes will be, take them to the admissions office and get them a college catalogue. Have them pick up some informational brochures to pore through when they return home. Make sure your high school–aged children pick up a campus newspaper. They can read articles that college students have written and learn what issues college students see as important. When you take your older children with you to your campus, you're giving them a tour of their own futures.

If you're attending a traditional college that has a physical campus, show your children where the sports teams practice and play. Show them the counseling center where students make plans for careers. Read plaques and look at statues on campus to better understand the college and its history.

Show your kids the actual classrooms where you attend class. Walk your children through your schedule, and in between classroom visits, tell them a little bit about each class.

Be prepared: your children will ask a lot of "why" questions about your return to college. They will try to make the new information you're providing fit with what they already know about school and learning. Your new information is broadening their view of "school" and how it works. With each new piece of information you provide, your children will be integrating what you say into their experience.

When children ask "why" questions, it merely means that they don't yet have enough information to allow what you've said to fit in with their knowledge and experiences. "Why" means: clarify! So, clarify. Think back to your own preconceived notions about college. You can likely anticipate what your children will ask or what additional information they need. If you don't know the answer to one of your children's questions, tell them so, and work together to find the answer.

Get Children Involved in Your Education

Few things can make children prouder than sporting a t-shirt or ball cap bearing the logo of their parents' college. When you begin college, your children will develop a sense of ownership with the campus simply because you are there.

Student Center
Dee Ann was a 29-year-old single mother when she returned to college. Her daughter Noel was in second grade and often went with her to campus and soon came to know the campus as well as her mother did. After Dee Ann graduated with her degree, her daughter often referred to the time when her mother was in school as "back when *we* were in college." Noel felt like a part of her mother's time on campus and now attends the same university where Dee Ann got her degree.

Buy your kids a t-shirt, a notebook, or ball cap bearing the college logo. Continue to involve your children by taking them to football or basketball games or cultural events on campus.

Campus Activities for Children

Some activities you can investigate to help your child become a part of your college campus include:

◆ Art institutes in music, painting, drawing, sculpture, and other arts

◆ Summer math and/or science academies where students work with college faculty and do real research

◆ Band camps, cheerleading camps, and football or basketball camps to help younger students hone their skills for the upcoming school year

◆ Bridge programs for older high school students to help orient them to a college campus and make the transition from high school to college a smooth one

Most of these activities are at least a week in duration and may run as long as four weeks during summer semesters.

The Right Way to Take Children to Class

There will probably be times when you don't have anyone to watch your children during class. A husband or wife works late and can't watch the children; a babysitter backs out at the last minute.

Some professors or instructors will allow you to bring your child to class when you have no other options. Others will not. As you begin your course work, it will become clear to you which classes and which instructors are more amenable to having a young person in the classroom. Above all, be sure to *ask* your instructor before you bring a child to class.

Don't be offended if you ask a professor if you can bring your child to class and she says no. It's likely that she has had an unpleasant experience with children in class before. It's equally likely that the professor is merely making sure that the classroom is not disrupted by having a child there. Some classes are simply not suitable for children.

It would be better to miss class than to show up in class with an infant in tow. You won't enjoy the class, and neither will your child. Even if your infant is quiet, your fellow students will want to play with your baby and make goo-goo noises, and that's distracting, even if it *is* fun.

Student Center

Terri, a mother of three school-aged children, was working on her degree in education. She often involved her older daughter and younger son in presentations and skits that she created and performed for her classmates. Terri says that her professor has never forgotten her—and is now a friend and colleague—because her children added so much value to the presentations. "The kids have never forgotten it, either" Terri adds, noting that her daughter is now working on her own teaching degree.

If you do have to bring your child to class, it's your responsibility to make sure that he doesn't disturb other students—and, of course, you need to do that while also getting something out of the class yourself!

Use your judgment before bringing a toddler to class. You know best if your toddler is comfortable around adults, can sit still for an hour and/or can entertain himself with quiet toys, a sippy cup, and some Cheerios. If there's any doubt about your toddler's ability to remain quiet, it's better to stay home and get notes from someone else.

With school-aged children, make sure they have crayons and paper, a puzzle, or some other activity they can do without disturbing others. Older school-aged children may even have homework of their own to bring.

Above all, if you bring a child to class, do your best to reduce the likelihood of distraction. Sit in the back of the room or near a door. If your child begins to disturb others, quietly leave the room.

Be sure to go over the ground rules of the classroom in advance. Tell your child that you expect him to stay quiet, to play with the toys you brought for him, and to whisper to you if he needs to go to the restroom. A little veiled bribery can help, too. Tell your child that if he behaves as expected, you'll stop on the way home and get ice cream or some other treat.

No matter how hard you work to make your transition back to college an easy one for your children, problems will pop up. For example, there will be times that your course schedule interferes with a parent-teacher conference or with a program your son or daughter is in. You will feel quite conflicted when these issues occur. Many faculty members are also parents, so provided you make arrangements in advance, you will most likely find that faculty will help you be a parent first when your children need you. Don't abuse this special treatment, however. If, for example, you know that an activity with your children conflicts with a test date, your best option is to work out a time to take your test the day before it is scheduled, as opposed to taking it late.

Share What You Learn with Your Kids

Going to school "together" can be fun for parents and for children. You're all learning new things at the same time and can learn from each other's school experiences. Younger children often bring their work home from school in special folders once a week. The folders often contain not only the work children have completed throughout the week, but also papers for parents to sign. Make your weekly review of your child's work a time for your child to also review *your* work!

Go the extra mile for your children by making your own weekly school folder. Do this even if it doesn't really help you organizationally, just to show them that you're learning and doing schoolwork as well. Let your children thumb through your papers and tell them about your papers and other homework. Show them your textbook(s) and encourage them to ask questions about the pictures. Tell them stories about what you've learned that week, but make sure you tell the stories in language appropriate to your children's ages.

Extra Credit

Report card time for school children can be turned into report card time for parents as well. Ask your teachers for your grades at the same intervals in which your children get report cards. Report card time will be a better experience for your children if you're sharing your grades with them at the same time. Do well, or your kids may try to "ground" you!

Point out similarities in what you are studying with what your children are learning in school. Your college algebra homework problems might look a lot like your child's multiplication homework. Your reading assignments might look a lot like the assignments your child has in language arts, reading, or history.

Your older children, especially in middle and high school, can benefit from reading papers you write for class. In sharing your work with them, you can often help your older children learn from your writing examples! Ask your older children for their opinions on your papers. Ask them if what you have written for class is clear to them. Before you know it, your children may also show you their papers for class; you can improve together.

Study Together!

Parents attending college, especially if they're working and going to school, often struggle to find a good balance of study time and family time. One way to build study time into your day and show your children good study habits is to make studying a regular part of your family's daily routine.

It might seem impossible at first, but you can schedule a half hour for studying while dinner is in the oven. Schedule an hour to study together after dinner. If your children are older, study in the same room or at the same table; you can ask questions of each other. You can be there to help your children with their homework while doing your own.

Build a buddy system in which your children study while you make dinner; have them clear the dinner table while you study for your classes. Make sure weekends are part of your study schedule, too. Study together at the college library on the weekends if your children are old enough. Take your children and all your homework to the local coffeehouse for a good hour of study.

You can even study with your younger children. After reading a bedtime story from one of your children's favorite books, read aloud to them from the text you're assigned to read. Not only will you be able to read your own lesson (and be more likely to remember what you've read because you've also "heard" your reading), you'll be almost guaranteed to put your young ones to sleep!

When you have your routine rearranged to include college as part of your family's life, your children will adapt to your new role as college student. The important thing to remember is not to put college off because you have children. Parents can succeed in college, and children of all ages can benefit from your college experience.

The Least You Need to Know

- Prepare children for changes that will take place when you go to college.
- Talk to your kids about college in an age-appropriate way.
- Take your children on a tour of your college campus.
- Make children feel like they're a part of your college experience.
- Study with your children and learn together.

## Chapter 18

Studying When "Real Life" Happens

In This Chapter

- ◆ Solving work-school conflicts creatively
- ◆ Finding time to study
- ◆ Forming study groups
- ◆ Preparing for tests

You've already read about making sure your marriage gets the right kind of attention while you're in college (see Chapter 16). And you've learned some strategies for being parent and student at the same time (see Chapter 17). But what about work? You're relying on the paycheck, sure, but does that mean that work always has to come before school? As late night talk show host David Letterman says, "This is not a competition!"

But it sure can feel like it sometimes. Despite all the advice from your friends, despite all the planning, you're going to face challenges while in college. Not all the challenges will be academic, either.

Managing "real life" and the stress that's a natural part of going to school won't always be easy. But you can do it.

This chapter helps you meet the challenges that emerge during college head-on. Strategies for managing college and real life are not all that different from managing other kinds of life stressors you will encounter. You *will* get the hang of it, and that's a promise.

Balance, Balance, Balance!

It doesn't matter how old or young you are, college is a challenge. It's hard, and it's supposed to be. In the end, though, you'll walk across a dais, wearing a robe and a mortar board, with your parents and kids and maybe even grandkids clapping and celebrating your success right along with you.

There's nothing magical involved in balancing your role as mom or dad, husband or wife, college student, employee, and all the other things competing for your time. Think of taking the events in your life as running them through a personal triage system. You pay attention to the issue that needs the most immediate attention first; you also deal with less important issues, but some of them have to wait.

Make sure, however, that not everything coming at you is an emergency. Step back and look at what's going on objectively. Take a deep breath, and then act.

When School Trumps Work and Vice Versa

The best way to see how you should handle conflicts of school and work is to show you some conflict scenarios that might arise and suggest some ways to solve them. The purpose of the scenarios is for you to see the creativity involved in solving work-school conflicts in such a way that …

- Your employer, no matter how much he supports your educational pursuits, doesn't feel like you're not giving 100 percent to your job.

- Your professors see that you are doing all you can to avoid conflicts in advance, are shooting straight with them, and are keeping up with your schoolwork.

Put yourself in the place of the student/employee in each scenario and, before you read the proposed solutions, think about how you would solve the conflicts. Also, consider your own workplace and think through any analogous conflicts that might arise in your job.

The Workplace Emergency Maneuver

Suppose you have a big test coming up or even a big term paper due. Your boss tells you that he needs you to hop on a plane *tomorrow* and spend the next three days negotiating a make-or-break deal for the company five states away. You start to panic because the test or paper you're working on is *half* of your grade for the semester. You're also mad because you know that other people in the company—people who don't have college conflicts!—could just as easily make that trip.

What do you do?

If your boss's request means that you will miss school on the day of the test, pick up the phone and *immediately* tell your professor about the situation (send an e-mail to your professor as well, for backup). Although it's an inconvenience to the professor, they're human, too. Almost every professor you encounter will help make arrangements for you to take the exam when you return.

Your boss asked you to go on this trip, so obviously he thinks that you can get the job done. Don't lie or play sick just to get out of the trip. Don't suggest that one of your colleagues go in your place. Make the trip itself work to your benefit—for work *and* school. Take your schoolwork with you and study on the plane. It's amazing how easy it becomes to block out the noises in a plane and focus on your work.

If you're working on a paper, take it with you. Take your laptop and use it on the plane. If you don't own a laptop, ask your boss if you can borrow one from work. More often than not, you will impress your boss with your willingness to take one for the company while also working hard on your studies.

Cautionary Tales

Just as you shouldn't abuse the good nature of your professor by asking for special treatment because of work, don't abuse your employer by asking for special treatment because of school conflicts. Such conflicts will happen only rarely. Seek solutions to conflicts that you can manage on your own before asking favors of your boss or of your professor.

Extra Credit

You may not be the kind of person who can block out the noise on a plane and study. No problem. Several companies make noise-canceling headphones, which can run anywhere from $40 and up, and they really work! You can turn the headphones on to cancel the noise or plug them into your favorite study music. You can also just pop in ear plugs if you prefer absolute quiet.

And all is not lost because you've got to work with clients out of town for a few days. Even if you're expected to have dinner with them to negotiate your deal and your days end up being 12 hours long, there's always the chance to sit back in your hotel room, in the quiet, and study or work for a good hour before you fall asleep. Your hotel room might even be more conducive to study than your own home!

When your meeting is over, you've also got the plane ride home to study as well. Adults in college with demanding careers study on planes or in hotels all the time. It becomes second nature after a while.

This particular work situation requires that you be creative and enlist the help of both your professor and your employer. The trick to negotiating this and similar conflicts is to …

- Be honest with your employer and your professor about the conflict.

- Demonstrate your willingness to go the extra mile to both your employer and your professor.

- Find a way to study or write even when you're not in your typical studying/ writing environment.

- Complete the assignment/take the test as soon as possible to show good faith to your professor.

- Get the job done that your employer wanted out of your trip.

Cautionary Tales

What do you do if you run into a boss whose whole opinion about college is this: "I've gotten by just fine in life without college!"

How can you work with a boss who doesn't support your going to college? Don't confront this kind of supervisor. Many people who behave this way feel threatened by an employee who is pursuing a higher level of education than they have. You may even find yourself in a situation where your supervisor tries to sabotage your quest for a college degree. If so, try to realize where your supervisor or fellow employees are coming from. Recognizing their anti-college attitudes for what they are is important—it's not about you, it's about *them*. Don't let these people bother you (yes, it will be difficult), do your job well, and keep focused on your goals despite the "noise."

There will be times when you simply can't show up for class because of work. Similarly, you might need to ask your boss for a couple of hours off to study or write a paper. As long as your boss knows that you're in school when the semester begins, you'll probably be in a good position to negotiate the time you need for school. The best employers know that school will periodically be more important to you than a project you have at work and will try to help by adjusting your work schedule.

The Shifts Upon Shifts Strategy

Suppose you work in a factory or hospital, or any job in which you work set shifts. In three years, you've never had to switch shifts, so you plan your college classes accordingly. One day, your boss asks you to work an additional shift for a couple of weeks because there's a big job coming up and the company needs everyone to work double shifts.

There goes your carefully planned school schedule. You did your best to work out a schedule in which you'd never have school-work conflicts and, out of the blue, a conflict arises. Because your boss is asking you to make a commitment that could cause you to miss two full weeks of class, you find yourself in what feels like an impossible situation.

Put your thinking cap on. This is a manageable problem if you get creative. One solution is to ask to work a different additional shift—one that would still have you working doubles, but that won't conflict with school. Keep in mind that even if you are granted this request, you're going to have a couple of sleep-deprived weeks—part of your "free time" outside of your double-shift work will be spent in class or preparing for class.

You may also be able to negotiate lunchtime to coincide with your class. Be reasonable here, because commuting time plus class time is going to be longer than a typical lunch hour. If you can negotiate a longer lunch hour, add the missed work time to the end of your day; your employer is likely to approve such a situation if you come with a reasoned, reasonable request.

Another solution is to find out if your professor teaches the same class you are taking at another time of day. If so, ask him or her if you can attend the other class for a couple of weeks. Most professors try to keep sections of the same classes moving at the same pace. If you can attend a different section, the two weeks of conflict will be a nonissue.

If none of these solutions work, contact your note-taking buddy and let her know you will be missing class so you can get notes each day of class. Don't let the two weeks go by and then read the notes; keep up with class reading assignments and go through your buddy's notes in as close to real-time as possible. Let your professor know of your work conflict and see if she has additional notes, PowerPoint presentations, and/or handouts she can provide you while you're gone. If this is how you have to approach your missed classes, and the creative solutions fail, you'll probably find that you really do buckle down and accomplish more than you thought you could.

Studying at Odd Times and Places

We've already talked about studying in planes and hotel rooms. With the busy life that you're going to be leading, prepare yourself to develop study skills that will take you to a lot of other strange places, as well.

Here are a few examples I've gleaned from watching friends, family, fellow students, and colleagues over the years:

◆ Joey never makes a trip to the restroom at home without study materials; he regularly studies while "otherwise engaged" in the restroom. This is a guy who knows how to fill every spare moment! The bathroom actually has bookshelves loaded with history and philosophy texts.

◆ After her kids go to bed, Dawn likes to draw a nice bath, light a few candles, and do her reading in a luxurious, aromatic bath. She says she remembers what she's read in the bathtub better than any of her other reading places because she goes right to bed and drifts off to sleep thinking about what she just read.

◆ Kathy has a nifty, clear plastic book holder that attaches to the steering wheel of her car and holds pages open. Every day during her lunch hour, she heads for a different fast-food restaurant, parks, puts her study materials up on her book holder, and eats while she reads and studies. When she brings her lunch from home, she still eats in her car and studies in the shade of the parking garage.

◆ Quinn likes to study in her favorite rocking chair in her spare bedroom while Beethoven's Ninth Symphony plays on her CD player. A string musician herself, she knows the music so well that she can hear the music without actually having to actively listen to it. And the four movements of the symphony last long enough to give her a good, set time to read or catch up on her notes from class. She replenishes her mind through study and music.

◆ Sandy takes time each Saturday when the weather is nice to ride her horse up to a small pond near her home, her border collie right with her. She sits under a tree on a saddle blanket after tying her horse off, and her dog noses around the pond while Sandy studies. She says the outdoors, no matter where you live, is wonderful for helping you focus on your work and get some needed fresh air at the same time.

◆ Stephen lives in northern Virginia and works in Washington, D.C. He has a long Metro ride to and from work each day. He manages to get anywhere from an hour to an hour and a half of studying done during his commute.

These are just some examples of odd places and ways to study. Adult learners have to study where and when they can, often fitting studying into the nooks and crannies of their already busy lives. Most adults find that they've actually got quite a bit of wasted "downtime," such as Stephen's subway ride each day, that they can fill with reading or going over class notes.

Look through your days and find where you have periods of downtime. You'll probably find that you've got several "holes" in your day you can fill with schoolwork.

Study Groups

I've already encouraged you to find good note-taking buddies in your classes. It's just as important to build a good group of study partners who learn well together and bring different strengths to the group. It's often the case that studying with others is more beneficial than studying on your own.

Even if you've always been the kind of person who studies best on your own, don't instantly shy away from the notion of study groups. Study groups that function well don't preclude individual study; they're best used as test times draw near and are good for participants to test their understanding of the academic content against what their colleagues' understanding is.

Study groups can be fun and can even get heated with marvelous academic arguments. They can enhance your critical thinking abilities and help you see through others' eyes. However, as good as great study groups can be, they can also be more trouble than help. You want your study group to help you, to help clarify what you think you know, and to fill gaps in your understanding.

Choose Your Study Partners Carefully

As you meet other students in your classes, you will come to know which ones best complement you. This isn't the same as knowing which students will be your friends, or which students you can rely on to be your note-taking buddies. You're looking for different things when creating a study group.

A study group can be as effective with only two people in it as it can be with six. A group with more than six will likely become unwieldy. You want your study group to be manageable, small enough so that everyone benefits from the combined knowledge of the group.

Cautionary Tales _____

Even if you join a study group, you still need to study on your own. You should use the study group to reinforce what you learned in your individual study and to make sense of concepts that you're struggling with.

Sharing Meals, Sharing Knowledge

You've probably walked into coffee shops and seen groups of students, legs thrown over the sides of the chairs, all gathered around a small table, studying with oversized lattés and other coffee drinks in their hands. Caffeine? Sure, that can help you think, but it's not the only reason why students gather in coffee shops to study. They are comfortable places, places where you can get into good-natured arguments about the academic content you're studying.

There's something pleasurable about learning while sharing food and drink with your colleagues. Older students who form study groups don't always meet in coffee shops; they're as likely to take turns making dinner for their colleagues during the course of the semester, inviting the study group to their homes. When I was in school, my fellow students and I were all in pretty much the same situation—eternally broke— so we cooked simple, inexpensive meals for each other and studied in each other's homes.

When it comes to studying, age, gender, and generation gaps don't mean much.

Preparing for Tests

Campus student service offices often hold mini-courses on study skills, test preparation, and other strategies to help you do well in class. I share some of these same strategies in the following sections.

Study Tips for Any Class

You'll be surprised by how quickly you develop a study rhythm. How you study now probably won't be the same as when you were younger. You're coming to each class with a deeper and more mature sense of dedication than you did before.

But where do you start in developing good "studying hygiene"? It depends on the structure of your life, certainly, but the following activities, regardless of what kind of test you take, will help you be ready:

♦ After each class period, look through the notes you took while they are still fresh in your mind. At the end of your notes for that class period (or at the end of your page on your laptop), take each point that was made in class and summarize it into your own words. Rewrite your notes in summary form and underline or highlight key points that were made in class that day. Doing this after each class will make studying for tests so much easier.

♦ As you write notes in class, if you can think of real-life examples of certain points made in class, jot those out to the side to help you remember principles you're being taught. If your professor gives you real-life examples, write those down as well. The real-life examples will be the most important pieces in helping you understand (and not just memorize) what you've learned come test time.

♦ As you read material for class, add summaries of your reading to your notes. Assuming that you are reading ahead, go ahead and jot down questions you have about your reading that you can either ask in class or get help with during your professor's office hours.

♦ A couple of weeks before test time, go back over your notes and, for each section, outline what you learned on a separate piece of paper. Use whatever outline form works for you. Read back over your personal summaries of what you've learned and draw from them to complete your outline. Try to put at least one example into your outline. Try to become so familiar with your outline that when you see a single example, the entire concept comes to mind.

♦ The week before your test, take your whole outline and trim it again. See if you can create a single word in your outline that, after you say it to yourself, opens up all the facets of the concept. Use this as your study guide for tests. When you aren't certain what a single word means, refer to your previous outline.

♦ Anticipate questions you'll be asked and create sample tests. Put away your notes and write an essay answer to a question. The act of writing your answers ahead of time will help tremendously on test day.

Cautionary Tales

If you don't want to succeed, here's what not to do: don't take notes on what you read, and don't bother reviewing your class notes until the day before your test.

Your challenge will be to develop consistent study habits in the midst of a very busy life. With these few strategies, you can keep your learning consistent and minimize the amount of time you need to spend outside of class each day on your course work.

These strategies help you *know*—not just memorize—your material. Try them out!

Adult Learner Study Habits

You might think that the word *habit* is laughable as you return to college because so many things in your life can get in the way of your plans for study each day. But habit means more of a commitment to study, not the habit of doing a certain amount of studying at a particular time of day.

Try to formalize your study habits with strategies for study, not necessarily with places or times. Be responsible for your learning and don't wait for a study group to connect the dots for you. Fit study in where and when it best works for you, and make the most of the time you do have to study. If you take the time to study for your classes throughout the semester, you're setting yourself up to succeed.

The Least You Need to Know

- Conflicts between work and school require compromise but can be handled if you anticipate them.

- Treat your employer and your professor fairly and they will do the same for you.

- You can study anywhere, any time.

- Preparing for tests requires consistency in study, not cramming or memorizing right before a test.

- Train yourself to have good study habits.

## Chapter 19

You and Your New College Degree

In This Chapter

- ◆ Being patient in your job search
- ◆ Leveraging your degree to enhance your career and increase your earnings
- ◆ Dealing with disgruntled colleagues
- ◆ Helping other adults ease back into college

After reading this book, you probably have a lot to think about. If you were on the fence about whether you could succeed in college, I hope I've convinced you that you can.

Most adults want college degrees to advance in their careers (or to start an altogether new career) and earn a better living. No matter how you earn your degree, or when or where, your life will improve in tangible ways—and you might even walk a little taller because you've accomplished something *big*—you're a college graduate!

In this chapter I want to tempt you a little bit more by talking about all the doors that will open for you after you have your degree in hand. Of course, not everything will be easy just because you have a college degree. You'll face some obstacles, but it'll be a piece of cake after succeeding in college!

Making Your College Degree Work for You

Even before you graduate, I encourage you to start exploring what career doors will open for you when you have your new degree. No longer will you have to forgo applying for jobs that require a college diploma. A whole new set of career opportunities will soon be within your grasp.

Your new credentials make you competitive for more jobs, for advancement in your current job, or for changing your career path altogether.

Moving Up in Your Current Job

If your ultimate goal after getting your degree is to get promoted within your company, don't wait until you have your degree in hand to begin laying the groundwork for your advancement. Review internal job postings during your final semester of school. Go ahead and apply for any jobs that interest you, even if it will be a few more months before you get the required credentials. Inform your employer of your expected date of graduation and include a copy of your transcript with your application as evidence of how close you are to finishing your degree.

Extra Credit _____

During your final year in college, update your resumé to indicate that you have a college degree coming. Under the section in your resumé that indicates your educational experience, note the degree that you expect to receive, the college you are attending, and the date you expect to receive the degree, as in the following example:

B.A. in Psychology, Minor in Social Work, Appalachian State University, Expected May 2007.

Throughout college be sure to inform your employer of any new skills you can use in your job. That way you will already have demonstrated to your supervisors how motivated you are. They will be impressed with your self-discipline and hard work.

Beware of Workplace Dynamics

No matter where you work, you're going to encounter some resistance from your colleagues when you move up in your job.

> ### Cautionary Tales _____
>
> Watch for colleagues who might feel so threatened about your change in educational status that they *watch* closely to see if you're holding up your end on the job. The best way to thwart them is to be in constant communication with your supervisor about your college work, your job, and how you are handling both in such a way as to not diminish your work output. Here, a little offense beats having to play defense.

Don't be surprised if your colleagues aren't as enthusiastic about your degree as you are. Most of the time, their lack of enthusiasm masks their wish to be in the same place that you are—ready to move up the ladder. Meet their lack of enthusiasm with an offer to help any one of them do the same thing you have. Being helpful can disarm naysayers, and you might just help a few of them make it into college themselves.

Student Center

Lana found herself in a difficult situation shortly after she earned her college degree after years of attending school part-time while working full-time. Colleagues who had been her friends were all of a sudden distant because she now had a college degree and they didn't. (Remember the lesson on degree disparity between spouses in Chapter 16? It can occur in the workplace as well.) Seeing how her work environment was changing, Lana held a surprise party for her group at work. She spent a few dollars on a cake, gave small gifts to each of her colleagues, and used the party as a means to, very genuinely, thank her close colleagues for their support and encouragement during her time in college.

Lana was smart. She gave credit to her friends and colleagues for their part in her college degree. She also made sure that each of them walked away knowing that they could come to her for help should any of them consider returning to college.

Set Realistic Expectations

It's important to be realistic about what a college degree will do for you. Having the diploma in your hand doesn't mean that you will automatically be promoted within

Extra Credit _____

If you haven't already done so, make use of the campus career center during your final year of college. The professionals who work there can help you market yourself as a college degree holder and assist with other job placement needs.

your organization. Even the federal government allows you six months after you graduate before you have to start paying loans. It's simply a fact that it takes time to secure a job commensurate with your degree.

It doesn't matter if you want to move up in your current job or hope to change companies altogether, the degree will not mean that, on the day after graduation, you'll be slotted in a higher-responsibility, higher-paying job.

Seeking a New Line of Work

If you plan to change careers when you get your degree, then a good relationship with the campus career center is a must. Each spring career centers hold job fairs where company recruiters show up on campus to interview candidates who are graduating at the end of the semester. Make sure the career center knows your career goals and informs you about the career fair and other employment opportunities. Career counselors can also arrange one-on-one interviews between students and employers.

Cautionary Tales _____

If you have no intention of relocating and you've been asked to interview for an out-of-state job, don't attend the interview just for the sake of gaining interview experience. It's unprofessional and wastes the hiring company's time and resources.

When you're changing careers, the career center is one free service you can't afford to ignore, especially because you are an adult student. Recruiters are often bombarded with students in their early 20s at these fairs who, like you, are looking for work. As an adult graduate, you bring not only your education to the table but your existing life and work experiences as well. A recruiter is likely to view your additional "seasoning" in the real world as a positive thing.

Be Fair to Your Current Employer

If your current employer has helped foot the bill for your college degree, play fair. Don't quit your current job the day you get your degree, thinking that the company of your dreams is going to snap you up the day after graduation. Remember, it can take time.

You'll probably need to remain at your current job until you find more suitable employment, but avoid slacking off at work even if it is no longer interesting to you.

You might go through periods in which you feel like you're overqualified for your current job. You wouldn't be the first person to feel this way. But remember, you're going to need a good reference from your current employer when you're applying for and interviewing for new jobs.

And when you do land an interview, don't lie and call in sick to attend the interview. Instead, take vacation time or personal time or make up the time another day. In short, don't burn bridges with your current employer. You never know when you'll need them.

> **Cautionary Tales**
>
> For a while, especially as you near graduation, you may feel as though you no longer belong in your current job, yet you're not quite qualified, at least on paper, for jobs higher up on the food chain. Be patient and continue to do your job well; you can't abandon the good work history you've built over time just because you're about to earn your degree.

Show Me the Money

Probably one of the primary reasons you went back to college in the first place was to earn more money. If you've researched your desired career, you probably have a pretty good idea of the average starting salary. So what happens when you're offered a job in your career area that barely exceeds what you were making before you got your degree? Don't get discouraged if at first your new job doesn't pay as much as you'd hoped.

Even if you're not making that much money right now, your degree is your ticket to making more—a lot more—money over a lifetime than if you'd not gotten a degree. You will be able to advance more quickly through the system with your degree (supported by the quality of your work), and you won't run into an "education ceiling" that people without college degrees hit.

Remember all those jobs you've looked at that require a degree? Remember reading the salary ranges and practically drooling with envy because you didn't have the required credentials? It will never happen again. Your degree opens doors. Of course, it's up to you to knock on those doors, and to make sure you've done everything you can to prepare for your dream job.

Graduate School?

For some career areas obtaining a Bachelor's degree isn't enough to step out and enter into the professional workforce. For example, if you want to become a college professor, you're going to need to continue your studies in graduate school. If you hope to become a doctor, lawyer, or pharmacist, you will need to go to college for much more than four years.

If you want to work in such careers, you can get a job in career-related positions while in graduate school. If you're working on a doctorate in psychology, for instance, you can work as an intake counselor in a hospital. If you are interested in a doctorate in pharmacy, you can work as a pharmacy technician. In both of these cases, you'll be getting good on-the-job experience, which will complement your academic pursuits in graduate school.

Sharing What You've Learned with Others

After getting a college degree, a surprising number of adult students want to share what they've learned so that other adults can make it through the college systems and earn their own degrees. After all, when you've been through the process, you're an expert on the subtleties involved in making it through college as an older student.

There are all kinds of ways you can help others succeed in college.

Mentoring Adult Students

You can mentor other adult students, even if it's volunteering to help your Human Resources director at work provide advice to other employees in your organization.

Some adult students gather together and create a support group for adult learners within their churches. Others do public speaking on the importance of college to civic organizations. You can even stay involved on your campus by leading small group discussions for adult learners.

If nothing else, you can exercise your new desire to help other adult students by making yourself available to friends and colleagues who are considering returning to college.

Helping Younger Students Learn the Ropes

Another way you can help others is by working with middle school or high school students who are not sure if college is in their future.

Many high schools have programs to help students learn about college, and they can always use volunteers. Spend a day each spring working with your local high school to help younger students find their way to college, so they don't have to wait until they're adults to learn the benefits of having a college degree.

What You Can Take with You

Going to college is like anything else in life. There are good days and bad days.

If you've done many of the things that you've learned in this book, then you should have the kind of support network in place that can help you through any problem. Your family is with you, and you have developed mutual support networks between and among other adult students. Maybe you've joined an adult student or nontraditional student network on campus.

Keep this book and refer back to some of the strategies identified for when problems creep up during the course of your academic path to your college degree. Many of the answers to problems you might encounter on campus can be found here.

The Least You Need to Know

- ◆ Don't wait until you have your degree to start laying the groundwork for your new career.

- ◆ Be prepared for it to take some time to find a job in your chosen field.

- ◆ If you plan to change companies, do what you can to stay on good terms with your current employer.

- ◆ Make use of the services offered by your college's career center.

- ◆ After you earn your degree, you can help others succeed in college, too.

Appendix A

Finding the Right College No Matter Where You Live

The following list of state-level entities for public and private colleges and universities serves as a starting point for choosing the right college to match your needs, no matter what state you live in. The primary agency listed under each state is the official State Agency for Higher Education as determined by federal law. These agencies not only guide public higher education policy in each state; they also may have responsibilities for accrediting private or independent colleges.

Although the e-mail addresses of each agency head are included if available, the best means of locating information is to use the website first, a general e-mail address (if provided) for information inquiries next, and as a last resort, a direct e-mail to the agency head.

Other entries within each state are sites that will guide you to choices of private or independent colleges. See Appendix C for national entities that provide information on colleges nationwide by college type (for example, community colleges, private colleges, and so on).

Alabama

Alabama Commission on Higher Education
PO Box 302000
100 North Union Street
Montgomery, Alabama 36130-2000
Tel: 334-242-1998
Fax: 334-242-0268
www.ache.state.al.us

Alabama College System
Department of Postsecondary Education
401 Adams Avenue (36104)
PO Box 302130
Montgomery, Alabama 36130
Tel: 334-242-2900
Fax: 334-242-0214
www.acs.cc.al.us

Alaska

Alaska Commission on Postsecondary Education
3030 Vintage Boulevard
Juneau, Alaska 99801-7109
Tel: 907-465-6740
Fax: 907-465-3293
alaskaadvantage.state.ak.us

University of Alaska System
910 Yukon Drive, Suite 202
PO Box 755000
Fairbanks, Alaska 99775-5000
Tel: 907-450-8000
Fax: 907-450-8002
www.alaska.edu

Arizona

Arizona Board of Regents
2020 North Central Avenue, Suite 230
Phoenix, Arizona 85004-4593
Tel: 602-229-2500
Fax: 602-229-2555
www.abor.asu.edu

Arizona Board for Private Postsecondary Education
1400 West Washington Street,
Room 260
Phoenix, Arizona 85007
Tel: 602-542-5709
Fax: 602-542-1253
http://azppse.state.az.us

Arkansas

Arkansas Department of Higher Education
114 East Capitol Avenue
Little Rock, Arkansas 72201
Tel: 501-371-2000
Fax: 501-371-2003
www.arkansashighered.com

California

California Postsecondary Education Commission
770 L Street, Suite 1160
Sacramento, California 95814-2932
Tel: 916-445-1000
Fax: 916-327-4417
www.cpec.ca.gov

Colorado

Colorado Commission on Higher Education
1380 Lawrence Street, Suite 1200
Denver, Colorado 80204-2059
Tel: 303-866-2723
Fax: 303-866-4266
www.state.co.us/cche_dir/hecche.html

Connecticut

Connecticut Department of Higher Education
61 Woodland Street
Hartford, Connecticut 06105-2326
Tel: 860-947-1800
Fax: 860-947-1310 or 860-947-1311
www.ctdhe.org

Delaware

Delaware Higher Education Commission
820 North French Street
Wilmington, Delaware 19801
Tel: 302-577-3240
Fax: 302-577-6765
www.doe.state.de.us/high-ed

District of Columbia

D.C. Office of Postsecondary Education
441 4th Street, NW, Suite 350N
Washington, D.C. 20001
Tel: 202-724-7739
Fax: 202-727-2739

Florida

State University System of Florida
Turlington Building, Suite 1614
325 West Gaines Street
Tallahassee, Florida 32399
Tel: 850-245-0466
Fax: 850-245-9685
www.flbog.org

Georgia

Georgia Board of Regents
University System of Georgia
270 Washington Street, SW
Atlanta, Georgia 30334
Tel: 404-656-2202
Fax: 404-657-6979
www.usg.edu

Georgia Foundation for Independent Colleges
Suite 1730, Resurgens Plaza
945 East Paces Ferry Road
Atlanta, Georgia 30326
Tel: 404-233-5433
Fax: 404-233-6309
www.georgiacolleges.org

Hawaii

Hawaii Board of Regents
University of Hawaii
2444 Dole Street
Bachman Hall 202
Honolulu, Hawaii 96822
Tel: 808-956-8207
Fax: 808-956-5286
www.hawaii.edu

Idaho

Idaho Office of the State Board of Education
PO Box 83720
Boise, Idaho 83720-0037
Tel: 208-332-1591
Fax: 208-334-2632
www.idahoboardofed.org

Illinois

Illinois Board of Higher Education
431 East Adams, Second Floor
Springfield, Illinois 62701-1418
Tel: 217-782-2551
Fax: 217-782-8548
www.ibhe.state.il.us

Indiana

Indiana Commission for Higher Education
101 West Ohio Street, Suite 550
Indianapolis, Indiana 46204-1971
Tel: 317-464-4400
Fax: 317-464-4410
www.che.state.in.us

Iowa

Board of Regents, State of Iowa
11260 Aurora Avenue
Urbandale, Iowa 50322-7905
Tel: 515-281-3934
Fax: 515-281-6420
www2.state.ia.us/regents

Iowa Association of Independent Colleges and Universities
505 Fifth Avenue, Suite 1030
Des Moines, Iowa 50309
Tel: 515-282-3175
Fax: 515-282-9508

Kansas

Kansas Board of Regents
1000 SW Jackson Street, Suite 520
Topeka, Kansas 66612-1368
Tel: 785-296-3421
Fax: 785-296-0983
www.kansasregents.org

Kentucky

Kentucky Council on Postsecondary Education
1024 Capital Center Drive, Suite 320
Frankfort, Kentucky 40601-8204
Tel: 502-573-1555
Fax: 502-573-1535
www.cpe.state.ky.us

Louisiana

Louisiana Board of Regents
Mailing:
PO Box 3677
Baton Rouge, Louisiana 70821-3677
Street:
1201 North Third Street, Suite 6-200
Baton Rouge, Louisiana 70802
Tel: 225-342-4253
Fax: 225-342-9318
www.regents.state.la.us

Maine

University of Maine System
107 Maine Avenue
Bangor, Maine 04401-1805
Tel: 207-973-3240
Fax: 207-973-3296
www.maine.edu

Maryland

Maryland Higher Education Commission
839 Bestgate Road, Suite 400
Annapolis, Maryland 21401
Tel: 410-260-4500
Fax: 410-260-3200
www.mhec.state.md.us

Massachusetts

Massachusetts Board of Higher Education
One Ashburton Place, Room 1401
Boston, Massachusetts 02108-1696
Tel: 617-994-6950
Fax: 617-994-6397
www.mass.edu

Massachusetts Association of Private Career Schools
PO Box 407
North Reading, Massachusetts 01864-0407
Tel: 978-664-5146
Fax: 978-664-5154
www.mapcs.org/links.htm

Michigan

State of Michigan: Dept. of Career Development
201 North Washington Square
Victor Office Center, 7th Floor
Lansing, Michigan 48913
Tel: 517-241-4000
Fax: 517-373-0314
www.michigan.gov/mdcd

Minnesota

Minnesota Office of Higher Education
1450 Energy Park Drive, Suite 350
St. Paul, Minnesota 55108-5227
Tel: 651-642-0533
Toll-free: 1-800-657-3866
Fax: 651-642-0675
www.ohe.state.mn.us

Minnesota State Colleges and Universities
500 Wells Fargo Place
30 East 7th Street
Saint Paul, Minnesota 55101
Tel: 651-296-8012
Toll-free: 1-888-667-2848
Fax: 651-297-3312
www.mnscu.edu

Minnesota Private College Council
Bremer Tower
445 Minnesota Street, Suite 500
St. Paul, Minnesota 55101-2903
Tel: 651-228-9061
Toll-free: 1-800-PRI-COLL (774-2655)
Fax: 651-228-0379
E-mail: colleges@mnprivatecolleges.org

Mississippi

Mississippi State Institutions of Higher Learning
Board of Trustees
3825 Ridgewood Road
Jackson, Mississippi 39211
Tel: 601-432-6623
Fax: 601-432-6972
www.ihl.state.ms.us

Missouri

Missouri Department of Higher Education
3515 Amazonas Drive
Jefferson City, Missouri 65109-5717
Tel: 573-751-2361
Fax: 573-751-6635
www.dhe.mo.gov

Montana

Montana University System
46 North Last Chance Gulch
PO Box 203201
Helena, Montana 59620-3201
Tel: 406-444-6570
Fax: 406-444-1469
www.montana.edu/mus

Nebraska

Nebraska Coordinating Commission for Postsecondary Education
140 North 8th Street, Suite 300
PO Box 95005
Lincoln, Nebraska 68509-5005
Tel: 402-471-2847
Fax: 402-471-2886
www.ccpe.state.ne.us/PublicDoc/CCPE/Default.asp

Nevada

Nevada System of Higher Education
System Administration North
2601 Enterprise Road
Reno, Nevada 89512-1666
Tel: 775-784-4905
Fax: 775-784-1127

System Administration South
5550 W. Flamingo Road, Suite C-1
Las Vegas, Nevada 89103
Tel: 702-889-8426
Fax: 702-889-8492

New Hampshire

New Hampshire Postsecondary Education Commission
3 Barrell Court, Suite 300
Concord, New Hampshire 03301-8543
Tel: 603-271-2555
Fax: 603-271-2696
www.nh.gov/postsecondary

University System of New Hampshire
Dunlap Center
25 Concord Road
Durham, New Hampshire 03824-3545
Tel: 603-862-1800
Fax: 603-862-0908
www.usnh.unh.edu

New Jersey

New Jersey Commission on Higher Education
20 West State Street
PO Box 542
Trenton, New Jersey 08625-0542
Tel: 609-292-4310
Fax: 609-292-7225 or 633-8420
www.state.nj.us/highereducation

New Mexico

New Mexico Higher Education Department
1068 Cerrillos Road
Santa Fe, New Mexico 87505-1650
Tel: 505-476-6500
Fax: 505-476-6511
www.hed.state.nm.us

New York

Board of Regents, New York State Education Department
2nd Floor Mezzanine West EB
89 Washington Avenue
Albany, New York 12234
Tel: 518-474-3862
Fax: 518-486-2175
www.highered.nysed.gov

North Carolina

The University of North Carolina—Office of the President
910 Raleigh Road
PO Box 2688
Chapel Hill, North Carolina 27515-2688
Tel: 919-962-1000
Fax: 919-843-9695
www.northcarolina.edu
www.cfnc.org

North Carolina Independent Colleges and Universities
879-A Washington Street
Raleigh, North Carolina 27605
Tel: 919-832-5817
Fax: 919-829-7358
www.ncicu.org

North Dakota

North Dakota University System
600 East Boulevard Avenue, Department 215
Bismarck, North Dakota 58505-0230
Tel: 701-328-2960
Fax: 701-328-2961
www.ndus.nodak.edu

Ohio

Ohio Board of Regents
30 East Broad Street, 36th Floor
Columbus, Ohio 43215-3414
Tel: 614-466-6000
Fax: 614-466-5866
www.regents.state.oh.us

Oklahoma

Oklahoma State Regents for Higher Education
655 Research Parkway, Suite 200
Oklahoma City, Oklahoma 73104
Tel: 405-225-9100
Fax: 405-225-9230
www.okhighered.org

Oregon

Oregon University System
PO Box 3175
Eugene, Oregon 97403-0175
Tel: 541-346-5700
Fax: 541-346-5764
www.ous.edu

Pennsylvania

Pennsylvania State Department of Education
Postsecondary/Higher Education
Commonwealth of Pennsylvania
333 Market Street
Harrisburg, Pennsylvania 17126-0333
Tel: 717-787-5041
Fax: 717-783-5420
www.pdehighered.state.pa.us/higher/site/default.asp

Pennsylvania State System of Higher Education
2986 North Second Street
Harrisburg, Pennsylvania 17110
Tel: 717-720-4000
Fax: 717-720-4011
www.passhe.edu

Puerto Rico

Puerto Rico Council on Higher Education
PO Box 19900
San Juan, Puerto Rico 00910-1900
Tel: 787-724-7100
Fax: 787-721-6447
www.ces.gobierno.pr

Rhode Island

Rhode Island Board of Governors for Higher Education
301 Promenade Street
Providence, Rhode Island 02908-5748
Tel: 401-222-6560
Fax: 401-222-2545
www.ribghe.org

South Carolina

South Carolina Commission on Higher Education
1333 Main Street, Suite 200
Columbia, South Carolina 29201
Tel: 803-737-2260
Fax: 803-737-2297 and 803-737-2251
www.che.sc.gov

South Dakota

South Dakota Board of Regents
306 East Capitol Avenue, Suite 200
Pierre, South Dakota 57501-2409
Tel: 605-773-3455
Fax: 605-773-5320
Agency E-mail: info@ris.sdbor.edu
www.ris.sdbor.edu

Tennessee

Tennessee Higher Education Commission
404 James Robertson Parkway
Parkway Towers, Suite 1900
Nashville, Tennessee 37243-0830
Tel: 615-741-3605
Fax: 615-741-6230
www.state.tn.us/thec

Texas

Texas Higher Education Coordinating Board
Mailing:
PO Box 12788
Austin, Texas 78711
Street:
1200 East Anderson Lane
Austin, Texas 78752

Tel: 512-427-6101
Fax: 512-427-6127
www.thecb.state.tx.us

Utah

Utah System of Higher Education
Board of Regents Building, The Gateway
60 South 400 West
Salt Lake City, Utah 84101-1284
Tel: 801-321-7100
Fax: 801-321-7199
www.utahsbr.edu

Vermont

University of Vermont
Waterman Building
Burlington, Vermont 05405
Tel: 802-656-3186
Fax: 802-656-1363
www.uvm.edu

Vermont State Colleges
Mailing:
PO Box 359
Waterbury, Vermont 05676-0359
Street:
Park Street, Stanley Hall
Waterbury, Vermont 05676-0539
Tel: 802-241-2526
Fax: 802-241-3369
web.vsc.edu

Virginia

State Council of Higher Education for Virginia
101 North Fourteenth Street
Richmond, Virginia 23219
Tel: 804-225-2600
Fax: 804-225-2604
www.schev.edu

Washington

Washington Higher Education Coordinating Board
917 Lakeridge Way
PO Box 43430
Olympia, Washington 98504-3430
Tel: 360-753-7800
Fax: 360-753-7808
www.hecb.wa.gov

West Virginia

West Virginia Higher Education Policy Commission
1018 Kanawha Boulevard, East,
Suite 700
Charleston, West Virginia 25301
Tel: 304-558-2101
Fax: 304-558-5719
www.hepc.wvnet.edu

West Virginia Independent Colleges and Universities
Huntington Square
900 Lee Street, Suite 805
Charleston, West Virginia 25301
Tel: 304-345-5525
Fax: 304.345.5526
www.wvicu.org

Wisconsin

University of Wisconsin System
1700 Van Hise Hall
1220 Linden Drive
Madison, Wisconsin 53706-1559
Tel: 608-262-2321
Fax: 608-262-3985
www.wisconsin.edu

Wyoming

University of Wyoming
Thomas Buchanan, President
PO Box 3434
Laramie, Wyoming 82071
Tel: 307-766-4121
Fax: 307-766-2271
www.uwyo.edu

Wyoming Community College Commission
2020 Carey Avenue, 8th Floor
Cheyenne, Wyoming 82002
Tel: 307-777-7763
Fax: 307-777-6567
www.commission.wcc.edu

The source for these addresses is State Higher Education Officers (SHEEO) website: www.sheeo.org.

Appendix B

Sample FAFSA and SAR

Two essential documents associated with student financial aid are the Free Application for Federal Student Aid (FAFSA), which you must use to apply for all federal and most state financial aid; and the Student Air Report (SAR), which the government generates based on the information on your FAFSA. The SAR indicates what aid you are eligible for at the federal level. Sample copies of the FAFSA and SAR are included here.

2006-2007
FAFSA ON THE WEB WORKSHEET
WWW.FAFSA.ED.GOV

FEDERAL
STUDENT AID

DO NOT MAIL THIS WORKSHEET.

You must complete and submit a *Free Application for Federal Student Aid* (FAFSA) to apply for federal student financial aid and to apply for most state and college aid. Applying online with *FAFSA on the Web* at www.fafsa.ed.gov is faster and easier than using a paper FAFSA.

For state or college aid, the deadline may be as early as January 2006. See the table to the right for state deadlines. Check with your high school counselor or your college's financial aid administrator about other deadlines.

• Complete this Worksheet only if you plan to use *FAFSA on the Web* to apply for student financial aid.

• Sections in grey require parent information.

• **Submit your FAFSA early, but not before January 1, 2006.**

Apply Faster—Sign your FAFSA with a U.S. Department of Education PIN.
If you do not have a PIN, you can apply for one at www.pin.ed.gov before beginning *FAFSA on the Web*. You will receive your PIN within a few days, and then you can electronically sign your FAFSA when you submit your information. If you are providing parent information, one parent must sign your FAFSA. To sign electronically, your parent can also apply for a PIN at www.pin.ed.gov.

You will need the following information to complete this Worksheet:

❑ Your Social Security Number and your parents' Social Security Numbers if you are providing parent information;

❑ Your driver's license number if you have one;

❑ Your Alien Registration Number if you are not a U.S. citizen;

❑ 2005 federal tax information or tax returns (including IRS W-2 information) for yourself and spouse if you are married, and for your parents if you are providing parent information. If you have not yet filed a 2005 income tax return, you can still submit your FAFSA but you must provide income and tax information.

❑ Records of untaxed income, such as Social Security benefits, welfare benefits (e.g., TANF), and veterans benefits, for yourself, and your parents if you are providing parent information; and

❑ Information on savings, investments, and business and farm assets for yourself, and your parents if you are providing parent information.

WARNING!	NOTE:
Be wary of organizations that charge a fee to submit your application or to find you money for school. In general, the help you pay for can be obtained for free from your school or from the U.S. Department of Education.	If you or your family has unusual circumstances (such as loss of employment), complete FAFSA on the Web to the extent you can, then submit the application and consult the financial aid office at the college you plan to attend.

STATE AID DEADLINES

AK	April 15, 2006 *(date received)*
AR	For Academic Challenge - June 1, 2006 *(date received)*. For Workforce Grant - check with your financial aid administrator
AZ	June 30, 2007 *(date received)*
* CA	For initial awards - March 2, 2006 For additional community college awards - September 2, 2006 *(date postmarked)*
* DC	June 30, 2006 *(date received by state)*
DE	April 15, 2006 *(date received)*
FL	May 15, 2006 *(date processed)*
IA	July 1, 2006 *(date received)*
# IL	First-time applicants - September 30, 2006 Continuing applicants - August 15, 2006 *(date received)*
IN	March 10, 2006 *(date received)*
# *KS	April 1, 2006 *(date received)*
# KY	March 15, 2006 *(date received)*
# LA	May 1, 2006 Final deadline - July 1, 2006 *(date received)*
# MA	May 1, 2006 *(date received)*
MD	March 1, 2006 *(date received)*
ME	May 1, 2006 *(date received)*
MI	March 1, 2006 *(date received)*
MN	30 days after term starts *(date received)*
MO	April 1, 2006 *(date received)*
# MT	March 1, 2006 *(date received)*
NC	March 15, 2006 *(date received)*
ND	March 15, 2006 *(date received)*
NH	May 1, 2006 *(date received)*
NJ	June 1, 2006, if you received a Tuition Aid Grant in 2005-2006 All other applicants - October 1, 2006, for fall and spring terms; March 1, 2007, for spring term only *(date received)*
* NY	May 1, 2007 *(date received)*
OH	October 1, 2006 *(date received)*
# OK	April 15, 2006 Final deadline - June 30, 2006 *(date received)*
# OR	March 1, 2006 *(date received)*. Final deadline - contact your financial aid administrator
* PA	All 2005-2006 State Grant recipients & all non-2005-2006 State Grant recipients in degree programs – May 1, 2006 All other applicants – August 1, 2006 *(date received)*
# RI	March 1, 2006 *(date received)*
SC	June 30, 2006 *(date received)*
TN	For State Grant - May 1, 2006 For State Lottery–September 1, 2006 *(date received)*
* WV	March 1, 2006 *(date received)*

For priority consideration, submit application by date specified.
* Additional form may be required.

Check with the school's financial aid administrator for these states and territories: AL, *AS, CO, *CT, *FM, GA, *GU, *HI, ID, *MH, *MP, MS, *NE, *NM, *NV, PR, *PW, *SD, *TX, UT, *VA, *VI, *VT, WA, WI, and *WY

Sample FAFSA.

SECTION 1 – STUDENT INFORMATION

- *Use of this Worksheet is optional. It should not be submitted to the U.S. Department of Education or to your school.*
- *Not all of the questions from FAFSA on the Web appear in this Worksheet, but questions are generally ordered as they appear online.*
- *Once you are online, you may be able to skip some questions based on your answers to earlier questions.*

Your last name

Your state of legal residence

Your Social Security Number

Your driver's license number (optional)

Are you a U.S. citizen?

If you are neither a citizen nor an eligible noncitizen, you are not eligible for federal student aid. However, you should still complete the application, because you may be eligible for state or college aid.

If you are in the U.S. on an F1 or F2 student visa, or a J1 or J2 exchange visitor visa, or a G series visa (pertaining to international organizations), you must answer "Neither citizen nor eligible noncitizen."

❑ U.S. citizen

❑ Eligible noncitizen

Generally you are an eligible noncitizen if you are:
- A U.S. permanent resident with a Permanent Resident Card (I-551);
- A conditional permanent resident (I-551C); or
- The holder of an Arrival-Departure Record (I-94) from the Department of Homeland Security showing any of the following designations: "Refugee," "Asylum Granted," "Parolee" (I-94 confirms paroled for a minimum of one year and status has not expired), or "Cuban-Haitian Entrant."

❑ Neither citizen nor eligible noncitizen

Your Alien Registration Number
If you are an eligible noncitizen, enter your eight- or nine-digit Alien Registration Number.

A

Your marital status as of today
"As of today" refers to the day that you complete your FAFSA online.

❑ Single, divorced, or widowed
❑ Married/remarried   ❑ Separated

Month and year you were married, separated, divorced or widowed
(Example: Month and year: 05/1995)

M M Y Y Y Y

Did you become a legal resident of your state before January 1, 2001?

❑ Yes   ❑ No

If "No," when did you become a legal resident of your state?
(Example: Month and year: 05/1995)

M M Y Y Y Y

Most male students must register with the Selective Service System to get federal aid. If you are a male between the ages of 18 and 25 and **NOT** already registered with Selective Service, answer "Yes" and Selective Service will register you.

❑ Yes   ❑ No

What degree or certificate will you be working on during 2006-2007?

❑ 1st bachelor's degree
❑ 2nd bachelor's degree
❑ Associate degree—occupa-tional/technical program
❑ Associate degree—general education or transfer program
❑ Certificate or diploma for completing an occupational, technical, or educational program of less than two years

❑ Certificate or diploma for completing an occupa-tional, technical, or educational program of at least two years
❑ Teaching credential—nondegree program
❑ Graduate or professional degree
❑ Other/Undecided

What will be your grade level when you begin the 2006-2007 school year?

❑ 1st year/never attended college
❑ 1st year/attended college before
❑ 2nd year/sophomore
❑ 3rd year/junior
❑ 4th year/senior
❑ 5th year/other undergraduate
❑ 1st year graduate/professional
❑ Continuing graduate/professional or beyond

SECTION 1 (CONTINUED) – STUDENT INFORMATION

Will you have your first bachelor's degree by July 1, 2006?	❏ Yes	❏ No
In addition to grants, would you like to be considered for student loans, which you must pay back?	❏ Yes	❏ No
Are you interested in work-study employment that is arranged or sponsored by the school you plan to attend?	❏ Yes	❏ No
Highest school your father completed Some states and schools offer aid based upon the level of schooling your parents have completed.	❏ Middle school/Jr. High ❏ High school ❏ College or beyond ❏ Other/unknown	
Highest school your mother completed Some states and schools offer aid based upon the level of schooling your parents have completed.	❏ Middle school/Jr. High ❏ High school ❏ College or beyond ❏ Other/unknown	

Have you ever been convicted of possessing or selling illegal drugs?
A federal law suspends eligibility for some students with drug convictions. Answer "No" if you have no convictions. Also answer "No" if you have a conviction that was not a federal or state conviction. Do not count convictions that have been removed from your record, or that occurred before you turned 18 years old unless you were tried as an adult.

If "Yes," you can complete an interactive worksheet when you complete the FAFSA online, or you can print a worksheet at www.fafsa.ed.gov/q31wksht67.pdf. Based on the worksheet questions, you will be able to answer whether you are eligible for federal aid when you complete your FAFSA online.

❏ Yes

If you have a conviction for possessing or selling illegal drugs, you should submit your FAFSA any-way. You may be eligible for non-federal student aid from state or private sources.

❏ No

SECTION 2 – STUDENT STATUS

For federal student aid purposes, you must provide parent information if you answer "NO" to ALL of the following questions.
If you answer "YES" to ANY of the following questions, you do not have to provide parent information.

Were you born before January 1, 1983?	❏ Yes	❏ No
At the beginning of the 2006-2007 school year, will you be working on a master's or doctorate program (such as an MA, MBA, MD, JD, PhD, EdD, or graduate certificate, etc.)?	❏ Yes	❏ No
As of today, are you married? (Answer "Yes" if you are separated but not divorced.) "As of today" refers to the day that you complete your FAFSA online.	❏ Yes	❏ No
Do you have children who receive more than half of their support from you?	❏ Yes	❏ No
Do you have dependents other than your children/spouse who live with you and who receive more than half of their support from you, now and through June 30, 2007?	❏ Yes	❏ No
Are (a) both of your parents deceased, or (b) are you (or were you until age 18) a ward/dependent of the court?	❏ Yes	❏ No
Are you a veteran of the U.S. Armed Forces?	❏ Yes	❏ No

Answer "No," you are not a veteran, if you (1) have never engaged in active duty in the U.S. Armed Forces, (2) are currently an ROTC student or a cadet or midshipman at a service academy, or (3) are a National Guard or Reserves enlistee activated only for training. Also answer "No" if you are currently serving in the U.S. Armed Forces and will continue to serve through June 30, 2007.

Answer "Yes," you are a veteran, if you (1) have engaged in active duty in the U.S. Armed Forces (Army, Navy, Air Force, Marines, or Coast Guard) or are a National Guard or Reserves enlistee who was called to active duty for purposes other than training, or were a cadet or midshipman at one of the service academies, and (2) were released under a condition other than dishonorable. Also answer "Yes" if you are not a veteran now but will be by June 30, 2007.

SECTION 3 – STUDENT FINANCES

- *Answer these questions as of the date you will submit your FAFSA.*
- *This section asks about your income. Refer to your IRS tax return when necessary.*
- *If you filed a foreign tax return, convert all figures to U.S. dollars, using the exchange rate. To view the daily exchange rates, go to www.federalreserve.gov/releases/h10/update.*
- *If you are married as of today, report your and your spouse's income, even if you were not married in 2005. Ignore references to spouse if you are single, divorced, separated or widowed.*

Have you completed a 2005 IRS income tax return or other income tax return?

❑ Already completed
❑ Will file
❑ Will not file

What income tax return did you file or will you file for 2005?

❑ IRS 1040
❑ IRS 1040A or 1040EZ
❑ A foreign tax return
❑ A tax return for a U.S. Territory or a Freely Associated State

---

If you filed or will file a 1040, were you eligible to file a 1040A or 1040EZ?

In general, you are eligible to file a 1040A or 1040EZ if you make less than $100,000, do not itemize deductions, do not receive income from your business or farm, and do not receive alimony.
You are not eligible if you itemize deductions, receive self-employment income or alimony, or are required to file Schedule D for capital gains. If you filed a 1040 only to claim Hope or Lifetime Learning tax credits, and you would otherwise have been eligible for a 1040A or 1040EZ, you should answer "Yes."

❑ Yes
❑ No
❑ Don't know

If you are providing parent information, you will see several parent questions on the Web at this point. Then you will be asked the following questions.

What was your (and your spouse's) adjusted gross income for 2005?
Adjusted gross income is on IRS Form 1040—line 37; 1040A—line 21; or 1040EZ—line 4.

$ _____

What was your (and your spouse's) income tax for 2005?
Income tax amount is on IRS Form 1040—line 57; 1040A—line 36; or 1040EZ—line 10.

$ _____

Enter your (and your spouse's) exemptions for 2005.
Exemptions are on IRS Form 1040—line 6d or 1040A—line 6d. On the 1040EZ, if a person checked either the "you" or "spouse" box on line 5, use EZ worksheet line E to determine the number of exemptions ($3,200 equals one exemption). If a person didn't check either box on line 5, enter 01 if he or she is single, or 02 if he or she is married.

_____

How much did you (and your spouse) earn from working (wages, salaries, tips, combat pay, etc.) in 2005?
Answer this question whether or not you filed a tax return. This information may be on your W-2 forms or on IRS Form 1040—lines 7+12+18; 1040A—line 7; or 1040EZ—line 1.

Student $ _____

Spouse $ _____

SECTION 4 – STUDENT HOUSEHOLD

- *If you answered "NO" to ALL the questions in Section 2, skip this section and go to Section 5.*
- *If you answered "YES" to ANY question in Section 2, complete this section and then go to Section 6.*

How many people are in your household?
Include in your household: (1) yourself (and your spouse, if you are married), (2) your children, if you will provide more than half of their support from July 1, 2006 through June 30, 2007, and (3) other people if they now live with you, you provide more than half of their support, and you will continue to provide more than half of their support from July 1, 2006 through June 30, 2007.

_____

How many people in the question above will be college students in 2006-2007? Always count yourself. Do not include your parents. Include others only if they will attend college at least half time in 2006-2007 in a program that leads to a college degree or certificate.

_____

SECTION 5 – PARENT FINANCES

- If you answered "YES" to ANY question in Section 2, skip this section and go to Section 6.
- If you answered "NO" to all the questions in Section 2, you must complete this section even if you do not live with your parents. Refer to your parents' IRS tax return when necessary.
  - Answer these questions as of the date you will submit your FAFSA.
  - Grandparents, legal guardians, and foster parents are not considered parents for this section.
  - If both of your parents are living and married to each other, answer the questions about them.
  - If your parent is widowed or single, answer the questions about that parent. If your widowed parent is remarried as of today, answer the questions about that parent and the person to whom your parent is married (your stepparent).
  - If your parents are divorced or separated, answer the questions about the parent you lived with more during the past 12 months. If you did not live with one parent more than the other, give answers about the parent who provided more financial support during the past 12 months, or during the most recent year that you actually received support from a parent. If this parent is remarried as of today, answer the questions about that parent and the person to whom your parent is married (your stepparent).

What is your parents' marital status as of today? "As of today" refers to the day that you submit your FAFSA online.	❏ Married/remarried ❏ Single ❏ Divorced/separated ❏ Widowed
Month and year your parents were married, separated, divorced, or widowed (Example: Month and year: 05/1995)	M M Y Y Y Y
Have your parents completed a 2005 IRS income tax return or other income tax return?	❏ Already completed ❏ Will file ❏ Will not file
What income tax return did your parents file or will they file for 2005?	❏ IRS 1040 ❏ IRS 1040A, 1040EZ ❏ A foreign tax return ❏ A tax return for a U.S. Territory or a Freely Associated State
If your parents have filed or will file a 1040, were they eligible to file a 1040A or 1040EZ? In general, a person is eligible to file a 1040A or 1040EZ if he or she makes less than $100,000, does not itemize deductions, does not receive income from his or her business or farm, and does not receive alimony. You are not eligible if you itemize deductions, receive self-employment income or alimony, or are required to file Schedule D for capital gains. If you filed a 1040 only to claim Hope or Lifetime Learning tax credits, and would have otherwise been eligible for a 1040A or 1040EZ, you should answer "Yes."	❏ Yes ❏ No ❏ Don't know
What was your parents' adjusted gross income for 2005? Adjusted gross income is on IRS form 1040—line 37; 1040A—line 21; or 1040EZ—line 4.	$
How much did your parents earn from working (wages, salaries, tips, combat pay etc.) in 2005? Answer this question whether or not your parents filed a tax return. This information may be on their W-2 forms, or on IRS Form 1040—lines 7+12+18; 1040A—line 7; or 1040EZ—line 1.	Father/Stepfather $ Mother/Stepmother $

SECTION 6 – STUDENT FAFSA WORKSHEETS A, B AND C

Complete the Worksheets on page 8 to answer the questions below.

Your amount from FAFSA Worksheet A	$
Your amount from FAFSA Worksheet B	$
Your amount from FAFSA Worksheet C	$

SECTION 6 (CONTINUED) – STUDENT ASSETS AND VETERANS' BENEFITS

- *Answer these questions as of the date you will submit your FAFSA.*
- *Investments include real estate (do not include the home you live in), trust funds, money market funds, mutual funds, certificates of deposit, stocks, stock options, bonds, other securities, Coverdell savings accounts, college savings plans, installment and land sale contracts (including mortgages held), commodities, etc. Investment value includes the market value of these investments as of today. Investment debt means only those debts that are related to the investments.*
- *Investments do not include the home you live in; the value of life insurance, retirement plans (pension funds, annuities, noneducation IRAs, Keogh plans, etc.), and prepaid tuition plans; or cash, savings, and checking accounts.*
- *Business and/or investment farm value includes the market value of land, buildings, machinery, equipment, inventory, etc. Business and/or investment farm debt means only those debts for which the business or investment farm was used as collateral.*

As of today, what is your (and your spouse's) total current balance of cash, savings and checking accounts?	$
As of today, what is the net worth of your (and your spouse's) investments, including real estate (not your home)? Net worth means current value minus debt.	$
As of today, what is the net worth of your (and your spouse's) business and/or investment farms? Do not include a farm that a student lives on and operates. Net worth means current value minus debt.	$
If you receive veterans' education benefits, for how many months from July 1, 2006 through June 30, 2007 will you receive these benefits? Use 01 to 12.	
What is the amount of your monthly veterans' education benefits?	$

SECTION 7 – PARENT INFORMATION

- **If you answered "NO" to ALL the questions in Section 2, complete this section and then go to Section 8.**
- **If you answered "YES" to ANY of the questions in Section 2, skip this section and go on to Section 8.**

What is your parents' e-mail address? (optional)	
What is your father's (or stepfather's) Social Security Number?	
What is your father's (or stepfather's) last name?	
What is your father's (or stepfather's) date of birth? (Example: Month, day and year: 05/07/1959)	M M D D Y Y Y Y
What is your mother's (or stepmother's) Social Security Number?	
What is your mother's (or stepmother's) last name?	
What is your mother's (or stepmother's) date of birth? (Example: Month, day and year: 05/07/1959)	M M D D Y Y Y Y
How many people are in your parents' household? Include in your parents' household: (1) your parents and yourself, even if you don't live with your parents, (2) your parents' other children if (a) your parents will provide more than half of their support from July 1, 2006 through June 30, 2007, or (b) the children could answer "No" to every question in Section 2 of this worksheet, and (3) include other people only if they live with your parents, your parents provide more than half of their support, and your parents will continue to provide more than half of their support from July 1, 2006 through June 30, 2007.	
How many people in the question above will be college students in 2006-2007? Always count yourself. **Do not include your parents.** Include others only if they will attend college at least half time in 2006-2007 in a program that leads to a college degree or certificate.	

SECTION 7 (CONTINUED) – PARENT INFORMATION

What is your parents' state of legal residence?

Did your parents become legal residents of the state before January 1, 2001?   ❑ Yes   ❑ No

If "No," give month and year legal residency began for the parent who has lived in the state the longest.   (Example: Month and year: 05/1995)

M	M	Y	Y	Y	Y

What was the amount your parents paid in income tax for 2005?
Income tax amount is on IRS Form 1040—line 57; 1040A—line 36; or 1040EZ—line 10.

$

Enter your parents' exemptions for 2005.
Exemptions are on IRS Form 1040—line 6d or 1040A—line 6d. On the 1040EZ, if a person checked either the "you" or "spouse" box on line 5, use EZ worksheet line E to determine the number of exemptions ($3,200 equals one exemption). If a person didn't check either box on line 5, enter 01 if he or she is single, or 02 if he or she is married.

Parent FAFSA Worksheets A, B and C. Complete the Worksheets on page 8 to answer the questions below.

Your parents' amount from FAFSA Worksheet A $

Your parents' amount from FAFSA Worksheet B $

Your parents' amount from FAFSA Worksheet C $

Parent Asset Information (See instructions on reporting assets, top of page 6)

As of today, what is your parents' total current balance in cash, savings, and checking accounts? $

As of today, what is the net worth of your parents' investments, including real estate (not their home)? Net worth means current value minus debt. $

As of today, what is the net worth of your parents' business and/or investment farms? Do not include a farm that your parents live on and operate.
Net worth means current value minus debt. $

SECTION 8 – SCHOOLS TO RECEIVE INFORMATION

Federal School Codes If you do not know the school code, write the school's name. You will have a chance online to search for the school code.	1st school code	2nd school code	3rd school code	4th school code	5th school code	6th school code
For each school code, indicate the corresponding housing plan.	1st school code ❑ on campus ❑ off campus ❑ with parent	2nd school code ❑ on campus ❑ off campus ❑ with parent	3rd school code ❑ on campus ❑ off campus ❑ with parent	4th school code ❑ on campus ❑ off campus ❑ with parent	5th school code ❑ on campus ❑ off campus ❑ with parent	6th school code ❑ on campus ❑ off campus ❑ with parent

For the 2006-2007 academic year, please report your expected enrollment status
(Enrollment definitions refer to undergraduate study).

❑ Full time—at least 12 credit hours in a term or 24 clock hours per week
❑ 3/4 time—at least 9 credit hours in a term or 18 clock hours per week
❑ Half time—at least 6 credit hours in a term or 12 clock hours per week
❑ Less than half time--fewer than 6 credit hours in a term or less than 12 clock hours per week
❑ Not sure

Go to **www.fafsa.ed.gov** and enter the information from this Worksheet.

Remember to apply for a PIN at www.pin.ed.gov.

Additional help is available online or you can call 1-800-4-FED-AID. TTY users may call 1-800-730-8913.

Visit www.studentaid.ed.gov for more information on federal student aid.

Talk with your school's financial aid office about other types of aid.

DO NOT MAIL THIS WORKSHEET.

FAFSA WORKSHEETS - CALENDAR YEAR 2005

**These worksheets are solely for completing the FAFSA Worksheet questions,
on page 5 for the student and, on page 7 for the student's parents.**

FAFSA Worksheet A—Report Annual Amounts

Student/Spouse For Page 5		Parents For Page 7
$	Earned income credit from IRS Form 1040—line 66a; 1040A—line 41a; or 1040EZ—line 8a	$
$	Additional child tax credit from IRS Form 1040—line 68 or 1040A—line 42	$
$	Welfare benefits, including Temporary Assistance for Needy Families (TANF). Do not include food stamps or subsidized housing.	$
$	Social Security benefits received, for all household members as reported in student's household size (or parents' household size), that were not taxed (such as SSI). Report benefits paid to parents in the parents' column, and benefits paid directly to student in the student/spouse column.	$
$	Enter in Worksheet A question on Page 5. Enter in Worksheet A question on Page 7.	$

FAFSA Worksheet B—Report Annual Amounts

Student/Spouse For Page 5		Parents For Page 7
$	Payments to tax-deferred pension and savings plans (paid directly or withheld from earnings), including, but not limited to, amounts reported on the W-2 Form in Boxes 12a through 12d, codes D, E, F, G, H, and S.	$
$	IRA deductions and payments to self-employed SEP, SIMPLE, and Keogh and other qualified plans from IRS Form 1040—line 28 + line 32 or 1040A—line 17	$
$	Child support you received for all children. Don't include foster care or adoption payments.	$
$	Tax exempt interest income from IRS Form 1040—line 8b or 1040A—line 8b	$
$	Foreign income exclusion from IRS Form 2555—line 43 or 2555EZ—line 18	$
$	Untaxed portions of IRA distributions from IRS Form 1040—lines (15a minus 15b) or 1040A—lines (11a minus 11b). Exclude rollovers. If negative, enter a zero here.	$
$	Untaxed portions of pensions from IRS Form 1040—lines (16a minus 16b) or 1040A—lines (12a minus 12b). Exclude rollovers. If negative, enter a zero here.	$
$	Credit for federal tax on special fuels from IRS Form 4136—line 15—nonfarmers only	$
$	Housing, food, and other living allowances paid to members of the military, clergy, and others (including cash payments and cash value of benefits)	$
$	Veterans' noneducation benefits such as Disability, Death Pension, or Dependency & Indemnity Compensation (DIC), and/or VA Educational Work-Study allowances	$
$	Other untaxed income not reported elsewhere on Worksheets A and B, such as workers' compensation, untaxed portions of railroad retirement benefits, Black Lung Benefits, disability, etc. Tax filers only: report combat pay not included in adjusted gross income. Don't include student aid, Workforce Investment Act educational benefits, combat pay if you are not a tax filer, or benefits from flexible spending arrangements, e.g., cafeteria plans.	$
$	Money received, or paid on your behalf (e.g., bills), not reported elsewhere on this form	XXXXXXXXX
$	Enter in Worksheet B question on Page 5. Enter in Worksheet B question on Page 7.	$

FAFSA Worksheet C—Report Annual Amounts

Student/Spouse For Page 5		Parents For Page 7
$	Education credits (Hope and Lifetime Learning tax credits) from IRS Form 1040—line 50 or 1040A—line 31	$
$	Child support you paid because of divorce or separation or as a result of a legal requirement. Don't include support for children in your (or your parents') household.	$
$	Taxable earnings from need-based employment programs, such as Federal Work-Study and need-based employment portions of fellowships and assistantships.	$
$	Student grant and scholarship aid reported to the IRS in your (or your parents') adjusted gross income. Includes AmeriCorps benefits (awards, living allowances, and interest accrual payments), as well as grant or scholarship portions of fellowships and assistantships.	$
$	Enter in Worksheet C question on Page 5. Enter in Worksheet C question on Page 7.	$

UNITED STATES DEPARTMENT OF EDUCATION

1-800-4-FED-AID (1-800-433-3243 or TTY: 1-800-730-8913)

We Help Put America Through School

www.fafsa.ed.gov

OMB No. 1845-0008
Form Approved
Exp. 12/31/2004

FINAL 12/30/02

000117C041

CHRISTOPHER E. STUDENT
1234 ABCDEFGHIJKLMNOPQRSTUVXYZABCDE
ABCDEFGHIJKLMNOPQ, MD 12345

June 27, 2003
EFC: 00000 * C

Dear CHRISTOPHER E. STUDENT,

Thank you for submitting your information for federal student aid to the U.S. Department of Education.

This is your Student Aid Report (SAR) for the **2003-2004** award year. Keep a copy of this SAR for your records.

You (the Student)

Here is where you are this year in the process of applying for student financial aid:

1. You applied for financial aid by completing a Free Application for Federal Student Aid (FAFSA).

2. **Now you should check your SAR information. If it is correct, you do not need to return it to us.**

3. * You will be asked by your school(s) to provide copies of certain financial documents to verify information you reported on your application.

U.S. Department of Education

Here is where we are in collecting, processing, and storing your information for the 2003-2004 award year:

1. We received your information and processed it. Our results are below.

2. We sent your information and our results to you and the school(s) you listed in Step 6.

3. We will update your federal student aid record with any changes you make.

Based on the information you have submitted, we have used the standard formula to calculate your EFC, which is 00000. Your school will use this number to determine what types of aid and how much you are eligible for based on your educational costs.

School(s)

Here are the steps your school(s) will take to put together your 2003-2004 financial aid package:

1. Your school(s) received your information and our results.

2. Your school(s) will ask you to verify your information.

3. Your school(s) may put together or change an aid package and notify you.

The amount of aid you receive from your school(s) will depend on the cost of attendance at your school(s), your enrollment status (full-time, three-quarter-time, half-time, or less than half-time), Congressional appropriations, and other factors. Review your financial aid notification from your school(s) or contact your financial aid administrator.

Please read the important information on page 2, and then go to page 3 to see what you need to do next.

DRN: 2401
X9XX999999   999

PAGE 1 OF 8

1 2 3 4 5 6 7 8 9 S T 0 1

Sample SAR.

2003-2004 Student Aid Report (SAR)

THE OFFICE OF MANAGEMENT & BUDGET WANTS YOU TO KNOW:

☞ According to the Paperwork Reduction Act of 1995, no persons are required to respond to a collection of information unless it displays a valid OMB control number. The valid OMB control number for this information collection is 1845-0008. The time required to complete this information collection is estimated to be an average of 15 to 30 minutes, including the time to review instructions, search existing data resources, gather the data needed, and complete and review the information collected. If you have any comments concerning the accuracy of the time estimate(s) or suggestions for improving this form, please write to: U.S. Department of Education, Washington, DC 20202-4651. If you have any comments or concerns regarding the status of your individual submission of this form, write directly to: Federal Student Aid Information Center, P.O. Box 84, Washington, DC 20044.

☞ By answering questions 87 through 98, and signing the Free Application for Federal Student Aid, you give permission to the U.S. Department of Education to provide information from your application to the college(s) listed in Step Six. You also agree that such information is deemed to incorporate by reference the certification statement in Step Seven of the financial aid application.

WARNING: If you are convicted of drug distribution or possession, your eligibility for Title IV student financial aid is subject to suspension or termination. If your drug conviction status changes at any time during the 2003-2004 award year, you must update your answer to question 35.

For Financial Aid Office Use Only

This information will be used by your Financial Aid Administrator to determine your eligibilty for student aid.

```
SAR C Flag: C              Dependency Status: I          Reprocessing Code: X
Application Source: 5      System Generated Indicator: X Rejects Met: X
Record Source Type: R      Dependency Override: X        Application Receipt Date: 06/19/2000
Processed Record Type: X   Early Analysis Flag: X        Transaction Receipt Date: 06/19/2000
Verification Flag: Y       FAA Adjustment: X             Subsequent Application Flag: X

MONTHS:         1     2     3     4     5     6     7     8     9     10    11    12
PRIMARY EFC:   00000 00000 00000 00000 00000 00000 00000 00000 00000 00000 00000 00000
SECONDARY EFC: 00000 00000 00000 00000 00000 00000 00000 00000 00000 00000 00000 00000
PC:   99999
SIC:  99999

Auto Zero EFC Flag:        SNT Flag: N      Pell Eligible Flag: Y

MATCH FLAGS:
    SSN Match Flag: 4      Selective Service Registration Flag: X   Selective Service Match: X
    INS Match Flag: X      INS Verification #: XXXXXXXXXXXXXX        SSA Citizenship Code: X
    INS Sec. Conf. Flag: X NSLDS Database Results Flag: 1           NSLDS Transaction Number: 01
    NSLDS Match Flag: 2    VA Match Flag: 1

COMMENTS: 001 002 003 004 005 006 007 008 009 010 011 012 013 014 015 016 017 018 019 020
```

X9XX999999   999   PAGE 2 OF 8

1 2 3 4 5 6 7 8 9 S T 0 1

2003-2004 Student Aid Report (SAR)

COMMENTS ABOUT YOUR INFORMATION

Based on the information we have on record for you, YOUR EFC IS 00000. Your school will use this number to determine what types of aid and how much you are eligible for. You may be eligible to receive a Federal Pell Grant and other federal student aid.

ISSUES AFFECTING YOUR ELIGIBILITY

If you want to register with Selective Service, you may answer "yes" to both items 27 and 28 on this SAR, complete a Selective Service registration form at your local post office, or register online at www.ssa.gov. Selective Service will not process your registration until 30 days before your 18th birthday.

The Social Security Administration (SSA) did not confirm that you are a U.S. citizen. You need to provide your school with documentation of your citizenship status before you can receive federal student aid.

WHAT YOU MUST DO NOW

Your school will ask you to provide copies of certain financial documents for you and your parent (s).

We assumed certain information to calculate your eligibility for federal student aid. We printed the assumption we made and the word "assumed" in the "You told us" column for each of these items. If our assumptions are correct, do not change them.

Be sure to review the items printed in darker print on this SAR and make corrections if necessary.

NOTE: You reported a value(s) that exceeds the amount of space allowed on the SAR. We printed all nines in darker print for these fields.

OTHER INFORMATION YOU NEED TO KNOW

If your parents have now filed their 2002 tax return, correct this SAR to reflect the information as reported on their tax return. If your parents still haven't filed, notify your Financial Aid Administrator once they file.

You did not tell us your state of legal residence are. We assumed that it is the same as your mailing state (or your parents' state if you were a dependent student).

ATTENTION: You did not list any schools or the schools you listed are not in our eligible school file. To receive federal student aid, you must attend a school that participates in the federal student aid program.

If you need additional help with your SAR, contact your school Financial Aid Administrator (FAA) or the Federal Student Aid Information Center at 1-800-4FED-AID (1-800-433-3243). If your address changes, send in the correction on your SAR or call 1-800-4FED-AID to make the correction on your record.

X9XX999999   999   PAGE 3 OF 8

123456789ST01

2003-2004 Student Aid Report (SAR)

You may need this information to answer Question 29 on page 6.

Codes for Question 29: TYPE OF DEGREE/CERTIFICATE

1 - 1st Bachelor's degree
2 - 2nd Bachelor's degree
3 - Associate degree (occupational or technical program)
4 - Associate degree (general education or transfer program)
5 - Certificate or diploma for completing an occupational, technical, or educational program less than two years
6 - Certificate or diploma for completing an occupational, technical, or educational program of at least two years
7 - Teaching credential program (non-degree program)
8 - Graduate or professional degree
9 - Other/Undecided

If you need a copy of the worksheets used to answer questions 44-46 or 79-81, you can go to the U.S. Department of Education's web page (www.fafsa.ed.gov/worksheets.htm).

Your Financial Aid History Information

Total Loan Amounts:

FFELP/Direct loans:	Total principal balance:	Remaining amount to be disbursed to you:	Total:
Subsidized loans:	$ 123,456	$ 123,456	$ 123,456
Unsubsidized loans:	$ 123,456	$ 123,456	$ 123,456
Combined loans:	$ 123,456	$ 123,456	$ 123,456
FFEL Consolidation loans:	$ 123,456		$ 123,456

Perkins loans:

Outstanding principal balance:	$ 123,456
Current year loan amount:	$ 123,456

Defaulted/Discharged Loan Detail Information:	Net loan amount	Loan begin date	Loan end date	Grade level
Loan type: FFEL Stafford Unsubsidized	$ 123,456	08/30/1999	05/14/2000	2
Status code ID as of 08/30/1999 Outstanding balance $ 123,456 as of 03/31/2000				
Loan type: FFEL Stafford Subsidized	$ 123,456	08/30/1999	05/14/2000	2
Status code ID as of 08/30/1999 Outstanding balance $ 123,456 as of 03/31/2000				
Loan type: Federal Perkins	$ 123,456	08/30/1999	05/14/2000	2
Status code DU as of 12/23/96 Outstanding balance $ 123,456 as of 09/29/1988				
Loan type: FFEL Stafford Unsubsidized	$ 123,456	08/30/1999	05/14/2000	2
Status code DU as of 04/06/1996 Outstanding balance $ 123,456 as of 08/26/1999				

Use your U.S. Department of Education PIN to see more information about your financial aid history at www.nslds.ed.gov on the Internet. For more information about your PIN, go to www.pin.ed.gov

X9XX999999   999   PAGE 4 OF 8

1 2 3 4 5 6 7 8 9 S T 0 1

2003-2004 Student Aid Report (SAR)

OMB No. 1845-0008
Form Approved
Exp. 12/31/2004

Check your SAR

☞ If you <u>find a mistake</u>, or an answer has changed, put the correct answer in the boxes or completely fill in an oval (example: ●).

☞ Look for arrows (---> or ↴) in the area next to your information. For these items, you must give us a new answer, or if your current answer is correct, rewrite the same information exactly.

☞ If you want to <u>delete an answer</u>, draw a line through your answer and through the empty boxes or ovals (example: 10. Permanent Home Phone Number (301) 555-1212).

Processed: 06/27/2003

123-45-6789 ST-01 DRN: 1234

Step One: You (The Student)

1. Last Name	2. First Name	3. Middle Initial
STUDENT	CHRISTOPHER	N

FOR INFORMATION ONLY DO NOT SUBMIT

4. Permanent Street Address
1000 NORTH LIBERTY STREET

5. City	6. State Abbreviation	7. ZIP Code
IOWA CITY	IA	20724

8. Social Security Number
123-45-6789

9. Date of Birth
(BLANK)

Use MM/DD/CCYY format (e.g., 05/01/1980)

10. Permanent Home Phone Number
(301) 555-1212

XXX – XX – XXXX   / / 1 9

11. Driver's License Number
ST17983-IA-000123008

12. Driver's License State Abbreviation
IA

13. Citizenship Status
U.S. CITIZEN

U.S. Citizen ○ 1   Eligible Noncitizen ○ 2   Neither ○ 3

Remember to completely fill in the oval as follows: ●

14. Alien Registration Number
(BLANK)

A

15. Marital Status
(BLANK)   --->

Single, Divorced or Widowed ○ 1   Married/Remarried ○ 2   Separated ○ 3

16. Date of Marital Status
DECEMBER 1999

/   Use MM/CCYY format (e.g., 05/1996)

	Full time/Not sure	3/4 time	Half time	Less than half time	Not attending
17. Summer 2003 FULL TIME/NOT SURE	○ 1	○ 2	○ 3	○ 4	○ 5
18. Fall 2003 FULL TIME/NOT SURE	○ 1	○ 2	○ 3	○ 4	○ 5
19. Winter 2003-2004 FULL TIME/NOT SURE	○ 1	○ 2	○ 3	○ 4	○ 5
20. Spring 2004 FULL TIME/NOT SURE	○ 1	○ 2	○ 3	○ 4	○ 5
21. Summer 2004 FULL TIME/NOT SURE	○ 1	○ 2	○ 3	○ 4	○ 5

	Middle school/Jr. High	High school	College or beyond	Other/unknown
22. Father's Educational Level UNKNOWN	○ 1	○ 2	○ 3	○ 4
23. Mother's Educational Level UNKNOWN	○ 1	○ 2	○ 3	○ 4

X9XX999999   999   PAGE 5 OF 8

1 2 3 4 5 6 7 8 9 S T 0 1

You Told Us	Write in Information for New or Corrected items only.
24. State of Legal Residence Abbreviation **MD**	
25. Did you become a legal resident of this state before January 1, 1998? **YES**	Yes ○ 1 No ○ 2
26. If you answered "No" to question 25, date you became a legal resident. **(BLANK)**	/ Use MM/CCYY format (e.g., 05/1980)
27. Are you male? **YES**	Yes ○ 1 No ○ 2
28. If you are male (age 18-25) and not registered, answer "Yes" and Selective Service will register you. **YES**	Yes ○ 1 No ○ 2
29. Type of Degree/Certificate **1ST BA**	Enter Code from Page 4
30. Grade Level in College in 2003-2004? **2ND/SOPHOMORE**	1st Never Attended....... ○ 0 2nd/Sophomore ○ 2 4th/Senior.. ○ 4 1st Yr. Graduate/Professional ○ 6 1st Previously Attended ○ 1 3rd/Junior........ ○ 3 5th or More ○ 5 Cont. Graduate/Professional ○ 7

You Told Us	Write in Information for New or Corrected items only.
31. High School Diploma or GED? **YES**	Yes ○ 1 No ○ 2
32. First Bachelor's Degree by 7-1-2003? **NO**	Yes ○ 1 No ○ 2
33. Interested in Student Loans? **YES**	Yes ○ 1 No ○ 2
34. Interested in Work-Study? **NO**	Yes ○ 1 No ○ 2
35. Drug Conviction Affecting Eligibility? **(BLANK)** DO NOT LEAVE THIS QUESTION BLANK	No...................... ○ 1 Yes (Part-Year).... ○ 2 Yes/Don't Know... ○ 3

Step Two: 2002 Student (and Spouse) Income and Assets

For 36-49, report your (the student's) income and assets. If you are married, report your and your spouse's income and assets, even if you were not married in 2002. Ignore references to "spouse" if you are currently single, separated, divorced, or widowed. Remember to completely fill in the oval as follows: ●

36. Filed 2002 Income Tax Return **ALREADY COMPLETED**	Have already completed ○ 1 Will file, have not yet completed ○ 2 Not going to file. ○ 3
37. Type of 2002 Tax Form Used **1040**	A. IRS 1040........................ ○ 1 B. IRS 1040A, 1040 EZ, 1040 Telefile.................... ○ 2 C. A foreign tax return.......... ○ 3 D. A tax return for Puerto Rico, Guam, American Samoa, the U.S. Virgin Islands, the Marshall Islands, the Federated States of Micronesia, or Palau.... ○ 4

For 42-43, answer the questions whether or not you filed a tax return. This information may be on your W-2 forms, box 1 and 8 or on IRS Form 1040-lines 7+12+18; 1040A-line 7; or 1040EZ-Line 1. Telefilers should use their W-2 forms, box 1 and 8.

42. Student's Income Earned from Work **$ (BLANK) (999,999 ASSUMED)**	$ [ ] , [ ]
43. Spouse's Income Earned from Work **$ (BLANK) (999,999 ASSUMED)**	$ [ ] , [ ]

38. If you filed or will file a 1040, were you eligible to file a 1040A or 1040EZ? **(BLANK)**	Yes ○ 1 No ○ 2 Don't Know ○ 3

For 39-51 (Student's Info.) and 74-84 (Parent's Info.), if the answer is zero or the question does not apply to you, enter 0. Report dollar amounts (such as $12,356.00) like this: **EXAMPLE** ➡ $ [1 2] , [3 5 6] **(no cents)**

44. Amount from FAFSA Worksheet A **$ 12,345**	$ [ ] , [ ]
45. Amount from FAFSA Worksheet B **$ 12,345**	$ [ ] , [ ]
46. Amount from FAFSA Worksheet C **$ 12,345 (00,000 ASSUMED)**	$ [ ] , [ ]

39. Adjusted Gross Income from IRS Form (IRS Form 1040-line 35; 1040A-line 21; 1040EZ-line 4; or Telefile-line I.) **$ (BLANK) (999,999 ASSUMED)**	$ [ ] , [ ]
40. U.S. Income Tax Paid from IRS Form (1040-line 55; 1040A-line 36; 1040EZ-line 10; or Telefile-line K(2).) **$ (BLANK) (00,000 ASSUMED)**	$ [ ] , [ ]
41. Exemptions Claimed from IRS Form (1040-line 6d; 1040A-line 6d; For 1040EZ or Telefile, see pg 2.) **02**	[ ]

47. Net Worth of Investments **$ 123,456**	$ [ ] , [ ]
48. Net Worth of Business/Investment Farms **$ 123,456**	$ [ ] , [ ]
49. Cash, Savings and Checking **$ 123,456**	$ [ ] , [ ]
50. How many Months Receive VA Education Benefits? **00**	[ ]
51. Monthly VA Benefits Amount **$ 1,234**	$ [ ] , [ ]

DRN: 1234

Step Three: Student Status
You Told Us

For 52-58, write in information for New or Corrected items only.

52. Born Before 1-1-1980?	Yes ◯ 1 No ◯ 2
NO (YES ASSUMED)	

You Told Us

53. Working on a masters or doctorate program in 2003-2004? NO	Yes ◯ 1 No ◯ 2	56. Have Dependents Other Than Children or Spouse? (BLANK)	Yes ◯ 1 No ◯ 2
54. Are You Married? **(BLANK) (YES ASSUMED)**	Yes ◯ 1 No ◯ 2	57. Are you an Orphan, or were you (until age 18) a Ward/Dependent of Court? NO	Yes ◯ 1 No ◯ 2
55. Have children you support? (BLANK)	Yes ◯ 1 No ◯ 2	58. Veteran of U.S. Armed Forces? YES	Yes ◯ 1 No ◯ 2

Step Four: 2002 Parental Information
Complete this section if you (the student) answered "No" to all questions in Step Three. If you do not live with your two parents, then provide information about the parent you lived with most during the past year (if that parent is married, provide information about the stepmother or stepfather to whom that parent is married).

59. Parents' Marital Status MARRIED/REMARRIED	Married/Remarried ◯ 1 Divorced/Separated ◯ 3 Single ◯ 2 Widowed ◯ 4	60. Date of Marital Status DECEMBER 1961

Use MM/CCYY format (e.g., 05/1980)

61. Your Father's/Stepfather's Social Security Number 123-45-6789	□□ - □□ - □□□□
62. Your Father's/Stepfather's Last Name FULLLASTNAMETEST	
63. Your Mother's/Stepmother's Social Security Number 123-45-6789	□□ - □□ - □□□□
64. Your Mother's/Stepmother's Last Name FULLLASTNAMETEST	
65. Parents' number of family members in 2003-2004 **(BLANK) (12 ASSUMED)**	

For 74-84, if the answer is zero or the question does not apply, enter 0. Report dollar amounts without cents. For 77-78, this information may be on W-2 forms, box 1 and 8 or on IRS Form 1040-lines 7+12+18; 1040A-line 7; or 1040EZ-line 1. Telefilers should use W-2 forms, box 1 and 8.

66. Parents' number of family members in college in 2003-2004 **(BLANK) (2 ASSUMED)**	
67. Parents' state of legal residence MD	

68. Parents' legal resident of the state before 1-1-1998? YES	Yes ◯ 1 No ◯ 2

69. If "No" to question 68, enter the date parent became legal resident. OCTOBER 1996	□□ / □□□□

Use MM/CCYY format (e.g., 05/1980)

70. Age of older Parent? 55	

71. Filed 2002 Income Tax Return WILL FILE	Have already completed ◯ 1 Will file, have not yet completed ◯ 2 Not going to file ◯ 3

72. Type of 2002 Tax Form Used 1040	A. IRS 1040 ◯ 1 B. IRS 1040A, 1040 EZ, 1040 Telefile ◯ 2 C. A foreign tax return ◯ 3 D. A tax return for Puerto Rico, Guam, American Samoa, the U.S. Virgin Islands, the Marshall Islands, the Federated States of Micronesia, or Palau ◯ 4

73. If your parents filed or will file a 1040, were they eligible to file a 1040A or 1040EZ? NO	Yes ◯ 1 No ◯ 2 Don't Know ◯ 3

74. Adjusted Gross Income from IRS Form (IRS Form 1040-line 35; 1040A-line 21; 1040EZ-line 4; or Telefile-line I) $ 123,456	$ □□□ , □□□
75. U.S. Income Tax Paid from IRS Form (1040-lines 55; 1040A-lines 36; 1040EZ-line 10, or Telefile-line K(2).) $ 123,456	$ □□□ , □□□
76. Exemptions Claimed from IRS Form (1040-line 6d; 1040A-line 6d; For 1040EZ or Telefile, see pg 2.) 02	
77. Father's/Stepfather's Income Earned from Work $ 123,456	$ □□□ , □□□
78. Mother's/Stepmother's Income Earned from Work $ 123,456	$ □□□ , □□□
79. Amount from FAFSA Worksheet A $ 12,345	$ □□□ , □□□
80. Amount from FAFSA Worksheet B $ 12,345	$ □□□ , □□□
81. Amount from FAFSA Worksheet C $ 12,345 (00,000 ASSUMED)	$ □□□ , □□□
82. Net Worth of Investments $ 123,456	$ □□□ , □□□
83. Net Worth of Business/Investment Farms $ 123,456	$ □□□ , □□□
84. Cash, Savings, and Checking $ 123,456	$ □□□ , □□□

X9XX999999 999

PAGE 7 OF 8

1 2 3 4 5 6 7 8 9 S T 0 1

Step Five: Student's Household Information

85. Number of Family Members in 2003-2004		86. Number in College in 2003-2004		**Housing Plans:**
02		2		1 -- on campus 2 -- off campus 3 -- with parent

Step Six: Student's School Information

You Told Us	NEW Federal School Code **or** NEW College Name, City, State		
87. First College Name, City and State ABCDEFGHIJKLMNOPQRSTUVWXYZ ABCDEFGHIJKLMNOPQRSTUVWXYZ			88. Housing Plans WITH PARENT
89. Second College Name, City and State ABCDEFGHIJKLMNOPQRSTUVWXYZ ABCDEFGHIJKLMNOPQRSTUVWXYZ			90. Housing Plans ON CAMPUS
91. Third College Name, City and State ABCDEFGHIJKLMNOPQRSTUVWXYZ ABCDEFGHIJKLMNOPQRSTUVWXYZ			92. Housing Plans OFF CAMPUS
93. Fourth College Name, City and State ABCDEFGHIJKLMNOPQRSTUVWXYZ ABCDEFGHIJKLMNOPQRSTUVWXYZ			94. Housing Plans (BLANK)
95. Fifth College Name, City and State ABCDEFGHIJKLMNOPQRSTUVWXYZ ABCDEFGHIJKLMNOPQRSTUVWXYZ			96. Housing Plans (BLANK)
97. Sixth College Name, City and State ABCDEFGHIJKLMNOPQRSTUVWXYZ ABCDEFGHIJKLMNOPQRSTUVWXYZ			98. Housing Plans (BLANK)

99. Student's E-mail Address	
CHRISTOPHERESTUDENT_UNIVOFMARYLAND.COLLGPRK@ED.GOV	

100. Date Completed JANUARY 10, 2003	DO NOT CORRECT
101. Signed By? STUDENT	DO NOT CORRECT
102. Preparer's Social Security Number REPORTED	If this form was filled out by someone other than you, your spouse, or your parent(s), that person must complete this part.
103. Preparer's EIN REPORTED	
104. Preparer's Signature SIGNED	

Application Receipt Date: 01/15/2003

Step Seven: Please read, sign, and date
You must read this Certification and sign below.

Certification:

If you are the student, by signing this application you certify that you (1) will use federal and/or state student financial aid only to pay the cost of attending an institution of higher education, (2) are not in default on a federal student loan or have made satisfactory arrangements to repay it, (3) do not owe money back on a federal student grant or have made satisfactory arrangements to repay it, and (4) will notify your school if you default on a federal student loan.

If you are the parent or the student, by signing this application you agree, if asked, to provide information that will verify the accuracy of your completed form. This information may include your U.S. or state income tax forms. Also, you certify that you understand that **the Secretary of Education has the authority to verify information reported on this application with the Internal Revenue Service and other federal agencies.** If you purposely give false or misleading information, you may be fined $20,000, sent to prison, or both.

Student Signature (Required to process your application. Sign in box below.)

1	Student	Date

CHRISTOPHER E. STUDENT

Parent Signature (one parent whose information is provided in Step Four)

2	Parent	Date

MDE Use Only

◯ P   ◯ *   ◯ L   ◯ E

SEND PAGES 5 - 8 OF THIS FORM TO: **Federal Student Aid Programs** **P.O. Box 7004** **Mt. Vernon, IL 62864-0074**	OR	You may also make corrections from the Department of Education's web page (www.fafsa.ed.gov). You must use your PIN to access your record online.

1 2 3 4 5 6 7 8 9 S T 0 1

Step Five: Student's Household Information

85. Number of Family Members in 2003-2004		86. Number in College in 2003-2004		**Housing Plans:** 1 -- on campus 2 -- off campus 3 -- with parent
02		2		

Step Six: Student's School Information

You Told Us   NEW Federal School Code **or** NEW College Name, City, State

87. First College Name, City and State ABCDEFGHIJKLMNOPQRSTUVWXYZ ABCDEFGHIJKLMNOPQRSTUVWXYZ			88. Housing Plans WITH PARENT
89. Second College Name, City and State ABCDEFGHIJKLMNOPQRSTUVWXYZ ABCDEFGHIJKLMNOPQRSTUVWXYZ			90. Housing Plans ON CAMPUS
91. Third College Name, City and State ABCDEFGHIJKLMNOPQRSTUVWXYZ ABCDEFGHIJKLMNOPQRSTUVWXYZ			92. Housing Plans OFF CAMPUS
93. Fourth College Name, City and State ABCDEFGHIJKLMNOPQRSTUVWXYZ ABCDEFGHIJKLMNOPQRSTUVWXYZ			94. Housing Plans (BLANK)
95. Fifth College Name, City and State ABCDEFGHIJKLMNOPQRSTUVWXYZ ABCDEFGHIJKLMNOPQRSTUVWXYZ			96. Housing Plans (BLANK)
97. Sixth College Name, City and State ABCDEFGHIJKLMNOPQRSTUVWXYZ ABCDEFGHIJKLMNOPQRSTUVWXYZ			98. Housing Plans (BLANK)

99. Student's E-mail Address
CHRISTOPHERESTUDENT_UNIVOFMARYLAND.COLLGPRK@ED.GOV

@

100. Date Completed JANUARY 10, 2003	**DO NOT CORRECT**
101. Signed By? STUDENT	**DO NOT CORRECT**
102. Preparer's Social Security Number REPORTED	
103. Preparer's EIN REPORTED	If this form was filled out by someone other than you, your spouse, or your parent(s), that person must complete this part.
104. Preparer's Signature SIGNED	

Application Receipt Date: 01/15/2003

Step Seven: Please read, sign, and date
You must read and sign this Certification.

Certification:

All of the information on this SAR is true and complete to the best of my knowledge. If I am asked, I agree to give proof that my information is correct. The proof might include a copy of the 2002 U.S. Income Tax Form filed by me or my family. I understand that if I purposely give false or misleading information on this SAR, I may be subject to a $20,000 fine, a prison sentence, or both.

If you made no changes:

☞ Do NOT send your SAR to either address given on this page.
☞ Follow the instructions on your SAR. You may need to contact your school.

If you made changes:

☞ You may make corrections from the U.S. Department of Education's web page (**www.fafsa.ed.gov**). You must use your PIN to access your record.

OR

☞ Read and Sign the Certification statement to the right.
☞ Send pages 5-8 to: **Federal Student Aid Programs**
       P.O. Box 7004
       Mt. Vernon, IL 62864-0074

Student Signature (Required to process your application. Sign in box below.)

1	Student	Date

CHRISTOPHER E. STUDENT

Parent Signature (one parent whose information is provided in Step Four)

2	Parent	Date

MDE Use Only

○ P   ○ *   ○ L   ○ E

If you need another copy of you SAR:

☞ Include your name, social security number, and signature.
☞ Write to: **Federal Student Aid Programs**
       P.O. Box 7005
       Mt. Vernon, IL 62864-0075

X9XX999999 999   PAGE 8 OF 8V

1 2 3 4 5 6 7 8 9 S T 0 1

Faculty and Student Perspectives

The comments in this chapter were originally sought for the purpose of providing anecdotes for the "Office Hours" and "The Student Center" sidebars in this book. I received so many rich comments from students and faculty, however, that I decided to include many of the extras in this appendix.

Perspectives from real students and real faculty members in community colleges, large research universities, smaller liberal arts colleges, and even from countries other than the United States demonstrate that the common fears that adult students have are just that—common. Also, returning adult learners can learn from the experiences other students have had. And it's good to know in advance how faculty members view adult students.

Some of the comments have been edited for length and appropriateness of language. All contributors were assured anonymity in order to generate frank feedback and discussion.

The Student Center

I was one of the youngest people in the program at the community college I attended. I also have a B.A. from a college where most of the students were straight out of high school. The experience of getting my B.A. was entirely different than my community college experience, simply because of the make-up of the classes. Attending classes with "nontraditional" students (though in some cases, I might be considered one) was, in my experience, hard.

One of my old professors taught remedial reading and writing to community college students and found that the older students had zero patience for anything that didn't directly correlate to a) their daily lives or b) their sought-after degree. And she's a good teacher—she has a very high success rate and has won numerous awards.

I was a good 10 years older than most of my classmates, but I never had any problems because of it. Then again, I earned major street cred in my first semester back when I talked the professor out of giving the final exam in one of my classes. Ahh, good times!

I'm what you would call a traditional college student in terms of age. I took a course in children's lit last year where there was one very outspoken mature student enrolled. This was a class of approximately 150 people, and somehow, when she spoke with the professor during class (and she spoke up a lot), she did so in a way that made me, as a younger student, feel excluded—it was as if she felt she was better able to relate to the material, to the professor, than we were as young students.

I started college at 18, at a medium-sized, private university. When I got married, near the end of what should have been my junior year, it became financially necessary for me to take two years off to work. Returning to the same university after being in the "real world" resulted in a serious situation-shock.

I had been working in my field, archaeology, and had in the course of my job been published multiple times, presented at conferences, and generally performed work intended to be completed by a degreed person. Coming back to taking undergraduate level courses with fresh out of high-school students was really difficult. I felt isolated from the other students. They were apathetic, disinterested in the subject, and overall tried to get by doing as little work as possible.

I felt isolated from the professors, too, even though I was married, carried a full load of coursework, and worked the equivalent of full-time hours in the field of my prospective degree. I had a husband, a house, and a mortgage. But often, the professors insisted on treating me as though I was still a child. I found myself talked down to, told that I was unlikely to succeed because of my age, and generally made to feel as if my presence was taking up a spot that another younger student could have used.

Eventually I transferred into a "General Studies" program, with a focus that allowed me to use my anthropological/archaeological coursework to fulfill many of the core requirements for graduation. I found that being out of a specific department removed a lot of the tension.

My college had a program that targeted nontraditional aged women. I always found these women inspiring—they were more engaged in the coursework and seemed to get more out of the experience. They actually appreciated the opportunity to learn what most of the rest of us took for granted. They also provided a unique perspective to our discussions.

Now that I am older and have been out in the "real world" I think that I, too, would have learned more and appreciated more about college if I had taken time off in between high school and college.

I'm 37, at a community college, soon to transfer to a business college in the fall to get my B.S. Most my classes are online but I do go to the classroom for some. My instructors, who are about the same age as me, have been fantastic in not talking down to me and even suggesting different ways for me to learn the information.

We nontraditional learners tend to look at our instructors as service providers for whom we are paying a fee. I don't put them on a pedestal just because they have a Ph.D. Teachers just know specialized material and they've learned processes to share it. I do judge them on their ability to teach me what I'm supposed to learn.

I was consistently one of the oldest people in my classes. A large part of me was profoundly grateful that I wasn't living the life of a typical college student. I didn't have to deal with dorms or parents or three part-time jobs. On the other hand, I *did* have a lot of concerns that were so far out of the realm of typical college students as to be incomprehensible to them. I had a husband and two small children. I had a mortgage and two car payments and grown-up responsibilities. Sometimes the fact that these responsibilities trumped the work I had to do for classes became problematic for me.

I think, though, that I came out ahead in most cases. I had a great deal of experience to bring to a college classroom. My writing was generally very well received by professors because it was far more mature and considered than much of my classmates' offerings.

For fun, at age 45 I'm taking classes in another discipline. I am in a group with people ranging from 22 to 50-something. At first I was very conscious of being "that" person, who always had something to say, and of the younger students eye-rolling when the older ones (3 of us) would talk a lot and ask lots of questions. Now that we all know one other, the younger students are acting more like us "oldsters," and we are meeting on the common ground of the material. We older students have learned not to monopolize as much class discussion, but we do take fuller advantage of the professor's office hours, which the younger ones don't do.

I'm 25, which is only just slightly older than most traditional students, but I have a 5-year-old son, a husband, a career, and I'm obviously pregnant. I'm also trying to overcome flunking out of college the first time around. It's been very difficult to get profs to understand how very different my life is compared to my classmates.

I got downsized by the Army in 1997 and went back to school with the GI Bill, a $21K (net) severance check, and a little Dodge Colt hatchback. I treated my return to university study as I would a job. I "punched in" at eight-ish, and "punched out" at six-ish. If I needed to work longer, I did, but that wasn't often. Bottom line, I had time to study *and* time to do fun things with my wife (who had a job) and eight-year-old son. I was 34.

Younger students would do well to follow that example. Applying the professional work ethic I acquired in the Army to my studies got me a 3.8 GPA, a magna cum laude on my diploma, countless interviews, and four solid job offers in the months prior to graduation.

Another thing the Army instilled in me was the sense that we were all in this together. So we all passed our courses, we all graduated on time, and everybody got decent jobs and lived happily ever after, as far as I know.

So I would say that older students are a net asset to a college class. I didn't see any know-it-all-ism among them, probably because that's something you have to overcome prior to deciding to go back to school. As for disrespect from the younger students, that pretty much melts away after the first midterm exam when the older students come out ahead of the curve.

My father finished his Bachelor's at the age of 51, after two "false starts" in college. The first time, he was fresh out of high school with a National Merit Scholarship, but flunked out of Caltech. The second time he had to quit because he didn't have time to support his family (two kids) and take classes. He was the second in his family, then, to graduate from college—after his second-oldest daughter, who did it a few years earlier.

He said that he didn't really develop the discipline needed to succeed in college classes until he was in his 30s. He went from being a kid who took a bet not to take a book home his last semester of high school to someone who diligently read and completed all his assignments—something I admit I had a lot of trouble with as a "traditional" student.

I think he did take with him an attitude more conducive to learning. He already had a job that technically required the degree he was earning, so he came to class out of a genuine interest in learning, rather than as a stepping-stone toward landing a job. Also, it was his own money invested in his education, rather than his parents'.

I'm 30, preparing to go back to college full-time in the fall to finish my degree, and I have to admit I'm nervous about the age difference issue. On the one hand, I'll be going to a small liberal arts college with a high percentage of nontraditional students and what they call "resumers," so students and profs ought to be used to the phenomenon.

On the other hand, last winter I took a couple of English lit classes to get my feet wet again and see if I could do this. I did end up being one of the most outspoken people in the class, to the point where I got embarrassed enough to experiment with *not* jumping in for a while. Only no one else took up the slack.

Two things help me deal with the jitters at going back full-time, though. One is the fact that I have always intended to do this, ever since I quit in my early 20s. In a lot of ways, I never stopped considering myself a student, always had the idea lurking at the back of my mind, even when I was married and couldn't see how I would ever make it back. The other is that, while I've been in the workforce for nearly seven years now, I'm also something of a nontraditional worker.

When I was an undergrad (mechanical engineering), one of the students in my design class had gone back to school after years of industry experience (he seemed really old at the time but I'm guessing he was only in his 30s). He was really great for brainstorming ideas and explaining things: he knew what would work and how things were put together, so I was almost wishing I'd done something like that first. The math and physics were probably easier for me because of coming straight out of high school, though.

After eight years as a professional writer and editor, I jumped back into school for a second degree, this time in the sciences. Turns out I was just of an age where the traditional undergrads asked me if I had ID and could help get a keg, while the grads and faculty just thought I was new in the department. I found that the group dynamics were the same as ever (my confidence in small group discussions inevitably wins me a leadership role), and yet my motivation was much, much higher for schoolwork since I no longer had dating and dorm life to distract me.

While I would never give up my traditional years of college, my return trip was more academically rewarding in that I was able to apply both good student skills and good workplace skills to every task. I found that I was much better able to manage my time, which helped me do independent research.

I was not a nontraditional student, but the small college I went to was known to be a friendly place for commuters and older students. As a result, I knew many nontraditional students. My experience was that they worked really hard and were acutely aware of the fact that this was a second chance to work toward a concrete goal. These people juggled spouses, kids, jobs, homework, and many of them still would make time to help a fellow student.

Furthermore, because these people had been around the block a few times, they had very clear ideas about what they wanted to do with their lives, and what they had to do to get there. I admire them greatly and wish The System would stop putting obstacles in their way: on-campus residence requirements; lack of financial aid for people who have completed a degree; bizarre class schedules. There's a big difference between a student who wants to learn things, and a student who is marking time—and that is true whether the student is 20 or 40.

Office Hours

As a community college instructor, I teach quite a few "older" students, in fact, sometimes ones that are old enough to be my parents. This can make things tricky, as I find that older students have very different expectations about professors or instructors as well as what happens in the classroom and how they will be assessed.

I've always had good experiences with nontraditional students. My undergraduate school was primarily nontraditional, so perhaps that affects how I approach nontraditional students in the first place. In general, I find that nontraditional students value their education more because they are usually the ones paying for it (not Mom and Dad) and because they are there because they want to be, not because they have to be.

I have only taught one course that included both traditional and nontraditional older students, and it was a great experience. I found my older students to be much less "grade-grubbing" and generally enthusiastic and engaged. I was probably younger [as a professor] than about 75% of the class and at no time did I feel that they tried to push me around. Some of them still contact me with ideas or questions that they have. I found that I had to be a little more flexible with make-up exams and such than I might be in a traditional classroom because these people had full-time jobs and family responsibilities. Older students are there because they want to be and they are footing the bill. I think both of these things make them more interested and willing to work harder.

I teach at a school that is primarily for upper-division transfers, mainly older non-traditional students who have gotten community college degrees and want to step up to a Bachelor's. I love teaching nontraditional students.

I've taught several courses cross-listed specifically for older, nontraditional students. The courses had a fairly even mix of nontraditional students, many who were just re-entering school, and younger students getting a requirement out of the way in the evenings. I never had any problems with authority with these students. The biggest problems came in pitching the material. The way I would teach to the young crowd, who were generally very good students and good at "being" students, was very different than what worked for the older students. Since they hadn't been in school for years, they didn't do well with the information-feed that many of the younger students really liked.

Young undergrads are still "trained to be students," and they know that role (sometimes to their own detriment). They know how to cull information from what the instructor says. The older students didn't know it, and sometimes got distracted by tangents that didn't seem that relevant to me; they didn't know how to figure out what was more or less relevant. Combining the two learning styles in a single class was hard. I've recommended to my department that these courses be separated but of course there's no way to do that (paying two instructors to do fewer students per class).

Walking into my lab as a 22-year-old teaching assistant, I was somewhat intimidated to find I was teaching a man my father's age. It was okay, but it can be difficult to get the interpersonal dynamic right in that situation. Likewise, I struggled with how to address the perpetual lateness of a single mom with a small child—I felt sorry for her, she was obviously having a difficult time.

The students worked in twos or threes, and after a couple of weeks I realized that the older guy did *everything* in his group. There were two quiet girls who sat at the same bench, but they never even spoke when I went over to see how they were doing. We had some awkward moments when I said that I'd noticed this and would like to see more active participation from the girls. It wasn't that he stopped them from contributing, just that *the girls* seemed to assume for some reason that he knew better than they what to do. He didn't, so I think it just came down to his greater confidence.

The older students (there were a few) in general were less forgiving when I couldn't answer a question immediately and said "give me a second to think." They seemed to expect me to have the answer to every single problem they might have right on my lips.

I've taught a lot of nontraditional students, ranging from ex-convicts getting themselves together to middle-aged women wanting to be more independent in their families. I really love non-trads because they bring so much more confidence and experience to the classroom. My younger students usually dislike the non-trads for their eagerness to speak and sincere interest in the material. The only really difficult experience I've had with a non-trad was with a middle-aged woman whose writing skills displayed a complete inability to organize thoughts. Her papers ranged all over the place and rarely contained any actual sentences. I urged her to get help, and she eventually did, before informing me that she had suffered some kind of brain damage during one of her eight childbirths, "from the pain," she said, but her husband had never allowed her to receive any treatment or diagnosis. Through an amazing amount of work with me and with tutors, she passed my very difficult intro to lit class.

I've had nothing but great experiences with older students, even when I was a first-year teaching assistant. I've taught at Big State U, at a small for-profit Adult Learning College, and at Urban Community College. In my estimation, they know why they're there, you don't have to worry about them doing the work (they know that if they don't, there are consequences, and they don't whine about it—but by and large, they do it), and they give props to you for knowing the subject matter. Even if you're a relatively new teacher, they get that your lack of pedagogical skills doesn't mean you don't know what you're talking about. And they give awesomely constructive feedback about how to do things better.

The students at For-Profit Adult Learning College were a little more difficult and critical than traditional students I've taught, primarily because a number of them had a lot of experiences of academic failure and they could be defensive if they felt they were being asked to do too much. The trick there is that you have to start pretty easy (give them stuff you're sure they can do), give lots of positive feedback, praise them for what they do know, and generally achieve trust before you can challenge them. And you have to make sure they know the small steps to taking a test/writing a paper/etc., so that they can manage their anxiety. I really like this kind of teaching, because it's so gratifying when they realize they can, in fact, succeed. I even had one much older woman end up applying to grad school in my field. I was touched.

As an undergrad I taught pre-college math at my university. This was offered by the university, but didn't give credit toward graduation. Generally I taught daytime sections of algebra classes, but one semester I had an evening section of arithmetic. The time, and to a certain extent the content, meant I had a large number of non-traditional students. Many of them were probably 40+, had day jobs, and hadn't done math in so long that they had to go back to basics. For this group, they had to get through first the arithmetic class, then the algebra class, then enroll in something that would count toward graduation.

One might expect a certain amount of resentment toward learning elementary school math from someone young enough to be their offspring, but there was none. They gave me the same respect they would give any teacher. They worked as hard in their classes as I did in mine. If they hadn't, they would have heard about it.

I've taught night classes in my university's extension school. About half the students come from surrounding colleges that don't offer these courses, and the other half are adults with full-time jobs.

Many of the adult students had quite specific ideas about how they wanted to learn. This was sometimes good—they knew what they wanted, and were able to make specific requests that I could work into my teaching style. They helped me become a much better teacher. On the other hand, knowing what they (thought they) wanted often also made them resistant to other teaching styles or activities.

My least favorite category of adult learners are what I think of as the "pay grade" students. They don't really want to be in school, they just want to go up a pay grade in a government job or hold on to a job for which they now need a degree unlike when they first were hired. These students often (but not always) don't want to be there, are trying to squeeze school in around full-time work and life, and aren't fully engaged. Maybe they didn't like college the first time around, which is why they didn't finish in the first place, and are doubly resentful. On the other hand, some of these students are glad for the chance they never had earlier (but now their job is paying for their education, for example) and make the most of it.

Overall, I've loved having older students in my classes. They are generally more dedicated, more experienced, more confident, and from a teacher's perspective, more interesting. But when they are not (like the guy who gets his secretary to write his paper, or the one who believes that "those who can, have jobs and those who can't, teach") they can be the worst.

I teach biology at an extension school as part of a Biotechnology Certificate. My students are mostly older and they have very different reasons for taking the class. While many students are conscientious and hardworking, many of them also expect special exemptions because of their special situations. Although I'm willing to be flexible, I'm not willing to give someone a passing grade when they were unable to demonstrate basic understanding of the material on any assignment or exam just because they really need (want) the certificate and don't plan to use it for "real" biology. I *am* willing to give them a re-test or answer any questions they might have, but anything else is unfair to my other students who do manage to learn and demonstrate that in my course.

I find the older students have a good idea of what they want from their courses. This means they are not afraid of asking questions during class and criticizing the subject or method. And they are motivated to get their money's worth from the lectures. They also benefit from previous education and general life experience, so they can place new knowledge in context.

I've had a few older (middle-aged or above) students in the classes I teach. I always hope to get one or two in a class, because I've found they mostly aren't as self-conscious as the 18-year-olds, so will generally be brave enough to talk and answer questions even if they know they haven't completely "got" the material yet. That goes a long way toward breaking the ice with the other students, too, and can generate some really interesting discussions.

I teach at a Big 10 U (English and web design) and the older students usually completely set the tone in my English classes. I think this is largely to do with the sort of person who chooses to come back to school and pursue humanities-related studies. They tend to be more engaged.

In technology-based classes, though—where the task at hand is to learn advanced web design—I find much more resistance and even antagonism from adult students. I attribute this to the fact that, unlike their younger peers, they have not grown up immersed in interactive technology and software tools. This breeds frustration, which can translate into negative attitudes toward me and the class.

I've only ever had positive experiences teaching students who are considered nontraditional because of age. They have always been much more diligent and respectful than their younger peers. I was very young (19) when I started teaching, and I always got much more respect from students old enough to be my parent than from students who were roughly my age.

My older students are consistently among my best. They are attentive, thoughtful, and handle criticism with grace. My own thought on this is that they are more dedicated because they're typically paying tuition themselves: they are, quite literally, invested.

I'm teaching a night class right now, and most of my students are nontraditional. I actually love it and find the students are warm and engaged in a way that I don't usually encounter. One way I find they differ most is in their time management. Most of them work full-time and are a) more skilled in managing their time and b) more realistic about what can get done and what obstacles they'll have to work around.

On the second day of class this semester, one of the students came up to me and asked if that week's reading load was typical. I said yes and that I thought it was pretty reasonable. She nodded and then said, "I don't have time for that." She wasn't complaining, just stating the facts. I told her she'd need to do the reading to be prepared for discussion and exams, and she nodded and moved on.

I relate this not as a story of a student who didn't take the assignments seriously or who couldn't commit to the work. I actually found it incredibly refreshing. She was aware of her limits and took them as such. She wasn't whining or asking me to solve her problems. And she's come to almost every class prepared to discuss and engage with the material, which shows me that even given her time constraints (I've since learned she's a single mother) she is able to grasp enough of the reading to get something out of it. I don't expect any of my students to read every single page every single week. I do expect them to be organized and mature enough to figure out their own limits and how to work within them, and this class is the best I've ever taught at that.

I've taught at urban and suburban community colleges with wide age ranges in the classroom, and returning/nontraditional students are by far my favorite to have in class mainly because they tend to be more invested in their education and in the world in general. I'm a young instructor who looks younger than I am, and I've never had returning/nontraditional students question or challenge my "authority" in class—they are almost always super hard workers who take what I say seriously and are able to interact with material in a more mature fashion. Perhaps unfairly (I don't know), I tend to look to my older students as leaders in many class situations because I feel like they have a lot to bring to my classroom, and I hope they feel I respect them as much as they seem to respect me.

I've been a young teacher with much older students; also been an older student. I generally found my older students to be very easy to work with and probably more respectful than was warranted. Did they sometimes go off on tangents? Sure, but they were sharp listeners and relatively easily reined in. The reining-in conversations were consistently the most interesting ones I had with students, because even though they were off my point, their tangents were usually rooted in vivid experience at points in their lives when they had something serious to lose.

Resources for Adult Students

The websites listed in this appendix can help you through every aspect of returning to college. The sites are listed alphabetically, with a brief description of the services available through each site. If you go no further than the sites listed here, you'll have access to everything you need to …

- ◆ Plan for college.

- ◆ Gain access to and apply for financial aid.

- ◆ Choose a college that's right for you.

- ◆ Practice assessments that will help you choose courses and careers.

- ◆ Find other adult students and learn from their experiences.

- ◆ Get advice that will help you make it through college and obtain your degree.

- ◆ Learn about internships available nationwide.

- ◆ Take your college learning experiences into the workforce.

The sites listed here are a mere drop in the bucket when it comes to higher education sites on the Internet. If you type the words *adult learners* into any search engine, you'll get thousands of options for investigation. It's difficult to narrow those search parameters to get a meaningful list (based on where your life or your interests or financial aid needs are, and so on), so if you start with these sites and let them draw your attention to additional links on the web, you'll be heading in the right direction.

ACT, Inc.

www.act.org

ACT does so much more than just administer the well-known college admissions assessment. Their website has much to help adult learners plan for and link college planning with career advancement. The website has the largest database in the United States, identifying skills needed for certain jobs.

ACT develops WorkKeys assessments (such as Reading for Information; Locating Information; Applied Mathematics; and others, including assessments of soft skills such as Teamwork), which you can use to match your work and career background, interests, and skills with an academic program that will build your skills to the levels needed for your desired job.

ACT also makes the DISCOVER career guidance and exploration system available to colleges and individuals; develops the ASSET and COMPASS-ESL assessments for colleges to use for placement purposes; creates assessments to measure learning following college general education courses; and more.

The ACT site is easy to navigate and has sections dedicated to students. Many of the college campuses that you will investigate deliver some of the ACT academic and career assessments—check with your local campus testing center, particularly if you want to use the DISCOVER system or would like to have a battery of WorkKeys assessments to help chart your college path.

American Association of Community Colleges (AACC)

www.aacc.nche.edu

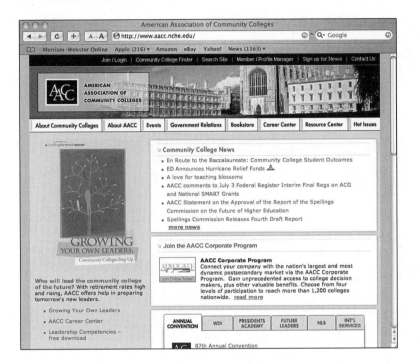

The American Association of Community Colleges is a national advocacy and support organization for community colleges. Among the features of interest to students are hot topics that highlight areas in which jobs are growing—such as nursing.

The AACC site also provides direct links to community colleges around the country and includes enrollment data and other information about each state's community colleges.

The American Council on Education (ACE)

www.acenet.edu

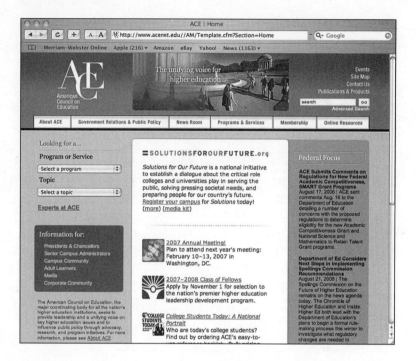

ACE helps adults navigate higher education programs and services. It offers a number of services to adult students, including the ACE Transcript Service and the College Credit Recommendation Service, or CREDIT.

ACE has helped thousands of adult learners through the years organize and gain college credit for learning on and off college campuses. ACE's services and informational expertise covers all forms of education.

The College Board

www.collegeboard.com

The College Board is the organization that develops the SAT test, as well as Advanced Placement (AP) assessments and training. The site also has samples of SAT exams you can take and tips for taking the SAT. Test dates are published on the site, as well as locations where you can take the SAT.

The College Board's site also provides information on which states and colleges require the Writing portion of the SAT. Not all states or colleges require the SAT Writing exam for admission. You can also access additional financial aid information, as well as information that helps you choose the right college.

The Council on Adult and Experiential Learning (CAEL)

www.cael.org

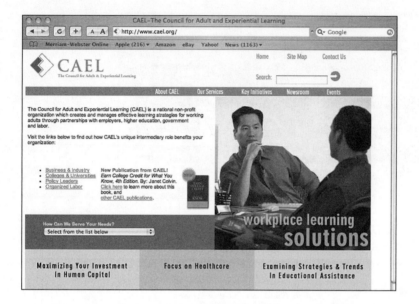

CAEL is a not-for-profit organization dedicated to helping adult learners get the education and training they need to be successful, contributing citizens.

CAEL helps adult students locate colleges that are the "best of the best" when it comes to serving adult learners. CAEL also helps companies, unions, and employee groups gain training that can be translated into college credit.

CAEL also teaches colleges and universities how to conduct Prior Learning Assessment (PLA). It's through PLA that colleges review portfolios or documentation of work-based or life-based learning and grant college credit for those learning experiences. You can learn more about PLA and how to present your credentials for PLA evaluation at the college of your choice by visiting CAEL's site.

Fastweb

www.fastweb.com

Fastweb is a must if you're looking for scholarship dollars to help pay for college. The site notes that more than 1.3 million different scholarships are available. You can fill out a secure online questionnaire to help identify scholarship opportunities. This site does for free what many companies or consultants charge you for.

In addition to being a fabulous resource for local and national, Fastweb also has a section that enables you to compare colleges.

And if you need to locate a part-time job, on or off campus, you may even find employment by using the portion of the site devoted to matching students with jobs. The site also identifies internships that are available, something important for upper-division courses for many fields.

Free Application for Federal Student Aid (FAFSA)

www.fafsa.ed.gov

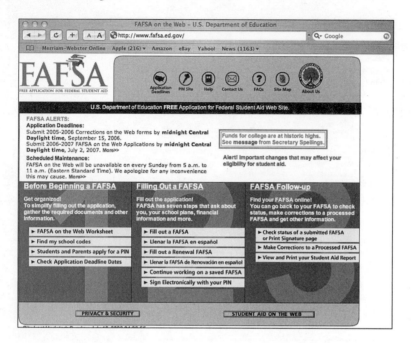

This link takes you directly to the site within the U.S. Department of Education's web portal through which you can fill out your FAFSA electronically (and therefore get your FAFSA processed more quickly).

This site takes you through the entire process of filling out your FAFSA. You can also learn the school codes for the institutions you want to have your financial aid information sent to.

When your FAFSA is filled out and processed, you can access your Student Aid Report (SAR) and check the status of your application throughout the entire process.

Mapping Your Future

http://mapping-your-future.org/adult

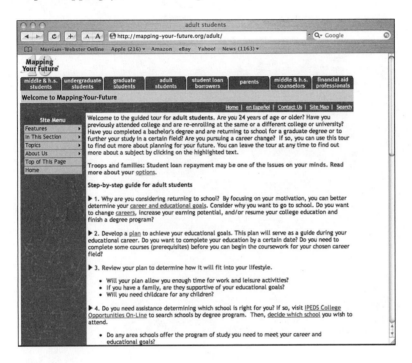

The Mapping Your Future site is sponsored by state guaranty agencies for student loans and provides comprehensive information on all aspects of preparing for college, including a special portion of the site devoted to adult students.

Through this website, you can link to all federal grant and aid programs, the FAFSA, and also learn the pros and cons of different ways to pay for college. The site is maintained by highly knowledgeable professionals who are up-to-date on all the latest federal regulations, laws, and policies.

The National Association of Independent Colleges and Universities (NAICU)

www.naicu.edu

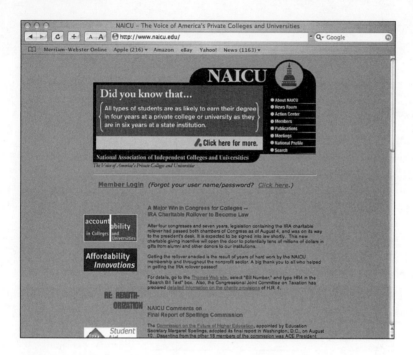

NAICU's site is the best nationwide portal for private, independent colleges and universities. In this one website, you have the nation's independent colleges and universities at your fingertips.

The National College Access Network (NCAN)

www.collegeaccess.org/NCAN

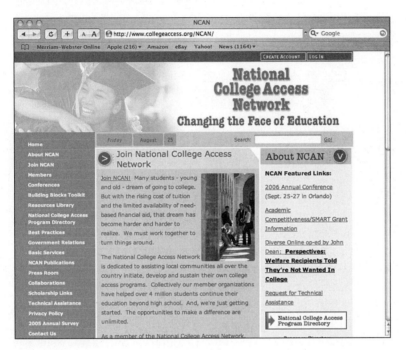

NCAN is changing the face of education. The staff at the network has been building college access programs all over the nation; their homepage has a link where you can see if there's a NCAN college access program in your area. While many of their services are for first-time students, underrepresented student groups, and first-generation students in the traditional age range, their adult services are growing daily.

The Student Center

www.adultstudentcenter.com

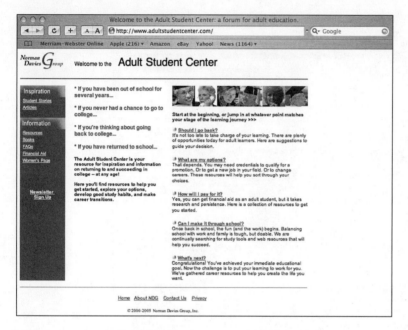

This is a virtual adult student center. Even if your campus is one that doesn't pay particular attention to adult students, you can find a "home" here.

Not only can you find wonderful and inspiring stories about adult learners just like you, who are either in college or who have completed a degree, you can also find special resources to help you through the various steps toward your college degree.

The site has a section devoted to Inspiration and Information and you can access everything from articles to research to stories from students like you.

You can sign up for a regular newsletter issued by the site owners, and there is even a special section devoted to women.

Southern Regional Education Board (SREB)

www.sreb.org

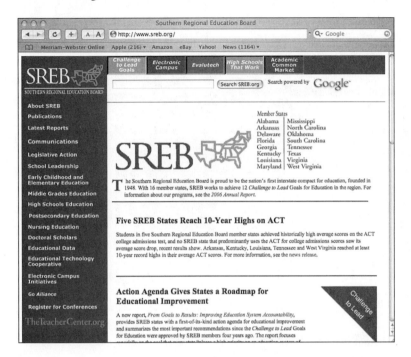

The SREB is a regional education organization that serves 16 southern states—from Maryland and Virginia southward; eastward to Arkansas and Oklahoma; and down through Texas and the Gulf Coast states. SREB, which is an organization that helps all levels of education, focuses on serving adult learners.

Within the SREB website adult students can locate online learning opportunities and be linked with colleges and university systems in the southern states that might serve their needs best.

The United States Department of Education (USDoE)

www.ed.gov

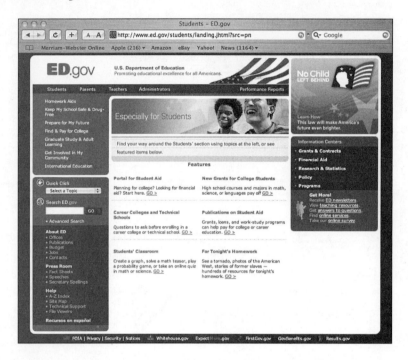

This is the website for the federal agency that oversees federal education programs. If you want to file a FAFSA online, you can do so through this site (though it is easier to use the FAFSA site listed previously in this appendix). You will be given a PIN number to use in all application information. The site maintains the highest security protocols, so you can feel comfortable in utilizing the FAFSA online.

College information is primarily located in the section of the site devoted to the Office of Postsecondary Education (OPE), though information on community college and vocational programs are located in the section of the site reserved for the Office of Adult and Vocational Education (OVAE).

Western Interstate Cooperative for Higher Education (WICHE)

www.wiche.edu

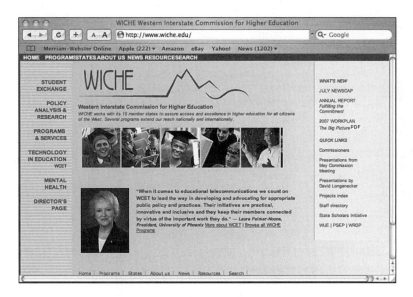

Like the SREB, WICHE is a regional education organization in the western United States. WICHE has performed numerous studies and written policy documents on tuition, cost of college, increases in college cost, and the linkages among state appropriations, tuition, and financial aid. WICHE can also link you to college and university systems. Their data and publications, though written for policy makers, are easy to read. You can learn a great deal about how colleges set tuition, raise tuition rates, and why. From WICHE's information, you can arm yourself with the right questions to ask on-campus—especially about tuition and aid.

Xap Mentor Sites (One-Stop Student Portals)

www.xap.com

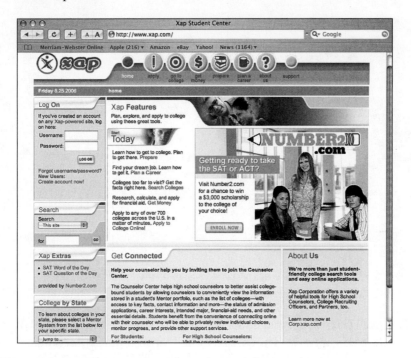

Many states and college systems within states have developed portals that allow you to do everything from managing your transcript delivery to applying for college on-line. In fact, you can apply for one college in your state and never have to retype the information again. Once you have an "account" (which is free), your information will pre-populate any form in your state's portal. This means that you can apply to multiple colleges with almost the touch of a single button!

The majority of student portals that have emerged have been developed by Xap. You can visit www.xap.com and select your state or college system from a menu on Xap's home page. Think of the Xap site as a portal for portals! Another positive feature of the Xap portals is this: not only can you apply for colleges in your own state once you create an account, you can also apply for other colleges in states where a Xap portal is being used. Xap's portals also pre-populate your personal information to the FAFSA should you choose to use this feature of the portal system in your state.

Glossary

academic certificates   Granted by community colleges or vocational/technical institutions upon completion of a specific project or learning outcome. For example, you may earn an Associate's degree in Business Management but also be awarded a certificate in word processing software.

Adult Learner Focused Institution (ALFI)   Designation coined by the Council on Adult and Experiential Learning (CAEL) that is an official designation for colleges and universities that meet certain criteria for serving adult learners.

adult student   Any college student age 25 years or older. See also *non-traditional student.*

articulation agreements   Agreements between colleges and universities that allow a degree or set of courses to transfer from one college to another for credit toward a higher degree.

assistant professor   A beginning professor in any content area. This is the lowest title in the tenure and promotion process.

Associate in Applied Sciences degree   A form of associate's degree in which technical and occupational courses form the core of the student's learning.

Associate of Arts degree   A two-year degree in which the field of study is largely based on liberal arts.

Associate of Science degree   A two-year degree in which the field of study is largely based on the sciences.

associate professor   The second rung in the tenure and promotion ladder, an associate professor has been judged by his peers as having completed necessary academic, research, and service activities to warrant promotion.

baccalaureate   Another word for Bachelor's degree; also sometimes refers to a ceremony in advance of graduation.

Bachelor's degree   A college degree that takes four or more years to complete; is usually comprised of 120 or more credit hours.

cohort   A group; in this case, a group of students who go through an academic program at the same time.

college   A place of higher learning accredited to deliver academic content that leads to a degree.

community college   Formerly called junior colleges, community colleges deliver academic content leading to an Associate's degree or general education courses that can transfer to a four-year college or university.

cost of attendance   A federal definition of the complete cost of attending college that includes not only tuition and fees, but also book costs, living expenses, and miscellaneous expenses.

credit hour   A unit of teaching. Most classes are three credit hours per semester; longer if laboratory time is included in the class. Tuition and fees are based on credit hours.

degree disparity   A social phenomenon that occurs within families (and even between friends and colleagues) when one person in a relationship has a college degree and the other doesn't. Also refers to when one person has a higher degree than the other. Risk of relationship crises are greatest when degree disparity is high; risk declines as each person in the relationship earns one or more degrees.

developmental courses   Courses or series of classes designed to help students become ready for college-level work. They are also called "remedial" courses on some campuses. Normally offered in the core academic areas of mathematics, basic sciences, reading, and English. These courses are zero-level, meaning that they don't count toward a degree.

doctorate   Also called a doctorate degree or a doctorate of philosophy (Ph.D.), this is the highest academic degree available. On top of the four-year Bachelor's degree, doctoral degrees take, at a minimum, an additional four years. Doctoral candidates also complete a dissertation, which they must defend before they can graduate.

estimated family contribution (EFC)   An amount discerned by filling out the Free Application for Federal Student Aid (FAFSA) form. The EFC is the amount you or your family are expected to contribute to your cost of attending college. EFC can be paid for with student loan funds.

FAFSA (Free Application for Federal Student Aid)   The federal form that must be filled out, either on paper or online, to qualify for federal financial aid, including grants and loans. The FAFSA is also used at the state and campus level to award grants, loans, and scholarships.

federal student loans   Low-interest loans made purely for the purpose of attending college and paying college expenses. Student loans are financial aid awards that must be paid back.

GED   The test most often taken by students who dropped out of high school and wish to attend college later on, this test measures whether you have the skills that are expected from a high school graduate.

general education courses   The "basics," or the general curriculum that every student is expected to complete, usually within the first two years of college, to obtain a Bachelor's degree.

grant   A form of financial aid that does not have to be paid back. Grants are normally awarded to families or students who have financial need.

high school equivalency   Normally granted by taking the GED exam, high school equivalency is how adults show that they are prepared for college if they never graduated from high school.

industry certifications   Certification awarded by academic or vocational institutions that are required by certain industry sectors. For example, the Automotive Service Excellence (ASE) exam is required in reputable automotive shops.

liberal arts college   A four-year college that doesn't specialize in any one academic area and provides a well-rounded curriculum that must be completed by all graduates.

loan forgiveness programs   Certain fields in which there is high demand for graduates sometimes have loan forgiveness available to them. In exchange for entering a high-demand field, students are granted forgiveness of some or all of their student loans.

major   The field of study that is emphasized and the title of the degree earned for a Bachelor's degree.

Master's degree   A graduate degree, required for some professions, that takes at least two additional years of study past the Bachelor's degree.

minor   A secondary field of study you undertake on the way to receiving your Bachelor's degree. The minor field of study can complement the major field or be a field completely unrelated to your major field of study.

net price   The actual price of college after the impact of financial aid is considered. Net price = published price – financial aid.

nontraditional student   Another term for adult student, often still used on campuses even when adults comprise the majority of students on campus.

open-entry and open-exit   Self-directed courses that can begin at any time during a semester and end at any time. The time a class takes is a function of individual time and effort.

Pell Grant   A federal grant provided for low-income students. Pell Grants require that a FAFSA is filled out and they are awarded on a sliding scale so that the lowest-income students reap the highest Pell Grants. They are only used for undergraduate study.

placement tests   Tests or assessments you take on campus to determine which courses in the core academic areas you're ready to be placed in. If you don't do well on placement tests, you may be required to take developmental or remedial courses.

podcasting   The delivery of audio content that can be received by small, handheld devices capable of capturing, saving, and playing back content.

published price   The actual retail price of college tuition. Sometimes refers to tuition plus fees and also refers to the total cost of attendance.

scholarships   Financial aid awards made based on merit or based on a student meeting certain criteria. Scholarships do not have to be paid back, but some may be taxable.

syllabus   The general outline for a course in college. Contains contact information for the professor, the rules of the class, and the sequence of information that will be covered during the course.

teaching load   The number of classes and/or credit hours that a given professor is teaching in any given semester.

terminal degree   A degree in which the Associate's or Bachelor's degree is the highest degree needed to enter a profession. Some degrees are nonterminal, such as a Bachelor's degree in psychology; you need a graduate degree in psychology to enter the profession and practice or teach.

traditional college student   A student who enters college directly after graduation from high school.

truth in tuition   When a college advertises what tuition really means—what proportion tuition is of the total cost of attending college. A college providing truth in tuition does not hide the fact that tuition is but a part of the total cost.

university   A higher education institution in which graduate and professional degrees are offered, in addition to lower degrees. Universities are typically larger and have research facilities on campus.

WorkKeys   A series of assessments created by ACT, Inc. that identifies a student's readiness for certain college-level learning and/or for certain jobs.

Index

X–Y–Z

Check Out These
Best-Sellers

Grammar and Style
SECOND EDITION

978-1-59257-115-4
$16.95

Buying & Selling a Home
FIFTH EDITION

978-1-59257-458-2
$19.95

Being a Groom
THIRD EDITION

978-1-59257-451-3
$9.95

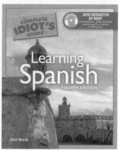

Learning Spanish
FOURTH EDITION

978-1-59257-485-8
$24.95

Investing
THIRD EDITION

978-1-59257-480-3
$19.95

Baby Sign Language

978-1-59257-469-8
$14.95

Total Nutrition
FOURTH EDITION

978-1-59257-439-1
$18.95

Positive Dog Training
SECOND EDITION

978-1-59257-483-4
$14.95

The Bible
THIRD EDITION

978-1-59257-389-9
$18.95

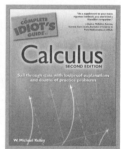

Calculus
SECOND EDITION

978-1-59257-471-1
$18.95

Music Theory
SECOND EDITION

978-1-59257-437-7
$19.95

The Perfect Resume
FOURTH EDITION

978-1-59257-463-6
$14.95

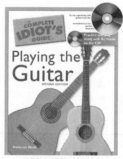

Playing the Guitar
SECOND EDITION

978-0-02864244-4
$21.95

Manga
ILLUSTRATED

978-1-59257-335-6
$19.95

Knitting & Crocheting
THIRD EDITION
Illustrated

978-1-59257-491-9
$19.95

More than *450 titles* available at
booksellers and online retailers everywhere

www.idiotsguides.com

ALPHA